MARITIME CORRIDORS IN THE INDO-PACIFIC

Geopolitical Implications for India

MARITIME CORRIDORS IN THE INDO-PACIFIC

Geopolitical Implications for India

Subhasish Sarangi

UNITED SERVICE INSTITUTION OF INDIA
NEW DELHI

PENTAGON PRESS LLP

MARITIME CORRIDORS IN THE INDO-PACIFIC:
Geopolitical Implications for India

Subhasish Sarangi

First Published in 2021

ISBN 978-93-90095-37-7

Published by
PENTAGON PRESS LLP
206, Peacock Lane, Shahpur Jat,
New Delhi-110049
Phones: 011-64706243, 26491568
Telefax: 011-26490600
email: rajan@pentagonpress.in
website: www.pentagonpress.in

Printed at Aegean Offset Printers, Greater Noida, U.P.

This book is dedicated to
those deployed on service for India on,
over and below the high seas

Contents

Foreword

The geopolitical implications of infrastructure development and connectivity became a major topic of discussion after China announced the Belt and Road Initiative in 2013. The vision document of the BRI was released on 28 March 2015, and the first Belt and Road Forum was held in May 2017. India did not join the BRI and was the first country to flag misgivings about the BRI. Its position has since been endorsed by many nations. A separate vision document for the Maritime Component of the BRI was released on 20 June 2017.

At this point in time, much had been written about the BRI but publications on the maritime component were scarce. While China's gradual ingress into the Indian Ocean Region and the massive expansion of the PLA Navy were being chronicled, the notions of what the 21st Century Maritime Silk Road was and what it implied were vague. This was also the time when the Indo-Pacific mapping had gained enough traction for even the USA to acknowledge and adopt it.

This book project was commissioned to focus on the development of maritime infrastructure across the Indo-Pacific Region and to analyse its geopolitical implications for India. The brief to the author was to write for a wider audience and present some clear conclusions and ideas from the Indian perspective.

The author has divided the book into three parts. The first provides the background and the historical perspective. The second provides an overview of all the national and regional initiatives in infrastructure development in the region. The third looks at the geopolitical implications for India and the options available for it.

The Indo-Pacific construct is one of the major developments of the last decade. Now, even Europe has 'pivoted' towards it. A snapshot of the maritime history of this region provides some lessons – the seas have been open and have been a conduit for trade and culture for centuries; the contribution to this flow of trade and culture has been by many peoples and nations; and no one country can claim ownership of this legacy. The intersection of technology and infrastructure with geopolitics is a common thread in history. Events similar to those happening today have played out in the past across centuries. The only difference now is that the notions of sovereignty and norms of international law are relatively stronger than in the past.

The BRI and its Maritime Component have run their course for the moment. Both have faltered on their great expectations of development that had built up due to the high-pitched marketing by China. Perhaps the expectations were too high. There is still no clarity on which projects constitute the BRI and how they are being funded. The opacity has exacerbated apprehensions and created a pushback. However, these are early days yet for the BRI that is supposed to run its course till 2049 as per China's timelines. India, for its part, has been pushing ahead in developing infrastructure within its territory and connecting up to its neighbourhood under its 'Neighbourhood First' policy launched in 2014. While this development is noteworthy, it has also exposed India's limitations in capacity and execution.

It is the third part that will be of particular interest to readers. The author has used a mix of history, technology and geopolitics to broad-base his conclusions. I am sure that this book will provide a lot of information and food for thought, not just for a wide audience but even for those who are working towards India's national security.

Maj Gen B. K. Sharma, AVSM, SM (Retd)
Director
The United Service Institution of India

Preface

The genesis of this book is the Maritime component of the Belt and Road Initiative, quixotically named as the Maritime Silk Road. The vision document had been released by China and there was curiosity about what this massive endeavour implied for the Indo-Pacific Region and for India.

Major General B.K. Sharma (Retd), the then Deputy Director, and now Director, recommended the flow of the book that I have substantially adhered to. Vice Admiral Satish Soni (Retd) guided this book project and nudged me whenever I went astray. Dr. Roshan Khanijo was the mentor providing much-needed discipline in adhering to timelines and guidelines. I have gained from my interactions with the richly experienced members of the United Service Institution of India – Major General Rajiv Narayanan (Retd) and Major General R.P.S. Bhadauria (Retd). Gaurav Dixit taught me several things that millennials and post-millennials tend to do better than those who came before them.

This book has been mostly written in 'lone wolf' mode but has drawn from the work of numerous scholars and commentators across the world who had written on the topics touched upon in the book. I have sincerely tried to ascribe credit where it was due.

I am thankful to the United Service Institution of India for having provided remarkable freedom to explore and study all avenues. I am also thankful to the Indian Navy for having provided me the opportunity to write this book.

I am thankful to Rear Admiral Monty Khanna (Retd) for his suggestions and corrections.

This book neither seeks to provide policy prescriptions nor construct theoretical frameworks. It is written for the young officers of the Armed Forces and students who like to browse through issues of strategic interest in their free time. Hence, it is written in an easy, readable form, avoiding convoluted language and high-brow formulations. However, the content is based on considerable research tempered by the experience of the writer, however limited it may be.

Finally, all shortcomings and errors in this book are entirely mine.

Abbreviations

A2AD	Anti Access Area Denial
ABC	Agricultural Bank of China
ADB	Asian Development Bank
AEI	American Enterprise Institute
AIIB	Asian Infrastructure Investment Bank
ASEAN	Association of Southeast Asian Nations
BCIM	Bangladesh-China-India-Myanmar
BoC	Bank of China
BRI	Belt and Road Initiative
BRICS	Brazil-Russia-India-China-South Africa
BRO	Border Roads Organisation
CCB	China Construction Bank
CCCC	China Communications Construction Company
CDB	China Development Bank
CDRI	Coalition for Disaster Resilient Infrastructure
CEE	Central and Eastern Europe
CELAC	Community of Latin American and Caribbean States
CGIT	Chinese Global Investment Tracker
CHEC	China Harbour Engineering Company
CMEC	China Myanmar Economic Corridor
CMHI	China Merchant Holding International
CMLV	Cambodia-Myanmar-Laos-Vietnam
CM Port	China Merchants Port Holding Company

CMREC	China-Mongolia-Russia Economic Corridor
CNPC	China National Petroleum Corporation
COPHC	China Overseas Port Holdings Company Ltd
COSCO	China Ocean Shipping Company
CPC	Communist Party of China
CPEC	China Pakistan Economic Corridor
CRBC	China Roads and Bridges Corporation
DFC	Dedicated Freight Corridor
DFCCIL	Dedicated Freight Corridor Corporation of India Limited
EAM	External Affairs Minister
EAS	East Asia Summit
EEU	Eurasian Economic Union
EEZ	Exclusive Economic Zone
EoI	Expression of Interest
EU	European Union
EXIM	Export-Import Bank
FDI	Foreign Direct Investment
FOCAC	Forum on China-Africa Cooperation
FTA	Free Trade Agreement
FY	Financial Year
GMCP	Greater Male Connectivity Project
HSR	High Speed Rail
ICBC	Industrial and Commercial Bank of China
IDA	Island Development Agency
IMF	International Monetary Fund
IOR	Indian Ocean Region
IPR	Intellectual Property Rights
ISA	International Solar Alliance
IWAI	Inland Waterways Authority of India
JICA	Japan International Cooperation Agency
JMSDF	Japan Maritime Self Defence Force
KPA	Kenya Port Authority

KRC	Kenya Railways Corporation
LAC	Latin America and Caribbean
LAPSSET	Lamu Port-South Sudan-Ethiopia
LDC	Least Developed Country
LoC	Line of Credit
MIV 2030	Maritime India Vision 2030
MoU	Memorandum of Understanding
MSR	Maritime Silk Road
MTPA	Million Tonnes Per Annum
MW	Mega Watt
NDB	New Development Bank
NDRC	National Development and Reform Commission
NELB	New Eurasian Land Bridge
NHSRCL	National High-Speed Rail Corporation Limited
NICDC	National Industrial Corridor Development Corporation
NIP	National Infrastructure Pipeline
NSG	Nuclear Suppliers Group
ODA	Official Development Assistance
OECD	Organisation for Economic Co-operation and Development
PCA	Permanent Court of Arbitration
PDSA	Port de Djibouti SA
PEACE	Pakistan-East Africa Connecting Europe
PRC	People's Republic of China
PSA	Port of Singapore Authority
RITES	Rail India Technical and Economic Service
RTA	Regional Trading Agreement
SCS	South China Sea
SGR	Standard Gauge Railway
SLPA	Sri Lanka Port Authority
SOE	State Owned Enterprise
SPV	Special Purpose Vehicle

SREB	Silk Road Economic Belt
SWIFT	Society for Worldwide Interbank Financial Telecommunication
TEU	Twenty Foot Equivalent Unit
TICAD	Tokyo International Conference on African Development
UNSC	United Nations Security Council
USA	United States of America

Introduction

The Scenario

In 2013, in two separate speeches, President Xi Jinping announced the setting up of the Silk Road Economic Belt (SREB) and the Maritime Silk Road (MSR). These two enterprises were envisioned under the umbrella of the One Belt One Road (OBOR). In 2015, good one-and-half years later, China released a White Paper on this grand vision. This audacious move obviously garnered enormous attention from scholars and commentators world-wide. The crescendo was encouraged with regular dispersal of eye-catching announcements, a major one being the China Pakistan Economic Corridor (CPEC) announced in 2015 that was initially pegged at $ 46 billion and later topped to $ 62 billion. The slew of announcements was matched by the output of literature that dwelt on all aspects of the venture–the intent, the challenges, the economics (or, rather lack of it), the funding and the security concerns. However, the initial burst of publications mostly dwelt on the terrestrial part of the venture – the SREB. The maritime component, the 21st century MSR, was hardly written about, primarily because there was considerable ambiguity on what it entailed and because there did not seem to be any tangible progress compared to the continental component. Somewhere along the way, this grand vision got christened as the Belt and Road Initiative (BRI). It also decisively moved the scholarly focus of international relations towards infrastructure development and connectivity as a 'pivot' of geopolitics. The Belt and Road Forum for International Cooperation was held on 14-15 May 2017 in Beijing to officially roll out the BRI. Twenty-nine Heads of State and Government attended the event. India was one of the major absentees that refused to join the endeavour on account of, amongst other things, the disregard to its sovereignty with the CPEC running through its territory occupied by Pakistan. However, India was an outlier in this since even nations with misgivings on BRI, that did not sign on later, attended the event.

The vision document of the MSR, now re-christened as the Maritime Component of BRI, was released in June 2017. Although it provided some more pointers to what the endeavour hoped to achieve, the ambiguities on the exact contours of this component persisted.

A month earlier, in May 2017, Japan and India had announced their intention to create the Asia Africa Growth Corridor (AAGC). India and Russia had announced formation of a Chennai-Vladivostok sea route in September 2017. Hence, it was a good time to examine the maritime corridors from the Pacific Ocean to the east coast of Africa, and to look at how they were shaping up for India.

The one major factor that defined the times was the rise of China. It was China that made the first move, with the world reacting to it. China broke out in ways not anticipated by many. It gave up its policy of 'hide your capacity and bide your time' to become more assertive. Its creeping assertiveness in the South China Sea, its use of economic coercion, instances of interference in internal affairs of other nations, increasing forays into the Indian Ocean Region (IOR) and its rapid naval expansion, forced a re-think on its intentions in creating the land and maritime corridors. China also started becoming more authoritarian in its internal administration. Xi Jinping consolidated his power substantially. His vision of the BRI was incorporated in the Communist Party Constitution. The restriction of two terms for the presidency was removed to enable him to continue further. The supremacy of the Communist Party of China (CPC) over all the organs of the State, and indeed the nation, was stated and reinforced unequivocally.

In 2018, after its initial marketing success, the BRI faced headwinds. The watershed event was the transaction that resulted in the Hambantota port of Sri Lanka being handed over to a Chinese State Owned Enterprise (SOE) on a 99-year lease. This triggered the narrative of the Chinese 'debt trap' that awaited nations that signed on without examining the economic viability of infrastructure projects and reading the fine print of the contract. This narrative echoed across the globe from Tonga in the South Pacific Islands to Pakistan in South Asia to Montenegro in Europe to Zambia in Africa and to Ecuador in South America. Nations started to relook at the terms and conditions for easy Chinese loans. Malaysia, Nepal, Pakistan and Myanmar are some the countries that either cancelled announced projects or re-negotiated the financial terms. In April 2018, 27 of the 28 European Union (EU) nation ambassadors in Beijing, with the exception of Hungary, signed a report sharply criticising the BRI. The Indian position, that unequivocally expressed reservations about many aspects of the BRI, was echoed by more nations as the year progressed.

The capacity of China to fund the BRI was never clear. In 2018, it seemed to become more difficult than ever. The Chinese economy started slowing. Although it achieved the targeted GDP growth of 6.5 per cent, there were major concerns. The high levels of debt in the economy meant that a fiscal stimulus, as was resorted to after the 2008 financial crisis, could not be resorted to. The march of the BRI juggernaut continued nevertheless. The 'Silk Road' continued to be appended to new sectors – Digital Silk Road and Space Silk Road. The MSR, after evolving from two to three branches, was stretched to Latin America and the Caribbean (LAC), and six nations of the region signed bilateral Belt and Road Cooperation agreements with China. Arbitration courts were set up for the BRI. Financial instruments based on the Renminbi were devised to provide alternate funding. However, internal economic woes reached a point when there was rare criticism of the government, within China, for draining resources on external projects despite internal challenges.

Another watershed event in 2018 was the non-partisan consensus that emerged in the USA on countering the rise of China. The traditional consensus in the USA, after the rapprochement of the 1970s, was that once China gained economic prosperity, it would reform politically and blend with the Western instituted world order. Over the years, all Western predictions on China, of either reform or implosion, proved to be incorrect. The USA's National Security Strategy released in December 2017 set the hawkish tone and labelled China as a 'revisionist power'. China was disinvited from the RIMPAC 2018 naval exercise. Vice President Mike Pence delivered a combative speech at the Hudson Institute in October 2018 and followed it up with some more verbal jabs in his speech at the Asia Pacific Economic Cooperation (APEC) Summit in November 2018. As the year progressed, the USA initiated an increase in tariffs for imports from China to reduce the trade imbalance. Measures to prevent China from taking the lead in cutting edge technologies came along with the trade war. In December 2018, US legislators passed the ARIA Act that authorised $ 1.5 billion to be appropriated every year, for the next five years, to fund activities in the Indo-Pacific Region. Buffeted by these headwinds, the Chinese capacity to steer the BRI was tested.

As nations contemplated their moves to balance the rise of China, it became clear that a major element had to be the provisioning of a more attractive alternative for smaller nations to fund their infrastructure development and enhancement of connectivity. Since connectivity and economic integration have become vital elements of foreign policy, contending initiatives of connectivity and infrastructure development unrolled for land and sea. The announcement of the Asia Africa Growth Corridor (AAGC), the passing of the BUILD Act by the USA, formation of tripartite groups to focus on infrastructure development, announcement of the EU-Asia Connectivity Strategy and Australia's $ 2 billion infrastructure financing facility for the Pacific Island Countries were all part of this trend. The most credible player, albeit, a relatively silent one, has been Japan. It has used a combination of direct investment, technological support and economic aid to earn credibility in countries across Southeast Asia to Africa.

The Chinese infrastructure projects in India's neighbourhood became reminiscent of the strategic 'squeeze' characteristic of the Chinese board game 'Go'. The Chinese footprint became bolder in Pakistan, Nepal, Bangladesh, Myanmar and the Maldives. With it came the imprint of influence and possible political heft. The recent tumultuous political events in Nepal, Sri Lanka and the Maldives were seen as tussles between proxies running parallel to the run of internal politics in these nations.

India, on its part, embarked on a slew of initiatives to bridge the infrastructure gap and win the approval of smaller nations in the region. It also took measures at various levels to balance the strategic environment and augment its security posture.

The Book

This book explores the various infrastructure development and connectivity enhancement initiatives of the Indo-Pacific and attempts to decipher their implications for India. The genesis of this study was, of course, the 21st century MSR or the Maritime Component of the BRI. However, other contending initiatives were also being initiated and are relevant. The last three years saw an avalanche of literature on the BRI. It was a double-edged sword. On the one hand, it offered varying perspectives and copious amounts of data, which aided in creating a coherent picture. On the other, the challenge was to present a fresh perspective that had not been covered already. This book attempts to collate all the initiatives in aiding infrastructure development and examines them from an Indian perspective. It also seeks to examine the flow of trade and energy resources and perceive the trends for the future. A significant challenge in this endeavour was the resolution of the vectors of security and economics while examining the geo-political implications. Every project of infrastructure enhancement has the twin components of economics and security implications inextricably woven. Separating the two strands is never easy. Perceiving the weightage of either component, security and economic, in each case and elucidating it can be tricky and not always successful.

The geographical canvas that this book looks at for all this unfolding action is a mapping labelled as the 'Indo-Pacific'. It is a mapping that has proponents and sceptics in equal measure. The global economic centre of gravity has shifted decisively towards the Indo-Pacific. The region is now witnessing an interplay of cooperation and competition between numerous regional and extra-regional powers. Therefore, the first chapter looks at this strategic space. It first narrates the genesis of the 'Indo-Pacific' mapping and thereafter proceeds to describe it in geographic and economic terms. It briefly looks at the Indo-Pacific policies articulated by several nations and ASEAN. The chapter ends with an overview of contemporary points of view on the Indo-Pacific mapping.

The second chapter provides a brief historical perspective on the maritime trade in the region. In ancient times, when ships were powered by wind, the predictability of the monsoon winds ensured the flourishing of rich maritime trade between East Africa, West Asia, South Asia and Southeast Asia. The oceans were open spaces without any sovereign restrictions. The trade routes were the channels for exchange of not just goods but of intermingling of cultures and carriers of knowledge. Although the hoary past is invariably invoked by China, its maritime zenith was primarily in the 15th century. The BRI invokes the ancient Silk routes while the MSR marketing pitch exalts the naval expeditions of Zheng He. Historical claims are presented by the Chinese, albeit in a selective manner. Hence, it is instructive to rush through a primer on the maritime history of the region. It will highlight the fact that movement of goods across the oceans was a relay with several stops, and various players dominated each segment of the relay during different times in history. Moreover, the oceans of Asia became restricted spaces, with availability subject to the approval of the dominant powers, only with the arrival of the Europeans.

Provisioning of finance and assistance for infrastructure building has ascended as a primary element of foreign policy and influence. The awareness that nations require assistance for infrastructure development and the criticality of providing that avenue has acquired salience in recent times. The third chapter dwells on this intersection between technology and infrastructure with geopolitics. It picks up examples in weapons, communications and transport to show that infrastructure building for geopolitical purposes is not a recent trend. It was always there. Since the earlier chapter covers history till the arrival of the Europeans, this chapter takes up examples of the colonial era that followed.

The fourth chapter will narrate the unfurling of and present status of the BRI. The deliberate vagueness, ever-increasing scope of its envelope and filling in of details as time progressed became the hallmark of this gargantuan enterprise. The BRI became a label to be affixed to every Chinese infrastructure and connectivity project executed abroad – past, present and future. It was extended to projects in South America and infrastructure in the digital domain. In the three decades of its conceived execution, it is not clear as to when the contours of its scope of work will finally crystallise. The jury is still out on what the BRI is and what its implications are. The various views cover the full spectrum. One end of it is that it is an attempt by China to utilise its surplus capital and infrastructure building capability to escape the middle income trap. The other end of it is that this is a grand strategy to integrate Asia, Europe and Africa in a Chinese world order. As the myriad projects progress along the six routes of the BRI, they face headwinds all around. From the Hambantota port to a highway in Montenegro to a dam in Ecuador, multiple concerns have been raised – the economic viability of the projects, the questionable valuation, suspected corruption, the opacity of financial terms, the unilateral award of contracts to Chinese State Owned Enterprises, use of Chinese labour, the quality of design and construction, and the intent of the project. Some nations have either re-negotiated or cancelled projects. However, there are several nations that seem to be keen to avail the financial and technical avenues provided by China. This chapter will trace the routes of the BRI and give an account of this attempt to integrate Eurasia and the Indo-Pacific. It provides an overall picture on the entire BRI while the next chapter looks more at the maritime component.

The fifth chapter looks at the maritime component of the BRI and Chinese investments along the route from China to Africa and West Asia. The MSR was generally understood as Chinese projects related to port and maritime infrastructure. However, there was no central Chinese repository of what constituted this MSR. Databases were compiled by think tanks around the world, with each differing from the other. Even the maps drawn by these organisations differed with most showing Kolkata as part of the MSR even though India had unequivocally stated that it would not join the BRI. The Chinese did not seem to be particularly keen to clear these ambiguities. After the establishment of a military base at Djibouti in 2017, there was a general lookout for Chinese 'bases and places'. Reports of possible bases kept emanating regularly from diverse locations like Jiwani (Pakistan), Vanuatu, Manus (Papua New Guinea) and El Salvador. Chinese companies also invested heavily to acquire control of ports, port operations and shipping lines across the world. This chapter will trace Chinese investments along the maritime channel from eastern China to the shores of east Africa.

The sixth chapter lists the other infrastructure and connectivity projects that have been initiated in recent times. There were several projects that were announced and remained mere announcements. Few remember the New Silk Road announced by the US Secretary of State Hillary Clinton in 2011. The Master Plan of ASEAN Connectivity 2025 was adopted in September 2016. The Vision Document of the AAGC was released in May 2017. The EU unveiled an EU-Asia Connectivity Strategy in September 2018. It proposed expenditure of € 60 billion over seven years for connectivity projects. In the following month, the US Senate passed the Better Utilisation of Investment Leading to Development (BUILD) Act with the provision of spending up to $ 60 billion. USA, Japan and Australia formed a tripartite arrangement to fund infrastructure projects. The India, Japan and USA tripartite joint statements too mentioned cooperation for infrastructure development. Meanwhile, Japan continued to be quiet performer across the Indo-Pacific, and in Africa, in the provisioning of direct investment, and economic and technical aid. Infrastructure development is seen as a credible sign of successful development by national political leaderships and many nations have announced grand development plans. Indonesia has it as part of the Global Maritime Fulcrum while the Philippines has a 'Build, Build, Build'. South Korea and Taiwan have 'Southbound' policies that, though not concentrated on infrastructure, seek to enhance trade and set up manufacturing facilities in Southeast Asia and South Asia. Australia has woken up to the ramifications of Chinese influence in the South Pacific Islands and has augmented its aid and assistance package for the region.

The seventh chapter looks at India's response so far. The Indian response is greatly handicapped by capacity constraints and, hence, speed of execution. However, the contours of a response at several levels can still be discerned. The narrative of this chapter starts from within India and moves out to its immediate neighbourhood and the IOR to list out the initiatives being taken by India. SAGAR, or Security and Growth for All in the Region, is India's maritime vision for the region and the Indo-Pacific Oceans Initiative (IPOI) is the executable proposal of that vision. India's foreign aid disbursement, technical assistance and utilisation of financial instruments like Line of Credit (LoC) have also been on the ascent.

The eighth chapter tries to decode the ramifications of these infrastructural development and connectivity projects for India. The primary concern, of course, is that the increase of the Chinese footprint in the IOR has also been accompanied by an increase in Chinese influence. There has also been a corresponding rise in defence cooperation that includes the induction of Chinese military equipment and increasing forays of the PLA Navy into the IOR. This raises concerns about reduction in India's strategic space and limiting of its options. Greater Chinese economic interests in the region provide the justification for a military presence. The influx of investment will be accompanied by the proliferation of Chinese standards and technology. The present race for setting up 5G telecom infrastructure world-wide is among the many for enforcing standards that include railways, information technology, finance and, arguably, governance. The possibility of 'dual use' of the infrastructure and technology needs critical examination, especially considering the seamless fusion of civil and military engineering industrial complexes in China. The chapter ends with a look at the military implications of the increasing Chinese presence in the IOR.

The ninth chapter looks at what measures need to be undertaken for mitigating the risks arising in the maritime corridors of the Indo-Pacific. The three actions at the strategic level include ensuring economic growth, forging partnerships and making choices in politics, trade and technology. An immediate requirement is for India to improve connectivity in its immediate neighbourhood (with the exception of Pakistan for understandable reasons) and provide unfettered access to its markets and resources for its South Asian neighbours and to establish itself as an attractive partner in economic prosperity. Although, India lacks financial muscle, it has the capability to assist smaller nations in issues that are critical for their economic prosperity and security. India has much to offer the world in terms of frugal and effective public goods. However, India needs to step up in creating technological standards, drafting legal interpretations on global commons, and, most importantly, upgrading its maritime sector. Equally paramount is the necessity to ensure that regional architectures for stability are created across the Indo-Pacific. Given the strategic distrust between the major powers, it is imperative to stitch together a patchwork of regional groupings based on common guidelines to provide stability to the region.

Finally, the conclusion provides a condensed version of the enquiry on the maritime corridors of the Indo-Pacific.

PART I

THE BACKGROUND

1

The Indo-Pacific Region

Introduction

This book focuses on the unfolding drama of maritime infrastructure, connectivity and geopolitics in the Indo-Pacific Region. 'Indo-Pacific' is a term that arouses interest, support, scepticism and derision in equal measure but is definitely 'the flavour of the season'. It is a term that has been adorned with multiple appendices – strategic mapping, region, strategy, construct, concept and vision, to name a few. However you look at it, it is the most recurrent term in contemporary commentary on geopolitics. Much has been written and spoken about it in recent years. The list of nations and regional organisations that have articulated an Indo-Pacific vision or policy continues to grow. At the time of writing, it included Japan, France, Australia, India, the USA, ASEAN, Germany and the Netherlands. The UK was in the process of drafting a vision and it was widely expected that the EU will have one too. Hence, this book will begin by looking at the Indo-Pacific Region and try to explain the characteristics of contemporary narratives.

The Indo-Pacific Region

The Indo-Pacific Region is basically a combination of three regions that were till recent times being considered separately – Indian Ocean Region, Southeast Asia and Asia Pacific Region. Although the geographical spread is not completely agreed upon, the maximum version extends from West Asia and the east coast of Africa, till the west coast of the Americas. So, the Indo-Pacific Region consists of the maritime space of the Indian Ocean and the Pacific Ocean, all islands and littoral nations of the two oceans, and adjoining seas. This makes it a gigantic region with the count of nations in it varying from at least 38 to over 72 depending on the limits chosen. It is estimated that these nations share 44 per cent of the world's surface, have 65 per cent of world population, account for 62 per cent of world GDP and 46 per cent of the world's merchandise trade.[1]

Given the large spread of the region, it is inevitable that there is wide divergence between the nations of the region in terms of size, population, development, volume of trade, economic structures and political setup. There are a few developed countries (the USA, Canada, Australia, New Zealand and Japan), several Least Developed Countries (LDCs) (Comoros, Madagascar, Mozambique, Somalia, Tanzania, Yemen, Bangladesh, Cambodia, Lao PDR and Myanmar) and many developing countries.

The economic centre of gravity of the world is shifting to this region from the North Atlantic. Some of the largest economies in the world and many of the fastest growing ones are in this region. In 2017, countries of the region contributed about half of world merchandise trade, but the contribution was lopsided as a significant portion was from East Asia.[2] Intra-regional merchandise trade was almost 65 per cent in 2017, with East Asia accounting for almost half the exports. This means that 65 per cent of the region's exports went to countries in the region itself, thereby indicating a strong interdependency in trade.[3] However, most of the energy requirements of the major economies of East Asia traverse through the Indian Ocean from West Asia, Africa and beyond. Since most of the merchandise trade and the energy resources are transported by sea, the security of the Sea Lines of Communication is critical for all.

The region has significant trading blocs with a large number of Regional Trading Agreements (RTAs) and tariff rates have fallen. However, intra-regional tariffs are relatively higher compared to global levels, non-tariff measures are a major trade barrier and trade facilitation measures are uneven over the region.[4] Connectivity across the region is fragmented and there are serious infrastructure deficits. In many cases, the cost and time to connect to an adjacent country exceeds the cost and time to connect to a relatively distant one.[5] Due to all this, the cost of intra-regional trade transaction is high and inhibits its growth of trade in the region. Improvements in infrastructure, connectivity and trade facilitation will reduce these costs and can transform the region.[6]

The Genesis of the Indo-Pacific

The use of the term 'Indo-Pacific' is common in diverse disciplines including marine biology, perhaps emphasising the seamless nature of the oceans. The first instances of the use of the term date back to the eighteenth century. The earliest usage in a geo-political context is in the writings of Karl Haushofer, in the 1920s and 1930s, in which he refers to the region from the Bay of Bengal to the Western Pacific as *Indopazifischen Raum* (Indo-Pacific region/space).

Dividing the globe into regions is not a perfect science. It is determined by geography, historical linkages, economic logic, geopolitical outlook, administrative convenience, connectivity and, sometimes, mischief. The basic logic of looking at the Indian and Pacific Ocean regions as one is the understanding that they have strong linkages and that events in one region affect the other. Similar discourses prevailed in India in the early part of the twentieth century. One of them was to consider Asia as a distinct space.[7] In the early years of India's foreign policy, Jawaharlal Nehru propounded an Asian identity. The fight against colonialism expanded the map further to 'Afro-Asian Solidarity'. Historian Kalidas Nag stressed India's past cultural and religious links with Southeast Asia and the Pacific.[8] He described this region as 'Greater India' – a most politically incorrect label for present times.[9] These discourses got lost in the grim tussle of the Cold War. The region got fragmented. India too marked its primary maritime interests between the Suez Canal and the Strait of Malacca, putting itself firmly in the Indian Ocean Region.

The present discourse on the Indo-Pacific Region can be traced to the famous speech of Japanese Prime Minister Shinzo Abe to the Indian Parliament on 22 August 2007. He spoke of the "confluence of the two seas of the Indian and Pacific Ocean" and their "dynamic coupling as seas of freedom and of prosperity".[10] By 2010-11, most Indian commentators had started mentioning the Indo-Pacific Region. By the time US President Donald Trump used 'Indo-Pacific' rather than 'Asia-Pacific', as a description of the region, during his 12-day Asian tour in November 2017, the term had gained acceptability.

National and Regional Visions

Japan sources its energy requirements from West Asia and is concerned about the security of the sea lanes through which they traverse. The rise of China has been on the minds of the Japanese leadership. Prime Minister Shinzo Abe conjured a number of formulations for partnership across the region. In 2006, it was the "Arc of Freedom and Prosperity". In 2007 in India, it was "Confluence of Two Seas". After returning to the Prime Minister's office in 2012, he proposed "Asia's Democratic Security Diamond". On his visit to India in 2015, the India-Japan Joint Statement described the region as "Indo-Pacific" for the first time.[11] As per Japan's Ministry of Foreign Affairs (MoFA), Prime Minister Abe announced his vision for "Free and Open Indo-Pacific" in his keynote address at the Tokyo International Conference on African Development (TICAD) VI held in Kenya in August 2016. Curiously, the text of the speech does not really mention it.[12] By November 2016, it had become the "Free and Open Indo-Pacific Strategy" as noted in the India-Japan Joint Statement made during the visit of Prime Minister Narendra Modi.[13] Somewhere along the way, the 'strategy' tag was dropped and it was described as either a concept or a policy. Japan intends to develop a "Free and Open Indo-Pacific" through three measures – promotion and establishment of rule of law, freedom of navigation and free trade; pursuit of economic prosperity; and commitment to peace and stability.

The Indo-Pacific mapping is an eminently suitable concept for Australia since both the oceans wash its coasts, one on either side. This provides it a certain centrality in the concept. Not surprisingly, Australia was an early adopter in using the 'Indo-Pacific' to describe its region. A White Paper published in October 2012 mentioned the Indo-Pacific.[14] The 2013 Australian Defence White Paper noted the trends that are shaping the emergence of the Indo-Pacific as a single strategic arc – China's continued rise as a global power; the increasing economic and strategic weight of East Asia and the emergence over time of India as a global power.[15] The Foreign Policy White Paper of 2017 lists the promotion of an "open, inclusive and prosperous Indo-Pacific region" as an objective of fundamental importance to Australia's security and prosperity.[16]

The Indian establishment is traditionally averse to publishing policy documents on defence and foreign policy. The sole reference for the Indian concept of the "Indo-Pacific" is the keynote address delivered by Prime

Minister Narendra Modi at the Shangri La Dialogue on 1 June 2018.[17] Describing the Indo-Pacific as a "natural region" and a "geographical definition", he declared that "India does not see the Indo-Pacific Region as a strategy or as a club of limited members.... Nor as a grouping that seeks to dominate. And by no means do we consider it as directed against any country". He went on to list the six elements of India's vision for the Indo-Pacific Region. The first is that it is "a free, open, inclusive region". The second is the centrality of South East Asia and ASEAN in this region. The third is the evolution, through dialogue, of "a common rules-based order" that "must believe in sovereignty and territorial integrity, as well as equality of all nations", based "on the consent of all, not on the power of the few" and "on faith in dialogue, and not dependence on force". The fourth is "equal access as a right under international law to the use of common spaces on sea and in the air that would require freedom of navigation, unimpeded commerce and peaceful settlement of disputes in accordance with international law". The fifth is a "rule-based, open, balanced and stable trade environment in the Indo-Pacific Region". The sixth element is connectivity to "enhance trade and prosperity". Speaking at the East Asia Summit on 4 November 2018, Prime Minister Modi urged support for an "Indo-Pacific Oceans' Initiative".[18] In keeping with the vision of keeping the region free, open and inclusive, the Indo-Pacific Oceans' Initiative proposes an open architecture to address regional challenges.

France published its Indo-Pacific policy document in 2018 and updated it in 2019. It can claim to be a resident Indo-Pacific power since it has island territories in both the Indian and Pacific oceans. This means that the freedom to sail freely between its territories is critical for France. In the three years from 2016 to 2018 when French Defence Ministers addressed the Shangri-La Dialogue, each one invoked a 'rule based international order' and 'freedom of navigation', and spoke with unusual frankness on the need to uphold international maritime law in the South China Sea. The issues flagged by the Indo-Pacific policy document include security responsibilities of a 'resident power' (protection of its territories, Exclusive Economic Zones (EEZs) and population); threats to multilateralism and international order due to big power rivalry and weakening of rule of law; threats from terrorism, nuclear proliferation (North Korea) and climate change.[19] To counter these challenges, France intends to develop a network of strategic partnerships in the Indo-Pacific with countries like India, Australia, Japan, Malaysia, Singapore, New Zealand, Indonesia and Vietnam. It wishes to contribute to the building of a regional security architecture. The four main pillars of the French Indo-Pacific Strategy are enhancing involvement in regional security; strengthening partnerships with major regional players; increasing engagement with regional organizations; and promotion of global public goods.[20] France appointed its first ambassador for the Indo-Pacific in October 2020.

The official US version of the Indo-Pacific picked up momentum in end 2017. The National Security Strategy, released in December 2017, mentioned the Indo-Pacific in lieu of Asia Pacific. On 1 June 2019, the Department of Defence (DoD) released its Indo-Pacific Strategy Report.

ASEAN adopted its "ASEAN Outlook on the Indo-Pacific" after a year of negotiations in June 2019. It "envisages ASEAN centrality as the underlying principle for promoting cooperation in the Indo-Pacific region, with ASEAN-led mechanisms, such as the East Asia Summit (EAS), as platforms for dialogue and implementation of the Indo–Pacific cooperation". It envisions "an Indo-Pacific region of dialogue and cooperation instead of rivalry". The areas of cooperation include maritime cooperation, connectivity, UN Sustainable Development Goals 2030, and economic cooperation.

Germany released its "Policy Guidelines for the Indo-Pacific" in September 2020.[21] It recognised that the security dynamics of the Indo-Pacific Region will have an impact on Europe as well. It supported Europe's engagement in the region and sought to coordinate its efforts with other European nations on a wide range of issues. In November 2020, the Netherlands released its policy document on the Indo-Pacific.

The Story Till Now

Now that we have described the Indo-Pacific Region and looked at the countries that have found it necessary to articulate their policies on the region, some general points can be made.

The first point is to reiterate that mental or strategic mapping of the earth's surface is not fixed. It changes frequently in terms of nomenclature and spread. There was once a region called 'Indo-China', for instance. Such mapping is useful to provide coherence to a narrative and to comprehend complex scenarios. Historical memory, national borders, national interests, alliances, trade blocs, connectivity, and strategic perception are some of the factors that affect the evolution of the mapping. For example, like it is reasoned that events in the Indian and Pacific oceans are interlinked, it can be reasoned that events at sea are affected by events on land. Hence, maybe, we should look at the entire Asian landmass and adjoining seas as one.[22]

Although the 'Indo-Pacific' term has gained prominence over the last decade, what it represents varies as per the context – geopolitical, economical, maritime cooperation or maritime contestation, to name a few. It is not surprising that each nation that has articulated an Indo-Pacific policy seeks to envision it in a way that serves its interests. For India, it enables catering to its widening radii of national interests. It is useful for India in extending its neighbourhood, and for its claim as a stakeholder in the region beyond the Strait of Malacca. Within India, enthusiastic support for the 'Indo-Pacific' is due to the belief that is an inclusive term that reflects India's growing interests in South East and East Asia (although the 'Indo' in Indo-Pacific is the Indian Ocean and not India) and provides it with a strategic orientation that supports increased engagement with the extended region. The Asia-Pacific term was seen as exclusionary and an impediment to India's engagements to its east. For the USA, it is about strengthening its alliances with additional partnerships to counter the rise of China. For Japan and Australia, it is about being hubs of the US Alliance system in the region while also stepping up to cater for a relative retreat by the USA. For France, it is about securing its maritime territories and ensuring freedom to move between them. For the other European nations, it is about maintaining stability so that their investments and trade in the region do not suffer.

It is, therefore, not surprising that the geographical limits of the region set by various nations are not yet coinciding. In fact, nations have adjusted their geographical scope of the "Indo-Pacific" over time.[23] In his keynote address at the Shangri La Dialogue of June 2018, Prime Minister Narendra Modi described it as 'from the shores of Africa to that of the Americas'. Just two days before Prime Minister Modi's speech, the USA renamed its Pacific Command as the Indo-Pacific Command. However, its area of operations continued to be from the west coast of the USA to the west coast of India, described by that catchy phrase "from Hollywood to Bollywood". The Australian definition has enlarged over time from the Defence White Paper of 2013 to the Foreign Policy White Paper of 2017, as also the Japanese definition. France's definition is probably the largest and includes even the southern Indian Ocean.

The narrative of the genesis and chronology of the latest avatar of the Indo-Pacific varies depending on whom one asks. China and Russia see it as an USA dominated discourse that seeks to draw in India into its fold. However, it can be argued that the idea of the two oceans being one integrated region had always existed. It was followed by British India in practice. The Cold War had fragmented this integrated space. Now, it is getting reclaimed. As India's External Affairs Minister has often remarked – "Indo-Pacific is not tomorrow's forecast but yesterday's reality".[24] It is the nations in the region that first articulated this construct. The USA has picked it up after them. Although China and Russia oppose the Indo-Pacific terminology, it can be argued that they follow it in practice. China's Belt and Road Initiative, with its land and maritime components, can be seen as having a similar outlook of considering an integrated geographic space. Russia too is not averse to initiatives like the Chennai-Vladivostok maritime link that reinforces the notion.

These opposing narratives also bring out the debate about which nation is proposed to be included and which is proposed to be kept out. It is argued that like the Asia-Pacific mapping intended to include the USA with East Asia, the Indo-Pacific mapping seeks to include India to a region with the USA and its allies. The mention of China and strategic competition varies between the extremes of the USA and ASEAN versions. The USA clearly describes China as a revisionist power, as it can afford to. US allies like Australia mention the rise of China but also mention the centrality of US support. The Europeans voice their misgivings of great power competition. India maintains the stance that the region is open and for all. ASEAN too seeks to focus on cooperation rather than competition. Connected to it is the question of whether there is an Indo-Pacific Strategy or Policy. Prime Minister Modi said that "India does not see the Indo-Pacific Region as a strategy or as a club of limited members.... Nor as a grouping that seeks to dominate. And by no means do we consider it as directed against any country". However, the very next day at the same forum, the US Secretary of Defence, James Mattis, in his remarks spoke of the Indo-Pacific Strategy and pointedly mentioned that "China's policy in the South China Sea stands in stark contrast to the openness of our strategy". Some indication of alignment among nations is provided by the terms that have become the bellwethers in most national Indo-Pacific outlooks. Phrases such as "freedom of navigation and overflight", "protection and safeguarding of rule-based order", and "resolution of disputes peacefully in accordance with international law" clearly allude to the recent events in the East and South China Sea.

There is common agreement that this mapping acknowledges the shift in the global economic centre of gravity from the 'West' towards Asia. It also acknowledges the economic and energy linkages that bind the two oceans and the understanding that events in one have implications in the other. This means that if regional organisations and mechanisms need to be evolved for security, stability and free trade, ideally the entire 'channel' of the Indo-Pacific has to be considered as an integrated entity. However, the Indo-Pacific in its entirety is too big and unwieldy a region for any such endeavour. If taken to its limits, the nations at either boundary vary substantially to make forging of any understanding difficult. Meaningful grouping for any endeavour can only be achieved with a restricted domain of participants. Institutions for economic and security cooperation are sprinkled across the region but it is not foreseeable that any one institution can ever have the membership of all the nations. That would become like a smaller version of the United Nations with nations varying widely in many ways somehow coming together. The only hope is to link these multiple organisations together on the basis of common elements in agenda and outlook to provide stability to the region. It does not help matters that the region has its fair share of frictions, tensions and conflicts that include the perpetual upheavals in West Asia, the contestation of sovereignty over maritime features in the South China Sea and East Asia, and nuclear brinkmanship in the Korean Peninsula. These varied sources of instability obviously require different forums and mechanisms to be resolved.

Conclusion

It is difficult to encapsulate all that has been written about the Indo-Pacific region in the last decade. This region that spreads from the east coast of Africa to the west coast of the Americas is seen as the one in which the shape of tomorrow's international order will be decided. This is due to the growing economic and political importance of Asia and the increasing strategic rivalry between the USA and China. Nations that have adopted the Indo-Pacific mapping have their own perceptions and expectations about it, obviously driven by their national interests. Connectivity and globalisation has created strong global linkages and forced rethinking on considering hitherto separate regions as one. However, it is debatable as to how far this convergence should be advanced.

NOTES

1. VAdm Pradeep Chauhan (Retd) and Prabir De, "Indo-Pacific Partnership: Realising the benefits of economic and maritime cooperation" in *Indo-Pacific Report 2019* (New Delhi: National Maritime Foundation, 2019), 3.
2. Anusree Paul and Prabir De, "Trade in Indo-Pacific: Trends and Prospects" in *Indo-Pacific Report 2019* (New Delhi: National Maritime Foundation, 2019), 30.
3. Paul and De, "Trade in Indo-Pacific", 32.
4. Paul and De, "Trade in Indo-Pacific", 29-69.
5. Prabir De, "Maritime connectivity cooperation in the Indo-Pacific: Identifying the scope and opportunities" in *Indo-Pacific Report 2019* (New Delhi: National Maritime Foundation, 2019), 109.
6. Mohammad Masudur Rahman and Prabir De, "Indo-Pacific Partnership: What do trade simulations indicate?" in *Indo-Pacific Report 2019*, (New Delhi: National Maritime Foundation, 2019), 71-86.
7. Carolien Stolte and Harald Fischer-Tine, "Imagining Asia in India: Nationalism and Internationalism", *Comparative Studies in Society and History*, 2012; 54(1); 65-92.
8. Kalidas Nag, *India and the Pacific World* (Calcutta: Book Company Ltd., 1941).
9. Kalidas Nag, *Greater India* (Bombay: The Book Centre Private Ltd., 1960).
10. Ministry of Foreign Affairs (MOFA) of Japan, *Confluence of the Two Seas, Speech by H. E. Mr. Shinzo Abe, Prime Minister of Japan at the Parliament of the Republic of India*, 22 August 2007.
11. Ministry of External Affairs (MEA), *Joint Statement on India and Japan Vision 2025: Special Strategic and Global Partnership Working Together for Peace and Prosperity of the Indo-Pacific Region and the World*, 12 December 2015.
12. Ministry of Foreign Affairs (MOFA) of Japan, *Address by Prime Minister Shinzo Abe at the Opening Session of the Sixth Tokyo International Conference on African Development (TICAD VI)*, 27 August 2016.
13. Ministry of External Affairs (MEA), *India-Japan Joint Statement during the visit of Prime Minister to Japan*, 11 November 2016.
14. Australian Government, *Australia in the Asian Century*, White Paper, October 2012.
15. Department of Defence, Australian Government, *Defence White Paper* 2013, 2.
16. Australian Government, 2017 *Foreign Policy White Paper*, 3.
17. Ministry of External Affairs (MEA), *Prime Minister's Keynote Address at Shangri La Dialogue*, 1 June 2018.
18. Ministry of External Affairs (MEA), *Prime Minister's Speech at the East Asia Summit*, 4 November 2019.
19. Ministry of Defence, France, *France and Security in the Indo-Pacific*, 2018.
20. Ministry for Europe and Foreign Affairs, Republic of France, *French Strategy in the Indo-Pacific "for an inclusive Indo-Pacific"*, updated August 2019.

21 The Federal Government, *Policy Guidelines for the Indo-Pacific: Germany-Europe-Asia: Shaping the 21st century together*, 2020.

22. Manjeet S. Pardesi, "The Indo-Pacific: a 'new' region or the return of history?" *Australian Journal of International Affairs*, 2019, DOI: 10.1080/10357718.2019.1693496

23. Wada Haruko, "The Indo-Pacific Concept: Geographical adjustments and their implications", *RSIS Working Paper* No. 326, 16 March 2020.

24. Ministry of External Affairs, *EAM's remarks at CII Partnership Summit 2020*, 17 December 2020.

2

Perspective of Maritime History

Introduction

It can be tricky and illusive to provide a snapshot of five millennia of maritime history in five thousand words. The flow of history is neither linear nor uni-dimensional. It can be traced over multiple layers – geographical, political, religious, cultural, technological, commercial, to name a few. Migration of people, transportation of material and conveyance of ideas are never a one-way flow but a simultaneous movement towards either side. Dynasties that are conveniently bookmarked within certain years may have, in reality, originated much earlier in minor principalities, risen to rule mighty empires, failed and resurrected themselves several times, before fading into oblivion years later. Kingdoms marked clearly on a dated map would have seen their borders expand and contract multiple times before breaking up or getting subsumed into other kingdoms.

Maritime linkages have been provided over the ages by an assortment of sailors, adventurers, explorers, merchants, and navies. Some backed by the state, some by merchant guilds, and some on personal enterprise. These linkages have provided kaleidoscopic imprints on many facets of society. It would be foolhardy for one particular nation and its rulers to claim 'sole proprietorship' of this legacy.

The Journey

Since this book provides an Indian perspective, it gazes seaward from the shores of India and briefly traces the journey of mariners in the last two-and-a-half millennia.

Among the earliest evidence of maritime activity in the civilised world are the Harrapan sites of Lothal and Dholavira in the Gulf of Khambhat and the Gulf of Kutch, respectively. The Harappan civilisation was at its peak in the period from 2600 to 2000 BCE. The Rann of Kutch was underwater and Dholavira was located on an island.[1] It had a fortified acropolis and urban settlements. The most important evidence that the Harappans had large-sized vessels capable of being used at sea is the dock at Lothal dated to 2300 BCE.[2]

Around 2600-2500 BCE, maritime interconnections were established in the region from the coast of Gujarat to the Tigris-Euphrates river system of Mesopotamia, and Bahrain and Oman on the other side.[3] Mesopotamian tablets of the third century BCE mention commercial centres in Bahrain, Oman, and Harappa.[4] Items of Harappan origin have been found all across this region.[5, 6] Harappan weights and measures became the standard across the region. After 2000 BCE, the Harappa civilisation saw a decline and it came to an end by 1400 BCE. The failure of the Indus Valley and Harappa civilisations is attributed to several factors, primarily a change in climate and flow of rivers. It was followed by the 'Vedic Age' dated between 2000 BCE and 500 BCE. Vedic literature is replete with references to boats, ships and sea voyages.[7] From the knowledge of the type of ships of the time, it reasonable to conclude that sea voyages followed the coasts.

Meanwhile, in the Pacific Ocean, the Lapitas, ancestors of the Polynesians had commenced their island-hopping from around present-day Papua New Guinea. By 1300 BCE, they had reached Fiji. By the eighth century, they had reached Hawaii across the Pacific Ocean.[8]

Coastal trade in eastern India picked up around 800 BCE, led by the kingdom of Kalinga.[9] Odia-Bengali seafarers started visiting and settling in Sri Lanka from the sixth century BCE.[10] Ancient Indian literature in Sanskrit, Pali and Tamil provide evidence of relations with Southeast Asia. They mention toponyms for Southeast Asia like Suvaranadvipa, Java-dvipa and Dvipantara.[11] The *Maha Nidessa* (Third century BCE) refers to 24 places in Southeast Asia.[12] The earliest clear evidence of trade between India and Southeast Asia comes from Ban Don Ta Phet in west-central Thailand dated to the fourth century BCE.[13] Ships of the merchants of Kalinga would hug the coast of the Bay of Bengal and reach the Isthmus of Kra (of Thailand). The goods would be taken over land to the Gulf of Thailand from where they would be loaded again on ships for Cambodia and southern Vietnam.[14]

In 325 BCE, when the army of Alexander III was returning home from the Indian sub-continent, one section sailed back. The local sailors informed the Greeks that there was a direct route by sea. Admiral Nearchus acquired a flotilla of locally-made vessels and undertook a sea voyage of 1,500 miles.[15]

That was also the time when the Maurya Empire was founded by Chandragupta. The establishment of a large united empire across the sub-continent led to a spurt in internal and external trade. For the first time, a single empire had control of ports in both the east and west coasts. Regions within the Indian sub-continent were interconnected through grand routes or highways that ran across the land.[16] Port towns came into prominence all around the coastline of India. Ships sailed from ports in Gujarat along the coast till the Red Sea. In the east, the port of Tamralipti (in Bengal) was a major one. The use of the monsoon winds had still not been mastered by this time.

Kautilya's *Arthshastra* is a remarkable work that throws light on the elaborate administrative system during the reign of Chandragupta Maurya. It mentioned an Admiralty Division in the War Office headed by a *Navadhyaksa* (Superintendent of Ships). It also codified regulations to be followed in naval and mercantile marine affairs. It differentiated between river, coastal and oceanic routes. It also covered all duties to be paid, facilities provided and punishments for contravention of laws.[17]

Towards the beginning of the present era (BCE to CE), maritime traffic in the Indian Ocean Region grew substantially. The major discovery was the pattern of the seasonal monsoon winds that were predictable and could be used to plan voyages. This was typical of the Indian Ocean Region and Southeast Asia, thanks to the geography of the oceans being surrounded by land. Ships sailing between China, India, and Africa took advantage of the monsoon winds to sail out of a port and returned on the retreating monsoon winds to the port of origin. They awaited the change of monsoon winds in some sheltered harbour. This also created the need for entrepot ports around the Indian Ocean where goods could be stored from one monsoon season to the next. These ports became business hubs, some of which retain their strategic naval importance till date. Goods travelled in stages between China, Southeast Asia, India and West Asia. Obviously, they travelled in different ships for each stage rather than one ship from origin to destination.

Sailors from Kalinga reached Java by 75 CE and started settling down there.[18] Ancient ports of that time have been discovered along the coastline of Bengal and Odisha, with the prominent one being on the Chilka Lake. The route was to sail down the coast till Sri Lanka using the north-eastern monsoon winds that blow from November. In Sri Lanka, they would replenish their supplies. Then they would use ocean currents to sail across to reach Java/Bali by mid-January. The return journey would commence in mid-March to reach Sri Lanka by May. The south-west monsoon winds would then take them north to Kalinga.[19] The rituals of *Boita Bandana* in Odisha and *Loi Krathong* in Thailand commemorate this maritime tradition. Similar journeys to Southeast Asia were made by merchants from the Tamil, Andhra and Bengal coasts. Tamil literature provides accounts of rich coastal and inland centres. Madurai, the capital of the Pandyas, was a magnificent city in first century BCE. Trade links with Southeast Asia led to cultural exchanges and the impact of Indian civilisation can be seen across the region to this day in religion (Hinduism and Buddhism), language (Sanskrit), legend (*Ramayana* and *Mahabharata*) and architecture. The Mekong Delta witnessed the establishment of the first 'Indianised' kingdom of Southeast Asia, called the kingdom of Funan by the Chinese, in first century BCE.[20]

Just like maritime trade flourished with Southeast Asia in the east, it also flourished with the Greco-Roman world in the west. By the third century BCE, ports and markets in South Asia had emerged as important destinations for Greek and Roman goods.[21] South India became the interim for spices from Southeast Asia to reach West Asia and the Roman Empire. Indo-Roman trade was most prevalent from the second century BCE to the second century CE. The existence of Indo-Roman trade is now well established through archaeological evidence and ancient texts. Archaeological evidence includes pottery, amphorae, bronze ware, and Roman coins found in India.[22] The largest concentration of amphorae (a jar of Mediterranean origin) found in India has been at Arikamedu near Puducherry. These contained Greek and Italian wine, Spanish *garum* and northern Adriatic oil.[23] Details on maritime routes and ports along the coast of India are available through western sources like "*The Periplus of the Erythraean Sea*" (first century CE) written by an anonymous merchant of Egyptian-Greek origin, "*Geographica*" by Strabo (67 BCE-20 CE), "*The Natural History*" (77 CE) by Pliny, and "*Guide to Geography*" by Ptolemy (140 CE). Earlier, mariners would sail along the coast to reach western India. The discovery of the monsoon winds meant that they could also sail directly to southern India. Trade was carried through ports in Gujarat and Maharashtra. Ships flocked to the port of Muzeris (located in Kerala) for black pepper. This southern route was also the channel for the earliest migrations of Jews, Christians and Muslims to the Indian sub-continent. Tamil texts of the Sangam period also provide information on sea trade between the West and South India, including the presence of *Yavanas* (Westerners) in India.[24] Roman writers of that age provide accounts of envoys of Indian kings who reached the courts of the Roman emperors. Trade with Rome was through Egypt and was in the hands of Arab middlemen at Alexandria. Indian merchants rarely reached Rome.[25] Trade with the Roman Empire declined after 217 CE. Indo-Roman trade was heavily tilted in favour of India and the Roman Empire ran a persistent trade deficit as recorded by Pliny (23-79 CE). Until the advent of the Arabs in the second century, Indian merchants had a monopoly over maritime trade in the Indian Ocean.[26]

The trade routes of the Indian Ocean became more firmly established in the fourth and fifth centuries. This was the time when the Gupta Empire flourished in India. Once again, ports in Sind, Gujarat, Bengal and Odisha came under a single ruler. These ports received merchants, diplomats, scholars and pilgrims from China, Persia, Arabia, Ethiopia and the eastern Roman Empire.[27] Buddhist monasteries at Bodh Gaya and the Nalanda University, funded by foreign kingdoms, were established. A famous account of that period is by the Chinese scholar, Fa Xian, who visited India in the early fifth century. His return journey in 411-413 CE was by sea. He recorded that Java had an overwhelmingly Hindu population. In the fifth century, no Chinese lived or traded there.[28] The predominantly Hindu population was of Kalinga origin. This population retained contact with India and carried on trade with China. Merchants of South India joined the trade and spread their network through their guilds. The kingdom of Funan, in present southern Vietnam and Cambodia, reached its peak in the fifth century and declined in the sixth century.

In the sixth century, the Pallava dynasty rose in southern India under king Simha-Vishnu. Kanchipuram, the capital, and Mahabalipuram, the main port, were impressive cities. The port, which is now submerged under the sea, was busy with merchant fleets.[29] The Pallavas had personal and political links with Southeast Asia. The spread of Sanskrit, and architectural influence on Cambodia and Java is attributed to the Pallavas.[30] By the eighth century, there were a number of 'Indianised' kingdoms in Southeast Asia - the Sri Vijaya kingdom in Sumatra and the Malay Peninsula; the Khmers in Cambodia; and the kingdom of Champa in Vietnam. By this period, Indian merchant communities were living in southern Chinese ports.[31]

From the eighth to the thirteenth century, there were three parallel tracks that require to be traced – West Asian, Indian and Chinese. By this time, Muslim West Asian merchants and Chinese merchants had started to challenge the predominance of South Asian merchants.[32]

The eighth to eleventh centuries were a period of expansion of Muslim (Arab and Persian) commerce on all major routes in the Indian Ocean. Merchants from West Asia ventured more frequently down the Somali and Kenyan coasts till Kilwa.[33] They established trading colonies along the east coast of Africa. The trading networks and ports of east Africa were integrated into a wider Indian Ocean mercantile system.[34] They moved eastwards as well, initially settling in Konkan and Gujarat; southern India and Sri Lanka by the eighth century; the Coromandel Coast by the ninth century; and extending to Guangzhou in southern China. The tenth century saw the development of further trade linkages between the Middle East and Southeast Asia through these ports of the Indian subcontinent, with Arabs, Persians and Jews trading along these routes.[35] By the late twelfth century, the 'southern sea trade' from China was essentially in the hands of Muslim traders.[36]

By the eighth century, the Palas of Bengal and the Pallavas of Kanchi continued to trade with Southeast Asia and beyond. Southeast Asia remained a patchwork of Hindu-Buddhist kingdoms that were heavily influenced by Indian civilisation. The Shailendra dynasty of Java, believed to have its origins in eastern India, established itself in 782 CE.[37] Jayavarman II of the Khmer throne founded the Angkor Empire.

In 873 CE, the Pallava dynasty was defeated by the Cholas. Rajaraja Chola, who ascended to the throne in 985 CE, is regarded as the greatest ruler in Tamil history. The Cholas got control over ports on both the eastern and western coasts in south India. His successor, Rajendra Chola, who ascended to the throne in 1014 CE, is best known for his naval expeditions against the Sri Vijaya kingdoms of Sumatra and Malaya.

By the late tenth century, maritime trade boomed between the Song empire in China, the Cholas in south India and the Shite Fatimid caliphate that controlled Egypt and the Red Sea. This trade across the Indian Ocean was through a series of segmented voyages.[38] The Angkor state expanded in mainland Southeast Asia. This period saw diplomatic missions, gifts and donations, exchanged between the Southeast Asian kingdoms, and India and China. The region of present day Malaysia and Indonesia was divided between the Sri Vijaya empire in the west and the kingdom of Mataram in Java. The Sri Vijaya kingdom controlled the Strait of Malacca (between the Malay Peninsula and Sumatra) and the Java kingdom controlled the Sunda Straits (between Sumatra and Java). In 1016, the Sri Vijaya empire defeated the Javanese and got control over both the straits. They started extracting higher tolls from merchant ships. Rajendra Chola sent a small naval expedition in 1017 to Sumatra. In 1025, a larger fleet destroyed Sri Vijaya ports and defeated its army in Kadaram (Kedah province in Malaysia).[39] The Chola fleet raided 14 port cities on the Malay Peninsula and in Sumatra. The Sri Vijaya king accepted the supremacy of the Cholas and the kingdoms resumed their ties. In fact, the Chola fleet returned in 1068 to support the Sri Vijaya kingdom. Tamil merchant guilds were most powerful in the eleventh and twelfth centuries. Chola power declined in the late twelfth century but South Indian merchant guilds continued to flourish into the thirteenth century.[40] There is evidence of the presence of a large South Indian (Tamil) merchant community in China.[41] The largest discovery was in the port city of Quanzhou. Of the hundreds of sculptures and carvings excavated in the city and surrounding areas since the middle of the last century, many are now in the Quanzhou Maritime Museum (also called the Museum of Overseas Communication History). A block of stone with bilingual Tamil-Chinese inscriptions, dated to 1281 CE, records the consecration of a Shiva temple.[42] In the thirteenth century, the Hindus of Java went on to establish the Majapahit empire across the region of present-day Indonesia.

With economic prosperity during the era of the Tang dynasty (618-907 CE), Chinese merchants and mariners became more regular visitors to Southeast Asia, occasionally sailing as far west as Sri Lanka and South

India.[43] There is evidence of the presence of Chinese merchants in South India.[44] Although the Chinese navigated their coastal waters and nearby seas for centuries earlier, trade with Southeast Asia and the Indian Ocean was carried mostly in foreign (Southeast Asian, Persian and Arab) ships.[45] This changed during the Song Dynasty (960-1279 CE). The Song state set up maritime offices, constructed new ports and actively encouraged foreign traders to come to Chinese ports.[46] Trade with distant markets became vital for China's economy. Larger and more seaworthy vessels were built and by 1161 CE, were armed with a variety of early gunpowder weapons[47] By the twelfth century, Chinese vessels were venturing up to southern India. In 1290 CE, Italian traveller Marco Polo commenced his return journey from China by sea. The ship set sail from Quanzhou and made its way to Champa (Vietnam), island of Bintan, Strait of Malacca, Nicobar Islands, Sri Lanka, and along the western coast of India to Persia. From the late thirteenth century, an increasing amount of China's foreign trade was carried over the sea through Southeast Asia into the Indian Ocean.[48] Chinese merchants and mariners became active in the ports of Sri Vijaya and were found to have extended their reach till Calicut in Kerala. Calicut was the largest port in India's west coast after Muzeris was destroyed by a flood in 1341. Chinese merchants began establishing their own diaspora communities and merchant guilds in Southeast Asian ports.[49]

China's officially sanctioned private participation in overseas trade that had the formal recognition of the Song dynasty in the tenth century lasted till the Ming dynasty outlawed Chinese civilian investment in maritime commerce.[50] It was forbidden to cross the oceans other than on official purposes and those who sent people across the seas for trade were punished. The prohibition was reiterated several times perhaps showing that it was not effective.[51] From around 1400 CE, Chinese merchants and sailors, mostly from Fujian province in southeast China, went to Southeast Asia to trade with the connivance of local officials and leading families in Fujian. Chinese merchants were prominent in the ports of Java in the fourteenth and fifteenth centuries.[52] Traders from China were able to make direct trips to the South Asian coast in the fourteenth century. These direct voyages, however, lasted till the fifteenth century.[53] By the fifteenth century, Muslims from West Asia and South Asia were the dominant force in maritime trade across the Indian Ocean.[54]

Chinese naval might was at its peak in the fifteenth century during the reign of Emperor Zhu Di. This was the time that Chinese interactions with Southeast Asia were the most pronounced. A major element of these interactions was the "tribute missions".[55] Trade concessions and rewards were available for those who submitted "tribute". There were several eunuch-led maritime missions and the most well-known were those led by Zheng He. He led seven naval voyages between 1405 and 1433. These missions were intended to create legitimacy for the emperor, display the might of the Ming, bring the known polities to demonstrated submission to the Ming and thereby achieve a *pax Ming* throughout the known world and collect treasures for the court.[56] They were military missions with strategic aims although they are now sought to be projected as friendly voyages. Military men made up a significant portion of the crew and the ships were equipped with the best firearms of the time.[57] The history of the voyages is replete with accounts of use of force, intervention in local politics and instituting regime changes. The armadas were made up from the largest fleet in the world at that time. In order to enable these large fleets to sail into the Indian Ocean, staging points and garrisons were created at Malacca. The new kingdom of Melaka became a counterweight to the Majapahit of Java.[58] The founder of Melaka, Parameswara, converted to Islam.

After the voyages of the fifteenth century, there was a complete withdrawal of Chinese forces from the high seas. At the heart of the naval withdrawal was the court politics between the mandarin officials and the eunuchs. The last of the Chinese voyages of the fifteenth century was in 1431-33.

Southeast Asia too saw a collapse of the 'Indianised' kingdoms – the Majapahit of Java, the Khmers of Angkor and the kingdom of Champa (Vietnam).

The European onslaught took over the seas thereafter. Till then, the Arabs had successfully blocked information about the Indian Ocean from reaching the Europeans. Bartolmeu Dias left Portugal in 1487 and successfully went around the Cape of Good Hope. Vasco da Gama reached Calicut (India) on 14 May 1498. Within decades, the Portuguese ransacked or occupied ports along the western Indian Ocean Region – Muscat, Mombasa, Socotra and Hormuz. The Portuguese occupied Goa in 1510, Malacca in 1515 and Colombo in 1518. Sailing westwards,

Christopher Columbus reached the Bahamas in 1492. Ferdinand Magellan successfully crossed from the Atlantic to the Pacific Ocean. However, he did not live to see the successful circumnavigation by his crew as he died in the Philippines in 1521. The Portuguese were followed by the Dutch, French and the British. By the time the Suez Canal opened in 1869, the entire Indo-Pacific region had been colonised by Europeans.

Reminiscences

This account of five millennia has obvious limitations. However, there are still some conclusions that are clear.

The first is that the maritime journey across the Indo-Pacific was never a single one. It was more like a relay of journeys. Each segment was decided by the timing of the ubiquitous monsoon winds. Each segment had its leaders at different points in time. One way of conceptualising it is to see it as three 'circuits' – West Asia and East Africa to India; India to Southeast Asia; and Southeast Asia to China.[59]

The second is that no one civilisation can claim primacy of the seas over the ages. As we see, the honour changes hands numerous times between Indians, West Asians (Arabs, Jews and Persians), Chinese, and finally the Europeans.

The third is that maritime linkages, though often backed by the rulers, were not necessarily due to them. A heterogeneous mix of people contributed to it. Often, it was the merchant guilds that were at the forefront of trade-driven linkages.

Fourth, notwithstanding the rivalries around the Malacca, the oceans were open before the Portuguese arrived to close them down and assert ownership. The Indo-Pacific region had a vibrant maritime culture many centuries before the Europeans arrived.

Fifth, events on land impacted movement over the seas. Both China and India retreated from the seas due to internal events. Formation of mighty and secure empires such as the Roman Empire under Augustus and the Gupta Empire propelled maritime trade. On the other hand, the rise of the Ottoman Empire disrupted European trade and forced the Europeans to seek a sea route.

Maritime Silk Road?

China often invokes imagery of the hoary past in pronouncements on foreign policy and on launching of mega projects. The nomenclature of the BRI seeks to project Chinese ownership of the ancient silk routes, real and imagined. The naval expeditions of Zheng He are highlighted to provide the historical link to the quixotically named "Maritime Silk Road". There is undeniably a strong desire to give salience to such events which is reflective of a psyche of superiority as a civilisation. Today's Chinese see themselves as heirs of a civilisation that was a world leader in terms of science, technology and culture till its subjugation by colonial powers.

The attempts to claim ownership over the "Silk Roads" are rather dubious considering that the name itself was given by a German in the nineteenth century. The linkages over land were by a network of local traders across the continents forming a transportation chain. Not all goods were either silk or of Chinese origin. Invoking a "Maritime Silk Road" is similarly dubious as it never existed. The nomenclature suggests a uniform maritime link, of Chinese origin, from India to Europe. If such ownership must be alluded to by the Chinese, it could probably only be done for the maritime link between China and Southeast Asia. The goods that were traded over the waters of Asia since ancient times included silk and porcelain from China, cotton from India and, most importantly, spices from Southeast Asia and India. Five wrecks recovered in Southeast Asia provide an insight into the bewildering range of products traded from the ninth to thirteenth centuries.[60] Hence, there was neither a "road" nor was it about "silk". If the term is intended to portray all the routes that Chinese ships ever traversed in history across the globe, it needs to be reiterated that they were not the only ones doing so. Moreover, if archaeological evidence emerges about items of Chinese origin at a site, it does not automatically mean that it reached there through Chinese traders. Market linkages since ancient times have conveyed goods far away from their countries of origin to distant lands. It is a tribute to Chinese marketing ingenuity that not only has the term "Maritime Silk Road" witnessed widespread usage, the coinage has also been appended to conferences, publications, archaeological discoveries and beauty contests (yes, you heard that right).

The Chinese cause is helped by having the convenience of a historic figure to prop up – Zheng He. A single maritime leader with seven voyages over three decades lends well to heroic storytelling compared to the numerous, mostly nameless and faceless, mariners, merchants and naval leaders from other civilisations that sailed the seas over five millennia.

Conclusion

A historical perspective is essential since it has several lessons to offer. The notion of connectedness of Eurasia and Indo-Pacific is not necessarily a modern one. The economic and cultural links span millennia. All this, while civilisations and empires have risen and fallen, borders have been redrawn, rivers have changed course, and religions and languages have evolved. The maritime flow of goods and culture across the region was never a linear orchestration by people of one region. It was always a collective effort with different people leading each segment of the flow at different points in time. The goods of trade were numerous and changed drastically over the years. It is foolhardy for any one nation to try to allude to ownership of this maritime legacy. A Maritime Silk Road is as dissonant as a Cotton Route or Spice Route. Technology and infrastructure were among the key catalysts of change. The next chapter will delve into the intersection of technology and infrastructure with geopolitics.

NOTES

1. Sanjeev Sanyal, *The Ocean of Churn: How the Indian Ocean Shaped Human History* (India: Penguin Books, 2016), 44.
2. Rear Adm K. Sridharan, *A Maritime History of India*, Second edition (New Delhi: Publications Division, GoI, 1982), 13.
3. Philippe Beaujard, *The Worlds of the Indian Ocean: A Global History*, Volume 1 (Cambridge: Cambridge University Press, 2012), 102.
4. I.K. Sharma, "Indian Seafaring Traditions: Archaeological Perspectives" in *Maritime Heritage of India*, Ed. K.S. Behera (New Delhi: Aryan Books International, 1999), 1.
5. Sanyal, *The Ocean of Churn*, 46.
6. I.K. Sharma, "Indian Seafaring Traditions", 2.
7. U.N. Dhal, "Indian Maritime Activities: Vedic, Epic and Puranic Sources" in *Maritime Heritage of India*, Ed. K. S. Behera (New Delhi: Aryan Books International, 1999), 11-14.
8. Daniel R. Headrick, *Power Over Peoples: Technology, Environments and Western Imperialism, 1400 to the present* (Princeton and Oxford: Princeton University Press, 2010), 12
9. Sanyal, *The Ocean of Churn*, 65.

10. Sanyal, *The Ocean of Churn*, 82.
11. Kishor K. Basa, "Early trade in the Indian Ocean: Perspectives on Indo-South-east Asian Maritime Contacts (c. 400 BC-AD 500)" in *Maritime Heritage of India*, Ed. K. S. Behera (New Delhi: Aryan Books International, 1999), 44.
12. I. Wayan Ardika, "Ancient trade relations between India and Indonesia", in *Maritime Heritage of India*, Ed. K. S. Behera (New Delhi: Aryan Books International, 1999), 80.
13. Basa, "Early trade in the Indian Ocean", 29.
14. Sridharan, *A Maritime History of India*, 34.
15. Sridharan, *A Maritime History of India*, 21.
16. Basa, "Early trade in the Indian Ocean", 54.
17. Sridharan, *A Maritime History of India*, 21.
18. R.K. Mookerji, *Indian Shipping*, Kitab Mahal (Allahabad), 1962, 103.
19. Karuna Sagar Behera, *Kalinga-Indonesia Cultural Relations* (Orissan Institute of Maritime and Southeast Asian Studies, 2007).
20. Sanyal, *The Ocean of Churn*, 83.
21. Tansen Sen, "Maritime Southeast Asia between South Asia and China to the Sixteenth Century", *TRaNS: Trans-Regional and National Studies of Southeast Asia*, Volume 2, Issue 1 (January 2014), 31–59.
22. Kishor K. Basa and Karuna Sagar Behera, "India-Roman Trade" in *Maritime Heritage of India*, Ed. K.S. Behera (New Delhi: Aryan Books International, 1999), 15-28.
23. Basa and Behera, "India-Roman Trade", 16.
24. Basa and Behera, "India-Roman Trade", 23.
25. M.K. Dhavalikar, "Maritime tradition of western India" in *Maritime Heritage of India*, Ed. K.S. Behera (New Delhi: Aryan Books International, 1999), 109.
26. Sridharan, *A Maritime History of India*, 49.
27. Sanyal, *The Ocean of Churn*, 105.
28. Haraprasad Ray, "Orissa in Chinese historical records" in *Maritime Heritage of India*, Ed. K.S. Behera (New Delhi: Aryan Books International, 1999), 227.
29. Sanyal, *The Ocean of Churn*, 1.
30. Sridharan, *A Maritime History of India*, 34.
31. Geoff Wade, "An Early Age of Commerce in Southeast Asia, 900–1300 CE", *Journal of Southeast Asian Studies*, Volume 40, Issue 2 (June 2009), 221–265.
32. Kenneth McPherson, *The Indian Ocean: A history of people and the sea* (New York: Oxford University Press, 1993), 76.
33. McPherson, *The Indian Ocean*, 102.
34. McPherson, *The Indian Ocean*, 102.
35. Geoff Wade, "An Early Age of Commerce in Southeast Asia", 221–265.
36. Wade, "An Early Age of Commerce in Southeast Asia", 221–265.
37. B.S. Das, *Studies in the Economic History of Orissa: From Ancient Times to 1833* (Calcutta: Firma KLM Pvt. Ltd., 1978), 44; M.N. Das, *Glimpses of Kalinga History* (Calcutta: Century Publishers, 1949), 117.
38. K.N. Chaudhuri, *Trade and Civilisation in the Indian Ocean: An Economic History from the Rise of Islam to 1750* (Cambridge University Press, 1985), 39.
39. This account has been taken from Sanjeev Sanyal, *The Ocean of Churn: How the Indian Ocean Shaped Human History* (India: Penguin Books, 2016), Ch. 7, 134.
40. Hermann Kulke, "Trade and Politics in the Eleventh Century Bay of Bengal" in

Maritime Heritage of India, Ed. K. S. Behera (New Delhi: Aryan Books International, 1999), 220.

41. Kulke, "Trade and Politics in the Eleventh Century Bay of Bengal", 221.
42. Richard Pearson, Li Min and Li Guo, "Quanzhou Archaeology: A brief review", *International Journal of Historical Archaeology*, Vol. 6, No. 1 (March 2002), 38.
43. McPherson, *The Indian Ocean*, 77.
44. Kulke, "Trade and Politics in the Eleventh Century Bay of Bengal", 221.
45. Mark Elvin, *The Pattern of the Chinese Past* (Stanford: Stanford University Press, 1973), 137.
46. Wade, "An Early Age of Commerce in Southeast Asia", 221–265.
47. Srikanth Kondapalli, *China's Naval Power* (New Delhi: Knowledge World, 2001), Preface.
48. McPherson, *The Indian Ocean*, 112.
49. Sen, "Maritime Southeast Asia between South Asia and China to the Sixteenth Century", 31–59.
50. McPherson, *The Indian Ocean*, 112.
51. Geoff Wade, "Engaging the South: Ming China and Southeast Asia in the Fifteenth Century", *Journal of the Economic and Social History of the Orient*, Vol. 51, No. 4 (2008), 578-638.
52. Craig A. Lockard, "'The Sea Common to All': Maritime Frontiers, Port Cities, and Chinese Traders in the Southeast Asian Age of Commerce, ca. 1400-1750", *Journal of World History*, Vol. 21, No. 2 (June 2010), 219-247.
53. McPherson, *The Indian Ocean*, 77.
54. McPherson, *The Indian Ocean*, 78.
55. Wade, "Engaging the South: Ming China and Southeast Asia in the Fifteenth Century", 578-638.
56. Geoff Wade, "The Zheng He Voyages: A Reassessment", *Journal of the Malaysian Branch of the Royal Asiatic Society*, Vol. 78, No. 1 (288), (2005), 37-58.
57. Wade, "The Zheng He Voyages: A Reassessment", 37-58.
58. Louise Levanthes, *When China Ruled the Waves* (Oxford University Press, 1994).
59. Chaudhuri, *Trade and Civilisation in the Indian Ocean*, 1985.
60. Wade, "An Early Age of Commerce in Southeast Asia", 221–265.

3

The Intersection of Infrastructure, Technology and Geopolitics

Introduction

Infrastructure building and technology have been inextricably linked with geopolitics all through history. Connectivity led to the collapsing of geographies. On the one hand it resulted in flow of trade and culture, and on the other became a vital requirement to enhance security and project power. Paths created for merchants were followed by soldiers and administrators of empires. Empires thrived due to their infrastructure network, and prosperous empires created infrastructure. Foreign powers used infrastructure and technology to subjugate and extract benefits for themselves. This narrative could probably commence from the Greek city-nations of ancient times but since we have already traversed through history till the arrival of the Europeans to the seas of Asia, it is more convenient to pick it up from here. This was the age of colonisation that finally saw two world wars. This chapter provides some snippets on the weapons, transport and communications of that era.

Weapons, Transport and Communications

Within decades of arriving in the Indian Ocean in 1504, the Portuguese established control over ports/enclaves all along the East African coast, Socotra, west coast of India and Malacca. These coastal bases provided Portugal with the means to seize control over the Indian Ocean's maritime trade routes, to and from the Indian subcontinent, from the Arabs. Their arrival itself was facilitated by recent inventions and advances in maritime technology in Europe. Their conquests were facilitated by superior weapons. The Portuguese were followed by the Dutch, French and British. Each of them sparred with the others to mark out and control territories that served to provide resources to the homeland from Africa and Asia.

By the early nineteenth century, Britain had cemented its position in India and the Royal Navy firmly controlled the main trade routes with the Indian subcontinent. The French were eliminated as a naval rival with the surrender of the Mauritius naval base in 1810. Between the fall of Napoleon in 1815 and the outbreak of World War I, Britain created a world empire of profit. It could only be sustained by a maritime strategy that relied on industrial and technological leadership.

Technology is power. It is this power of technology that subdued people and extracted natural resources. On land, this imperialistic power was possible through changes in infantry weapons from muskets to machine guns. On water, it was the advent of the steamship and its military variant, the steam-powered gunboat. Steam-powered boats enabled the Europeans to move deep into Africa and Asia on the rivers. The boats could move fast, both up and down river, independent of the requirement of either wind power or rowing manpower. "Few inventions of the nineteenth century were as important in the history of imperialism".[1] Technological development between 1815 and 1890 profoundly altered the manner in which military force could be brought to bear on land from the sea. It enabled the means of waging "offensive war, not only against fleets, but harbours, fortresses, and rivers, not merely of blockading, but of invading and carrying the warfare of the sea to the heart of the land".[2] Armoured steamships could pass existing shore defences and their heavy artillery could destroy forts. The East India Company was one of the earliest users. By December 1838, the company had eight iron gunboats (five for the Tigris and Euphrates and three for the Indus) and ordered five more.[3] The *Nemesis* was the first British ocean-going iron hull warship. Interestingly, she was commissioned by the East India Company and not by the British Admiralty. She was propelled by coal-powered steam engines rotating paddle wheels. The Opium War in China was the first event whose outcome was determined by these gunboats. The Chinese had no defence against the *Nemesis*, with its two 32-pounder guns, five 6 pounders, ten smaller cannons and a rocket launcher.[4] It was ironic considering that the inspiration for the paddle wheel-propelled vessels came from China.[5] These gunboats penetrated up Chinese rivers and opened up the Chinese interior to British forces. Similar action took place in the Anglo-Burmese wars, and all across Southeast Asia. "The gunboat had become not just the instrument, but the very symbol of Western power along the coasts and up the navigable rivers of Asia".[6]

India was the prized possession of the British Empire and every effort was made to improve and secure communications between Britain and India. Two of the most important means of doing so was by steamship travel (that also carried mail) and the telegraph.

There were, historically, three routes between Europe and India. One across Egypt, down the Red Sea, and across the Arabian Sea; the second across Syria to Iraq (Mesopotamia), then down the Euphrates and the Persian Gulf to the Arabian Sea; and the third by circumnavigating Africa. One or the other route had taken precedence over the ages depending on the prevalent maritime technology available and the political climate of West Asia. We can capture some snippets of history along these three routes.

Three innovations enabled long-distance sea travel from Britain to Asia to become regular – iron hull, the propeller, and the high-pressure engine. The first iron hull steamer, the *Aaron Many,* came from the Horsley Iron Works in Staffordshire in 1820.[7] Iron shipbuilding began in earnest in the 1830s. Steel hulls followed thereafter. The screw-propeller was introduced in 1838.[8] In a high-pressure steam engine, steam is recycled back to the boilers in the form of salt-free distilled water. This saves the boilers from corrosion and allows them to operate at higher pressures. It was introduced onboard ships in the 1860s.[9]

Pluto (1822-30) was the first steam dredger in India and *Diana* (1823-36) was the first steam paddle boat.[10] *Diana* was extremely effective in the advance up the river Irrawaddy during the first Anglo-Burmese war. By the 1830s, steamers were operating in the Ganga River. A group in Calcutta offered prize money to any steamship that could make four consecutive voyages between Bengal and England at an average of seventy days per trip.[11] In 1825, the *Enterprise,* which employed both sails and steam power, sailed from London but took 113 days to reach Calcutta.[12] The sea route around Africa was favoured by the East India

Company in the early nineteenth century as it was the safest. However, the first successful steamship liner service used the middle route through the Red Sea. It was initiated by the Presidency of Bombay, acting against the advice of the Board of Directors of the East India Company. The steamship *Hugh Lindsay* was constructed in Bombay. It sailed from Bombay for Suez in March 1830. However, it ran out of coal by the time it reached Aden. Almost a third of the journey time was spent in loading coal. To provide the *Hugh Lindsay* with a coaling station, the ruler of the island of Socotra (off the Horn of Africa) was invited to sell his island to the Presidency of Bombay in 1835. When he refused, it was seized by force.

The *Hugh Lindsay* was joined by *Atlanta* and *Berenice* in 1837; *Semiramis* in 1838; *Zenobia* and *Victoria* in 1839; and *Auckland*, Cleopatra and *Sesostris* in 1840. Monthly steam ship service from Bombay to Egypt became a reality.[13] The *Atlanta* was the first ship to complete the London to Bombay route around Africa on steam power alone, in 68 days.[14] Aden was found to offer a better harbour and a healthier climate than Socotra for the Red Sea route. Its ruler was intimidated and bribed to give it up. When he did not yield, it was taken by force in 1839.[15]

Soon, private firms stepped in. The first firm to do so was the Peninsular and Oriental Steam Navigation or P&O. It started the Suez to Calcutta service in 1842. In 1845, the service was extended till Penang, Singapore and Hong Kong. In the 1850s, it launched the world's largest steamer, *Himalaya*, for the Suez-Bombay route. The earliest steamship lines were heavily subsidised by the British government. They also got paid for carrying mail between the territories. By the early 1860s, P&O had 39 ships serving India, Malaya, Singapore, China and Australia.[16] These steamers were requisitioned by the government for transportation in wartime. P&O liners were requisitioned in the Burma campaign of 1852, in the Indian Mutiny of 1857, and in the Sudan expedition of 1884; ships of the Calcutta and Burmah Steam Navigation Co. were requisitioned in 1857 and in the Abyssinian campaign of 1863; and Cunard liners were used in Cyprus in 1878, Egypt in 1882 and the Sudan in 1884-85.[17]

There was a tenfold increase in world trade between 1860 and 1900. This resulted in almost equal growth in the annual tonnage of shipping movements.[18] The increasing efficiency of the marine steam engine captured key trade from sailing ships. Earlier steam-driven ships had paddles but later the screw-propeller was developed. Warships, with engines for propulsion, depended upon access to bases for maintenance and fuelling (coal). The screw-propeller that now propelled ships needed to be maintained. Underwater fouling, which affected speed and range, could be removed only in a dry dock. This required a global network of naval bases and harbours linked by a communications network. Only ships with adequate bases for supply and repair could control the sea. Between 1815 and 1860, new bases were developed to meet the demand for naval support to British commercial interests. The construction of dry docks at Bombay in the mid-eighteenth century was indispensable to Britain's command of the Indian Ocean.[19] Before 1840, only Britain and Bombay had dry docks for British ships.[20] However, there was a rapid spread of dry docking facilities between 1860 and 1890.[21] This included Malta in 1848, Sydney in 1857, Singapore in 1859 and Hong Kong in 1860. Dry docks enabled the Royal Navy to send squadrons to any part of the globe. Marine technology kept evolving at a fast pace.

In the late 1870s, wrought iron was replaced by steel in the construction of merchant ships. The use of steel allowed operating boilers at higher pressures and this resulted in the triple-expansion engine, the successor to the earlier compound engine. This lowered fuel consumption and improved engine efficiency. By World War I, the steam turbine and diesel engine had started replacing it. As the ships got larger, harbours had to be deeper and larger as well. The Suez Canal had to be widened to allow passage of larger ships. Newer ports were built to serve the expanding traffic.

Getting back to the three routes between Britain and India, travel through the route through Egypt was the most successful. However, there was a short stretch of land journey in between to get from the Mediterranean to the Gulf of Suez in the Red Sea. This was to change soon. The Cairo-Suez Rail was built in the 1850s. On 30 November 1854, the Pasha of Egypt, Mohammed Siadgave, and the French consul, Ferdinand de Lesseps, signed the concession to build the Suez Canal.[22] Work started in 1859. Excavation was done manually till 1865, when steam driven dredgers were employed.[23] Construction by massive manpower was replaced by massive mechanical power. The British government was opposing the project all along but by 1869, it stopped its opposition and looked to using the canal and guaranteeing its safety.

The Suez Canal was inaugurated on 17 November 1869 after delays and cost overruns.[24] It was built mostly with Egyptian labour, and French money and machinery. However, after completion, it served mainly the interests of Great Britain. The voyage from London to Bombay was shortened by 51 per cent, to Calcutta by 32 per cent, and to Singapore by 29 per cent.[25] The first ship to pay a toll on the canal was British, and within a few years, three quarters or more of the ships that used it were of British registry.[26]

By 1882, the Canal started operating to capacity. However, no benefits accrued to Egypt as the host nation. Local manpower did not receive any training or new skills. Egypt received only 15 per cent of the Suez Company's annual profit even while providing the company major concessions. Egypt accumulated a steep external debt as it had borrowed heavily for infrastructure projects, including the Suez Canal itself. It sold its 45 per cent stake in the Suez Company to the British in 1875. When Egypt went bankrupt in 1876, representatives from Britain and France moved in to take control of its government revenue and expenditure.[27] In 1882, Britain invaded and colonised Egypt. The route from Britain to India was safeguarded with a string of naval bases at Gibraltar, Malta, Cyprus, Alexandria and Aden.

The spread of railways is yet another example of the interplay between infrastructure and geopolitics. Railway lines linked up regions of the far-flung empires. It served both military and economic purposes of the empire. Russia built the Trans-Siberian Railway connecting Moscow to Vladivostok that opened in 1904; the Trans-Caucasian Railway from Poti, on the Black Sea, to Baku, on the Caspian Sea, in 1883; the Trans-Caspian Railway from the Caspian to Samarkand (by 1888) and Tashkent (1898); and the Trans-Aral Railway from Kinel to Tashkent in 1906. The Ottoman Empire stretched from the borders of Austria-Hungary to the Persian Gulf. It was through this empire that a rail route was envisioned from Germany to the Persian Gulf. The Oriental Railway line from Vienna to Istanbul became operational in 1888. The existing railways in Asia Minor in 1888 were owned entirely by French and British financiers.[28] However, the Germans took over thereafter. In a period of 10 years, the German-owned Anatolian Railway Company constructed almost a thousand kilometres of railway lines in Asia Minor.[29] They were conceived and constructed by German engineers, with material provided by German factories, and financed by German bankers. It occurred alongside the expansion of German economic interests and political influence in the Ottoman Empire. The grandest project was connecting Berlin to Baghdad by rail, to be enabled by the Baghdad Railway. The rail line from Konya, in the Turkish highlands, to the Persian Gulf, was to be constructed by the Baghdad Railway Company set up in 1903. Ten per cent of the company was owned by the Ottoman government, 10 per cent by the Anatolian Railway Company and the rest by an international syndicate led by Deutsche Bank.[30] The Ottoman government not only agreed to pay for every kilometre built but also guaranteed minimum revenue for each kilometre open to traffic, in addition to other financial guarantees, tax exemptions and grants of public lands.[31] It included mining rights, establishment of brick works, construction of port facilities, and hydro-power stations. This was not the only instance when such one-sided guarantees were provided. In 1910, the French-backed Smyrna-Cassaba Railway too extracted hefty guarantees for the Soma-Panderma rail line.[32]

Work on Baghdad railway began in 1903. As we have seen, Britain was determined to control every important route to India. It was the dominant power in the Persian Gulf. The British made a clandestine agreement with the Sheikh of Kuwait as a consequence of which Kuwait, which was a part of the Ottoman Empire, became a protectorate of the British. Thus, a trans-continental rail link with a terminus at a deep-water port of the Persian Gulf was averted. This was just one episode in the many instances when a project became victim to the geopolitics of the age that included great power rivalry of Europe; desire of the West to maintain a firm grip on its vested interests in the east; and rival imperialistic ventures for raw materials and markets supported by respective governments. The biggest disruption was the outbreak of World War I. There were gaps in the rail line when the war commenced. At the end of the war, the Ottoman Empire disappeared, German economic and political power in the region was completely eliminated and a republican nationalistic Turkey had been formed. The ownership of the rail line got divided, like the entire region, and got built in parts over the next two decades.

After the establishment of scheduled oceanic steam shipping routes, the next revolution in communications was the establishment of a global telegraph network, with overland and underwater cables. This too was led by the British. The first attempt at underwater telegraphy seems to have been a cable laid across the Hooghly River in Calcutta in 1839.[33] Dover and Calais were linked by a submarine telegraph cable across the English Channel in 1851. In 1852, a cable linked England and Ireland. The British began connecting India's major cities in 1853. The first trans-Atlantic cable, laid in 1857-58, failed after a few messages were passed.[34] During the revolt of 1857 in India, the 4,500 miles of telegraph land lines in India helped the East India Company to mobilise its troops.[35] The cable laid in 1859 to connect Alexandria to Karachi was a failure. This prompted the formation of a committee to standardise the technology for underwater cables. A rush to install underwater cables followed when the committee completed its work in 1860. In 1865, Britain was connected to India, a year before the telegraph arrived in America.[36] By then, India had 28,000 kilometres of telegraph.[37] However, the Britain-India line had many problems. It was only in 1870, after two more lines were laid, that Britain and India were linked by an efficient telegraph line that regularly conveyed messages in about five hours.[38] In 1871, a cable linked India with Penang, Saigon, Hong Kong, and Shanghai, and another went from Singapore to Java and Port Darwin. Europe was now in contact with Southeast Asia, China, and Australia.[39]

Other regions were connected to the telegraph in Britain. North America was connected by 1867, Australia and Japan by 1872, Brazil and Argentina by 1873, and the rest of the world thereafter.[40] In 1879, a cable was laid from Aden to South Africa, along the East coast of Africa.[41] In 1885, two cables were laid from Europe to South Africa along the west coast of Africa. Between 1860 and 1890, the globe was effectively encircled by submarine telegraph cables laid, owned and operated by the British.[42] The industry also was consolidated into one giant monopoly by the 1870s under the Eastern and Associated Companies. Of the approximately 190,000 miles of submarine cables in the world in 1900, 72 per cent were British owned, mostly by Eastern and Associated.[43] The cable firms were supported by subsidies from the British government. The cables gave value to some deserted islands around the world when they served as relay stations for the telegraph network. The telegraph networks served the purpose of keeping the European empires together. The shipping companies could control the movement of their fleet of ships from a headquarters half a world away.

At the turn of the century, the British government developed a separate system of cables, known as the "All Red" routes, which touched only Britain and the territories it possessed.[44] Britain's largest telegraph company manufactured two-thirds of the cables used in the nineteenth century and almost half thereafter.[45] In 1896, there were 30 cable-laying ships in the world, of which 24 were British-owned.[46] This extensive network, and monopoly on cable-laying and manufacture, proved to be valuable during World War I. It allowed Britain to maintain continuous communications with its territories while monitoring and disrupting enemy communications. On 5 August 1914, a day after declaring war on Germany, Britain cut Germany's direct telegraph cables to the world outside Europe.[47] These cables remained disabled for the duration of the war, leaving Germany with only one indirect cable that ran through London and allowed British Intelligence to intercept its messages.[48]

The British built an extensive network of railways in the Indian sub-continent to enable them to transport natural resources, and troops in wartime. The first rail went into service in 1853 from Bombay to Thane. Many companies sprang up and all of them were guaranteed four-and–a half to five per cent profit with the Indian treasury paying for any deficit.[49] The shareholders of these companies were, of course, wealthy Britons. Of the 50,000 holders of Indian railroad shares in 1868, only 400 were Indian. The shares could only be traded in London. The exploitation and loss of Indian labour was huge. The construction of the rail line between Mumbai and Poona, through the Western Ghats of India, was considered as one of the most challenging engineering feats of the mid-19th century. The most difficult section was the Bhor Ghat Railway incline. Constructed between 1856 and 1863, it used tens of thousands of Indian workers up to an average daily maximum of 40,000 in 1860 and 1861. It is estimated that 25,000 Indian men, women and children died due to accidents and disease in the construction of the Bhor Ghat Railway incline.[50] By 1872, India had over 5,000 miles of track. By 1902, British India (including Burma) had 25,936 miles of railroads, more than the rest of Asia put together, and over three times as much as that of Africa.[51] It was the fourth largest railway network in the world.[52] However, it is estimated that 40 per cent of the capital raised for India's colonial-era railways was spent in England.[53] The policy was to hire British contractors and discourage Indian enterprise. Skilled workers and engineers were brought from Britain. Rail, locomotives, rolling stock and other iron products were all imported. Wooden sleepers and coal was also imported in some cases.

The Rhyme and Repeat of History

All the events narrated in this chapter are episodic and snippets of a particularly unique moment in history when a few nations from Europe could subjugate and control major portions of the globe among themselves. However, the rhyming and repetition of history can still be felt in present times in some measure. The world is still divided between "have and have not" nations. Less developed nations struggle to close the gap of development with developed ones. Some nations in East Asia achieved remarkable success but many others continue to struggle. Infrastructure development promises to provide that 'leap-frog' effect. However, infrastructure development requires finance. Finance is often deployed on the basis of viability and return on investment.

Rich natural resources do not automatically guarantee economic prosperity. It was true in the past, and it is true in the present. Venezuela, South Sudan and Congo are some examples that come to mind. Infrastructure development did not necessarily benefit the host nation. Egypt and the Ottoman Empire provided revenue guarantees, labour, land and other hefty benefits to companies undertaking the Canal and rail projects. They expected these projects to aid in providing economic prosperity and security. The infrastructure projects became part of the intense political competition in Europe at the time. Benefits, if any, accrued to foreigners. The companies used construction material and the expertise of their home industry. Financiers with the requisite capital and political leaders dictated terms. Of the 300,000,000 francs (£ 12,000,000) spent on the Suez Canal, one third went for political, promotional, and "incidental expenses" to lobby for and promote the Canal in Paris, London, Cairo and Constantinople.[54]

Major infrastructure projects can alter geography in ways that profoundly affect trade and security in the region, and beyond. The Suez and Panama canals are two such examples. China's bid to have accessible corridors through Pakistan and Myanmar to the Indian Ocean is a continuation of this endeavour to alter geography. Its reclamation on the maritime features in the South China Sea is another example. Remote regions that were not accessible may become attractive destinations. Remote islands may become important as docking stations for underwater cables or earth stations for space programs. Harbours with little or no hinterland can become bunkering stations.

Similarly, political redrawing of borders can alter connectivity and make existing infrastructure redundant. Like the Baghdad Rail project was disrupted with the division of the Ottoman territories, closer home on the Indian subcontinent, the partition of 1947 and subsequent wars blocked existing rail links. These rail links between India, Bangladesh and Nepal are now being revived decades later.

The possession of technology provides power and security. Lack of it breeds dependency and vulnerability. India knows it well, being one of the largest importers of military equipment in the world. The technology and the domain may have changed but the basic principle has not. If it was valid for infantry weapons and steam gunboats earlier, it is equally valid for cyber and space today. Surveillance technology and social media provide insidious methods to control populations without physically invading a nation or pointing a weapon at its population. The race for laying underwater cables still continues. Earlier, it was for the telegraph network, now it is for Internet and telecommunications. Whoever has physical access to the cables can possibly eavesdrop on the data passing through it, regardless of whatever form it may be.

The railways are the best example to explain the dependency of technology standards. If a nation sets up a railway line of a particular standard, its options for expansion get tied down to that standard. This includes the width of track, the traction, the signalling system, and so on. If there are railway tracks of different standards, they will not be compatible to run one train seamlessly on them. This is true for all industries and products. The present competition to capture 5G telecom standards is one of the many underway.

Infrastructure building, even if by private companies, had its share of intervention by the state, with its associated policies and politics. Companies that ran steamship liners and the telegraph services benefitted from subsidies of the state. The canal or the railway line was often important enough to be discussed and negotiated even at the level of heads of state.

It is a fair argument that we are no longer in the colonial era. The yoke of colonialism was overthrown in the twentieth century. International norms and international laws have progressed. Nations, howsoever large and powerful, still have to take cognizance of their international reputation. Some of the strategically located territories that were important centuries ago have returned to the limelight but with a difference. They are now sovereign nations. This provides these nations the opportunity to manoeuvre around the requirements of larger powers to extract benefits for themselves.

Conclusion

This first part of the book, consisting of three chapters, has provided the background for the chapters that follow. The first chapter looked at the Indo-Pacific Region. This is the region consisting of the Indian and Pacific oceans where great power rivalry between the USA and China is playing out. The way it ends will have ramifications over the rest of this century. The second chapter provided a snapshot of five millennia of maritime history in the Indo-Pacific region to stress the point that trade across the region was segmented and different people dominated trade in each segment at different times. No nation can claim primary ownership over this maritime tradition of five millennia. The third chapter looked at the intersection of technology and infrastructure with geopolitics to stress the point that the present debate over the motive of the BRI is not something new. Infrastructure development was something that great empires and powers have undertaken in the past. Invariably, it got intertwined with economic extraction and projection of power.

The next section of the book will look at all the infrastructure initiatives, primarily in the maritime domain, by regional and extra-regional nations in the Indo-Pacific Region.

NOTES

1. Daniel R. Headrick, *The Tools of Empire: Technology and European Imperialism in the Nineteenth Century* (New York and Oxford: Oxford University Press, 1981), 17.
2. Andrew Lambert, "The Pax Britannica and the advent of Globalization" in *Maritime Strategy and Global Order: Markets, Resources, Security*, Eds. Daniel Moran and James A. Russel (Washington, DC: Georgetown University Press, 2016), 8.
3. Headrick, *The Tools of Empire*, 33.
4. Headrick, *The Tools of Empire*, 48.
5. Headrick, *The Tools of Empire*, 53.
6. Headrick, *The Tools of Empire*, 54.
7. Headrick, *The Tools of Empire*, 144.
8. Headrick, *The Tools of Empire*, 145.
9. Headrick, *The Tools of Empire*, 147-148.
10. C.A. Gibson Hill, "The Steamers employed in Asian Waters, 1819-39", *Journal of the Malayan Branch of the Royal Asiatic Society*, Vol. 27, No. 1 (165) (May,1954), 120-162.
11. Headrick, *The Tools of Empire*, 134.

12. Hill, "The Steamers employed in Asian Waters, 1819-39", 120-162.
13. Headrick, *The Tools of Empire*, 138.
14. Hill, "The Steamers employed in Asian Waters, 1819-39", 120-162.
15. Headrick, *The Tools of Empire*, 133.
16. Headrick, *The Tools of Empire*, 138-139.
17. Headrick, *The Tools of Empire*, 171.
18. Lambert, "The Pax Britannica and the advent of Globalization", 8.
19. Lambert, "The Pax Britannica and the advent of Globalization", 11.
20. Lambert, "The Pax Britannica and the advent of Globalization", 12.
21. Lambert, "The Pax Britannica and the advent of Globalization", 12.
22. Headrick, *The Tools of Empire*, 151.
23. Headrick, *The Tools of Empire*, 154-155.
24. Headrick, *The Tools of Empire*, 150.
25. Headrick, *The Tools of Empire*, 155.
26. Headrick, *The Tools of Empire*, 156.
27. Jonathan E. Hillman, *The Emperor's New Road: China and the project of the Century*, (New Haven and London: Yale University Press, 2020), p. 22.
28. Edward Mead Earle, *Turkey, the Great Powers and the Baghdad Railways: A study in Imperialism* (New York, The Macmillan Company: 1924), 29-30.
29. Earle, *Turkey, the Great Powers and the Baghdad Railways*, 34-35.
30. Earle, *Turkey, the Great Powers and the Baghdad Railways*, 93.
31. Earle, *Turkey, the Great Powers and the Baghdad Railways*, 77-78.
32. Earle, *Turkey, the Great Powers and the Baghdad Railways*, 245.
33. Headrick, *The Tools of Empire*, 158.
34. Headrick, *The Tools of Empire*, 158.
35. Headrick, *The Tools of Empire*, 158.
36. Headrick, *The Tools of Empire*, 159.
37. Hillman, *The Emperor's New Road*, 29.
38. Headrick, *The Tools of Empire*, 160.
39. Headrick, *The Tools of Empire*, 161.
40. Lambert, "The Pax Britannica and the advent of Globalization", 11.
41. Headrick, *The Tools of Empire*, 161.
42. Lambert, "The Pax Britannica and the advent of Globalization", 19.
43. Headrick, *The Tools of Empire*, 162.
44. Jonathan E. Hillman, *Influence and Infrastructure: The strategic stake of foreign projects*, (Washington, DC: Centre for Strategic and International Studies (CSIS), 2019).
45. Hillman, *Influence and Infrastructure*.
46. Hillman, *Influence and Infrastructure*.
47. Hillman, *Influence and Infrastructure*.
48. Hillman, *Influence and Infrastructure*.
49. Headrick, *The Tools of Empire*, 184.
50. Ian Kerr, "The building of the Bhor Ghat Railway incline in western India in The mid-19th century" in *Railroads in historical context: Construction, costs and consequences*, Eds. Anne Mccants, Eduardo Beira, Jose M. Lopes Cordeiro and Paulo Lourenco, Vol. I (MIT Portugal: 2011), 343-346.
51. Headrick, *The Tools of Empire*, 187.
52. John Hurd and Ian J. Kerr, *India's Railway History: A Research Handbook*, (Brill: 2012), 2.
53. Headrick, *The Tools of Empire*, 188.
54. Headrick, *The Tools of Empire*, 152.

PART II

THE PRESENT

4

The Belt and Road Initiative

The Beginning

The Belt and Road Initiative (BRI) has two components – the continental Silk Road Economic Belt (or the Belt) and the Maritime Silk Road (or the Road). It is supposed to be the most expansive and ambitious vision being enacted in the 21st century with a timeline of four decades ending in 2049. As of January 2021, 140 countries had signed the Memorandum of Understanding (MoU) of the BRI.[1] Although estimates for the total investment in BRI over two decades range from $ 1 trillion to $ 8 trillion, investment tracking is not exact since the countries and projects that are considered part of BRI are hardly clear.

The popular narrative is to trace the BRI from two speeches made by President Xi Jinping in 2013. However, the genesis of the BRI can be traced to earlier times. The Chinese economy started its remarkable run of double digit growth for four decades after the initiation of reforms in 1979 by Deng Xiaoping. However, the economic prosperity was primarily concentrated in the coastal regions of the east. By the 1990s, the consequences of inequitable economic growth began to exercise the minds of the Chinese leadership. Social unrest amongst the minority communities in Tibet and Xinjiang Uyghur Autonomous regions lent further urgency to the issue. Several measures taken to address it included creating infrastructure and improving connectivity, one of which was the Great Western Development Plan launched in 1999-2000.

With agreement on its land borders with Russia, China started concentrating on improving its linkages with its neighbouring continental nations. China has always been wary of US intentions. Post the Cold War, it found its maritime space constricted by the presence of the USA and its allies in the 'chains of islands'. A line of thought called "Go West" prevailed. It advocated concentrating westward on land to increase China's strategic space without the risk of conflict, provide economic prosperity to the interior provinces and to provide connectivity with Europe. The lack of a strong US presence in the regions of Central and Eastern Europe was considered helpful for this endeavour. In 2001, PLA General Liu Yazhou proposed setting up trading hubs along the western border and connecting them to Central Asia and Europe.[2] Peking University's Dean of International Studies, Wang Jisi, proposed a similar plan called the "March West Strategy" in 2012.

China settled its land borders with the Central Asian countries, Vietnam and Laos, even giving up substantial claims in some cases.[3] With economic prosperity came the need for energy resources and the Central Asian countries promised to be a major source. China started to invest heavily in the sector in Central Asia, including construction of pipelines. All these projects were later amalgamated under the BRI umbrella.

The 2008 financial crisis was the point when the Chinese leadership sensed a weakening of Western institutions. China was already economically powerful, even providing a $ 586 billion economic stimulus to revive its economy post the financial crisis. The population was young but an ageing profile was looming ahead. Moreover, there were important anniversaries coming up. The Chinese leadership estimated that there was a strategic window for China to seize the initiative for primacy in Asia and its position on the world stage. The switch from 'hide your capacity and bide your time' to a more assertive policy commenced in the Hu Jintao era.

A study group for the BRI was set up before Xi Jinping assumed the highest office. China's Ministry of Foreign Affairs and the Chinese Academy of Social Sciences had started to jointly work on the idea in 2011.[4] Although everyone traces the BRI to the two speeches made by President Xi Jinping in 2013, the speeches were so inconspicuous that their import was not realised till much later. The speeches are, of course, the one made at Nazarbayev University in Astana on 7 September 2013 in which he mentioned the Silk Road Economic Belt, and the one made to the Parliament of Indonesia on 2 October 2013 in which he mentioned the Maritime Silk Road. The choice of Kazakhstan and Indonesia was unexceptional. One country is at the centre of the Eurasian land route and the other in the maritime route from the Pacific to the Indian Ocean. Both speeches conveyed the historical imagery of ancient times in which Chinese prosperity contributed to global prosperity in a peaceful and cooperative manner. They, in effect, claimed historical ownership over both these routes.

The import of the two announcements was comprehended only when the follow-up actions happened. The SREB and 21st century-MSR were officially endorsed at the CPC level.[5] With its integration into the central government's foreign and economic policies, all government agencies and entities, including related think tanks and academic centres, started to work on providing substance to the initiative laid out by the Chinese leadership. A central 'Leading Small Group' chaired by Vice Premier Wang Huning was formed in March 2015. An office was established in the National Development and Reform Commission (NDRC), China's top economic planning agency, to coordinate the work.[6] The lexicon of the BRI found its way into the highest levels of government by 2015. It was incorporated into the government's 13th Five Year Plan. Considerable diplomatic persuasion was expended in explaining and signing on nations to this initiative. Local governments, academic institutions and state enterprises were galvanised into the conduct of activities to support the BRI. Events were organised under the auspices of the BRI.

The vision paper of the BRI was released on 28 March 2015. The fact that it was unveiled 17 months after the initial announcements is symptomatic of the organic nature of this enterprise. The paper itself was a laundry list of good intentions that left more things unsaid than what it revealed. This mega vision announcement did not mention any specific projects or timeline or other details that would be considered mandatory in any such endeavour. In fact, there are no official maps either.

The Belt and Road Forum for International Cooperation was held on 14-15 May 2017 in Beijing to officially roll out the BRI. Twenty-nine Heads of State and Government attended the event.[7] There were certain

European nations that had reservations on the BRI but attended the event nevertheless. When the final MoU was signed, EU nations did not sign citing disagreement on the omission of social and environmental sustainability, and lack of transparency regarding public tendering. India was one of the major absentees that refused to join the endeavour on account of, amongst other things, the disregard to its sovereignty with CPEC running through its territory occupied by Pakistan. However, India was an outlier in this regard as even nations that later expressed misgivings on the BRI, attended the event.

On 18 October 2017, the BRI was included in the CPC Constitution as part of the "Thought on Socialism with Chinese characteristics for a New Era". In April 2018, China set up the State International Development Cooperation Agency (SIDCA) to coordinate foreign development collaboration. It was headed by Wang Xiatao who, as Deputy Director in the NDRC, had been involved with the BRI.

The Belt

The BRI is an audacious plan that seeks to integrate the Eurasian continental landmass, the Indo-Pacific maritime region and Africa into an integrated domain through hard and soft infrastructure. Further, the Maritime Silk Route has been extended to include the Latin American and Caribbean nations, several of which have signed on to the BRI. Since there are no fixed criteria for a BRI project, any project that is fully or partly financed by the Chinese earns the moniker. The part of the enterprise that traverses the Eurasian land mass is the Silk Road Economic Belt or, more simply, the Belt.

The White Paper describes six arms of this belt – New Eurasian Land Bridge (NELB), China-Mongolia-Russia Economic Corridor (CMREC), China-Central Asia-West Asia Corridor, China Pakistan Economic Corridor (CPEC), Bangladesh China India Myanmar (BCIM) and China Indo-China Peninsula Corridor.[8]

The NELB consists of a series of rail corridors from the east coast of China to cities in Europe traversing about 12,000 kilometres. The rail route passes through Urumqui in Xinjiang region and moves north-west through Kazakhstan and joins the Russian rail network at Yekaterinburg. It thereafter traverses through Belarus and Poland to reach Western Europe.

The CMREC has a central route, also known as "Prairie Road", which starts from the port city of Tianjin in North East China. It moves north-west to enter Mongolia at Erenhot and thereafter moves through Mongolia and enters Russia to join the Trans-Siberian rail at Ulan Ude.

The China-Central Asia-West Asia Economic Corridor starts from Xinjiang in China. It exits China at Alashankou and thereafter traverses through Kazakhstan, Kyrgyzstan, Tajikistan, Uzbekistan, Turkmenistan, Iran and Turkey.

The China Pakistan Economic Corridor (CPEC) runs between Kashgar in Xinjiang and Gwadar in Pakistan.

The Bangladesh China India Myanmar (BCIM) Economic Corridor was envisaged as a link between Kunming in Yunnan Province of China with Kolkata, passing through Dhaka (Bangladesh) and Mandalay (Myanmar). Originally called the Kunming Initiative, it has been under discussion since the 1990s and was renamed as BCIM Economic Corridor in 1999, much before the BRI. Despite India not joining the BRI, the maps continued to show Kolkata as part of the BRI. The Joint Communiqué of the 2nd Belt and Road Forum held in May 2019 did not mention the BCIM indicating that it was no longer considered as part of the BRI. It was replaced by the China Myanmar Economic Corridor (CMEC).

The China Indo-China Peninsula Economic Corridor extends from China's Pearl River delta to cover Vietnam, Cambodia, Laos, Thailand, Malaysia and Singapore.

The vision paper lists five major cooperation priorities – policy coordination, facilities connectivity, unimpeded trade, financial integration and people-to-people bonds.[9]

In keeping with the nebulous arrangement of the BRI, the projects have not been restricted to the routes mentioned in the vision document. The Himalayan Economic Corridor, a bilateral proposal between Nepal and China, is one such addition to the BRI.

The Belt traverses through regions with harsh terrain, political instability, territorial contestation, under-developed economies and poor security environment. All these factors add to the risks of the enterprise. Of the 68 nations that initially participated in the BRI, 33 were rated 'below investment' grade or non-rated.[10]

Financing

The capacity of China to finance this gargantuan enterprise valued at over $ 1 trillion has never been clear. Of course, it was never the case that China would finance it completely. The sources of funding were expected to be multiple, including existing multilateral financial institutions.

There are five types of financial resources deployed by China – pure aid, preferential loans, development finance, commercial loans and various special funds.[11] Pure aid is around $ 7 billion each year. Preferential loans, with repayment over 20 years and rate of interest about 2 per cent, are disbursed by EXIM of China at the rate of around $ 10 billion per year. Development finance is provided at rate of 3 to 4 per cent interest. China has also set up more than 20 special funds to finance the BRI that cumulatively promise $ 1,500 billion.[12]

Two state-owned banks, China Development Bank (CDB) and Export-Import Bank of China (EXIM of China), had received capital injections from the nation's foreign exchange reserve ($ 32 bn and $ 30 bn, respectively) to support the administration's overseas development plans better. Additionally, the four big state-owned commercial banks, Bank of China (BoC), Industrial and Commercial Bank of China (ICBC), China Construction Bank (CCB) and the Agricultural Bank of China (ABC), had also allocated capital to the CDB and EXIM of China to promote the implementation of BRI investment projects.[13]

The initial pledges of investment by China were impressive. A Silk Road Economic Fund was established on 29 December 2014 with a corpus of $ 40 billion contributed by Chinese state-owned banks and sovereign wealth funds (Chinese State Administration of Foreign Exchange, EXIM of China, the CDB and the China Investment Corporation). The CDB announced in May 2015 that it will invest over $ 890 billion.[14] It claimed to be tracking more than 900 projects in 60 countries worth nearly $ 900 billion.[15] One estimate is that by 2018, outstanding loans of CDB to BRI countries were $ 110 billion while that of EXIM of China was $ 140 billion. The other large component came from the four major state-owned commercial banks.[16]

During the fifth annual summit of the "16+1" held in 2016, Chinese Premier Le Keqiang formally launched a $ 11.1 billion investment fund run by the financial holdings of ICBC to finance infrastructure projects in Central and Eastern European (CEE) countries. The Asian

Infrastructure Investment Bank (AIIB) commenced operations in January 2016 and had a total corpus of $ 100 billion, some of which was expected to be used to finance the BRI. The New Development Bank (NDB) set up under the aegis of BRICS with a corpus of $ 100 billion was also expected to contribute. It was set up in July 2015 and commenced operations by July 2016. Other on-going projects were already being financed by organisations like the Asian Development Bank.

Timelines

The BRI is planned to be executed in three stages.[17] The mobilisation stage is from 2013 to 2016. The planning stage is from 2016 to 2021. The implementation stage is from 2021 to 2049.

Soft Infrastructure

The BRI is not just about physical infrastructure of roads, railways, pipelines, power stations and industries. It is also about the development and deployment of 'soft' infrastructure. This includes providing platforms for processing paperwork involved in multi-nation transit of trade – invoicing, payment, taxation and customs. It also includes traffic management systems, supply chain management systems and all other elements that create the ecosystem to facilitate trade and transport. On 5 July 2016, China acceded to the TIR Convention of the United Nations. The TIR system serves as a global customs clearance facilitator for international cross-border road transportation of goods for 73 nations, several of which are located along the Belt.

The BRI will also encourage the promulgation of Chinese standards in all fields – construction, finance, data management, transport, and so on. Ownership of standards in many cases means controlling access to technologies, generating revenue from royalties and licence fees, and getting a captive customer. For example, the initial project of high speed rail in a country clears the way for getting more since the subsequent tracks should match the standards of the previous ones. The current tussle over providing access to Huawei is more about control of 5G telecommunication standards. China is developing alternatives to all the present globally accepted systems such as the Society for Worldwide Interbank Financial Telecommunication (SWIFT) payment gateway.

China is also seeking to increase the international use of its currency

– the Yuan. In 2015, the International Monetary Fund gave the status of "reserve currency" to the Yuan and in October 2016 added it to the Special Drawing Rights basket. Financial instruments have been devised to encourage currency exchange in Yuan. Currency swap deals with local currency have been signed with a number of countries. The BRI will create opportunities for greater use of the Yuan in international transactions. Oil futures based on Yuan are being traded in the Shanghai Stock Exchange. This is all part of a larger design to provide a 'soft' infrastructure for the BRI. Payment gateways and electronic banking systems based on the Yuan have been developed. Although the Yuan is nowhere close to the dollar in terms of usage as an international currency, the intent of spreading its use is clear. The vision document too mentions the options for use of the Yuan.

China has also set up international courts for arbitration and settling disputes among companies participating in the BRI. The three courts are based in Beijing, Shenzhen and Xian.[18]

Digital Silk Road

The BRI plans a host of infrastructure and connectivity projects – roads, railways, pipelines, ports, power stations and industrial clusters. However, it is not just the 'steel and mortar' industries that will be exported. Telecom and IT industries will get a fillip. Routes for the rails and roads will have fibre optic lines that will form the backbone of the 'Digital Silk Road'. Telecom and IT infrastructure will enable the deployment of the soft infrastructure described earlier.

Over the last seven years, it is the Digital Silk Road that has gained traction even as the BRI slowed down. Like the BRI itself, the Digital Silk Road is an umbrella term with no common understanding of what it entails. There is no single policy document that describes what it encompasses. However, it can be broadly described as all projects related to IT and telecom connectivity. It includes hard infrastructure of telecom networks, data centres, terrestrial and undersea fibre optic cables, and satellite navigation system. Smart city infrastructure and surveillance systems for public security are another element. Riding on the infrastructure are services like e-commerce, fintech and e-governance. China is deploying Artificial Intelligence (AI) technology on a massive scale. The data required for furthering these deployments can be provided by this infrastructure.

In 2016, China's CITIC Telecom International acquired the Dutch company Linx Telecom and took over its extensive infrastructure across 14 nations in Europe and Central Asia.[19] Chinese companies are global industry leaders in telecommunications and are involved in setting up fibre optic networks across the world. The Beidou satellite navigation system is now available as a global option. By 2019, Huawei Marine had laid 59,000 km of undersea cable in 98 projects world-wide. It was sold to the Hengtong Group which is heading a consortium of telecom companies from Africa, Pakistan and Hong Kong to install the Pakistan East Africa Connecting Europe (PEACE) cable in the Indian Ocean and the Mediterranean. The backbone of the project will connect Pakistan, Djibouti, Egypt, Kenya and France. The 15,000-km cable is expected to start service by the end of 2021.

In Pakistan, a Landing Station is being constructed at Karachi. The laying of a fibre optic cable from Karachi and Gwadar to Rawalpindi is a $ 240 million project being implemented by the Pakistan Army's Special Communications Organisation along with China's Huawei Technologies.[20] The $ 37 million, 850-km fibre optic cable link from Xinjiang to Rawalpindi became operational in 2018.[21] Hence, the PEACE cable will enable China to connect up to Africa and Europe through Pakistan.

Economic Intentions

The economic intentions of the BRI are easier to fathom. First and foremost is the inequitable development of China. The nation consists of distinct zones with contrasting levels of development. One are of the eastern coastal areas (centred primarily on the delta regions of the Yangtze, Yellow and Pearl rivers) that are the densely populated, Han-majority, prosperous regions that benefitted immensely from the economic prosperity. The rest of the country lagged behind creating inequalities in regional per capita income. China has been aware of the consequences of this inequitable distribution of development. There is an official line of thought that the social unrest of the minorities in the western provinces can be quenched through economic development. Hence, there is a need to shift industries to these regions and provide connectivity to the seas and the markets in adjoining countries. The vision paper talks of Xinjiang region being the core area for the Belt and opening up westwards to Central, South and West Asia. The inner provinces of Shaanxi, Gansu,

Qinghai and Ningxia Hui Autonomous Region are to connect up to this core area. Yunnan province in the south-west will be the 'pivot' to South and Southeast Asia. Trade between Tibet and Nepal will be promoted.[22]

The second economic reason is the need to overcome the 'middle income trap'. In the cycle of economic growth, initial growth is achieved through mass production and exports. However, as time progresses, the return on investment starts diminishing due to rising production and labour costs. Hence, the growth slows down. In 2013, the wages of Chinese workers increased at nearly twice the growth rate of China's GDP.[23] China's working age population has started shrinking. In 2016, for the first time in its modern history, more capital flowed out of China than in. Outbound FDI was $ 183 billion and inbound FDI was $ 133 billion.[24] The corporate sector wants to diversify away from China. One way out of this trap is for the economy to switch over to manufacturing of niche technology items that are higher up the value chain. China has the option of shifting the industries, on which its growth depended till now, to either its western regions or to other countries.

Concurrent to this is the need for China to utilise the excess capacity of infrastructure development that it has built up. The huge fiscal stimulus, post the 2008 financial crisis, ensured massive infrastructure and real estate development within China. It also ensured setting up manufacturing capacity way beyond national requirements. This included the steel, cement and power sectors. These sectors also employ a large number of workers. One option was to cut down on this capacity. This would inevitably include retrenchment of workers. The other option was to shift this capacity to other nations.

The other asset that was lying idle was the huge volume of capital that had been deployed in low-return instruments. Deploying this in investments that could provide relatively greater returns was an incentive.

The State Owned Enterprises (SOEs) in China are massive industrial organisations that employ a large workforce and have been kept afloat with state intervention. China has approximately 150,000 SOEs accounting for 30-40 per cent of total GDP and about 20 per cent of China's total employment, with approximately 34 per cent owned by the central government and the remainder by local governments.[25] Reforms in these industrial organisations had been attempted. One aspect of those reforms entailed deploying these SOEs in projects abroad to provide them international exposure that would hopefully make them more efficient and thus create 'national champions' in various sectors.

The BRI was also seen as an attempt to rework the markets and supply chains by China. As mentioned earlier, it envisaged shifting of certain assets of production and creation of industrial clusters in other regions. At the same time, the transport corridors were primarily aimed at improving the connectivity of all regions in Asia, Europe and Africa with China. This had the twin objectives of providing accessibility to markets abroad, and accessibility to natural resources and energy required to sustain the Chinese economy. As of 2015, China was the leading global producer of 23 of the 41 elements that the British Geological Society believed were needed to "maintain our economy and lifestyle" and had a lock on supplies of nine of the 10 elements judged to be at the highest risk of unavailability.[26] China had diversified its energy sourcing and secured sources of natural resources across the globe. The BRI seeks to connect all these diverse locations to China.

Geopolitical Intentions

The economic intentions of the BRI, although not readily agreed to universally, are not fiercely debated. It is the accompanying geopolitical implications that have been the subject of much debate. The BRI reflects a change in China's foreign policy to a more active one that is aimed at shaping its external environment rather than merely adapting to it.

Much as the Chinese may disagree, the Belt has security implications and requirements woven into it. A primary concern of China that is quoted most often is what President Hu Jintao coined in November 2003 as the 'Malacca Dilemma'. Around 80 per cent of China's crude oil requirements traverse the Indian Ocean and transit through the narrow straits of Malacca, Lombok and Sunda to reach the South China Sea. The possible interdiction of these vital supply lines at these 'choke points' is an apprehension that the Chinese sought to address. Accessing oil and gas from diverse sources in Central Asia, Southeast Asia and the Arctic, apart from diversifying sources of supply, was also a step towards alleviating this concern. China is accessing oil from Kazakhstan and gas from Turkmenistan and Russia. The other step was to provide oil and gas pipeline links from the Indian Ocean littoral to China. Pipelines cannot match transport by sea in either volume or cost. Hence, the pipelines set up through Myanmar and those planned though Pakistan (if they ever come up) can never cater for China's requirements beyond a marginal level. However, it has still been touted as one of the objectives.

As was discussed earlier, the "Go West" strategy had two major objectives – to provide development to the central and western provinces and to increase strategic space by breaking through a region not dominated by the USA. The original thought that economic prosperity in the western provinces would rein in social discontent, was extended to the immediate neighbourhood. One of the antidotes to the fear of insurgents seeking refuge in neighbouring regions was to increase the presence and engagement in those regions. China desires to change the nature of its relations with these neighbours. In October 2013, President Xi Jinping hosted a Communist Party work forum in which this 'peripheral diplomacy' was outlined with four objectives – enhance political goodwill, deepen regional economic integration, increase China's cultural influence and improve regional security cooperation.[27] He spoke of "letting the awareness of *community of common destiny* take root in the neighbouring countries".[28]

The attempts for improving connectivity in Central Asia were concurrent to the setting up of forums like the Shanghai Cooperation Organisation (SCO) that were focused on security aspects like countering terrorism. The investments, assets and nationals in foreign regions allow the Chinese to claim 'residency' in the region and participate in regional forums and devise the architecture for stability for the region. In the White Paper on the Arctic, China calls itself a 'Near Arctic' power.[29] It takes a certain amount of imagination to believe that description.

Increasing Chinese investments overseas has the corollary effect of greater Chinese nationals working abroad. This in turn creates an additional responsibility for the government to work towards their security and to extricate them safely in case of any major incidents. The safe extrication of 35,000 Chinese nationals from Libya in March 2011 was the first such operation for China. Deployment of forces to undertake such an exercise at short notice obviously means that such a capability has to be built up and located in suitable places.

As the projects progressed through nations that had an unstable security environment, the security of the projects became an issue. To protect these investments, private security agencies have recruited guards for deployment along the BRI. The US firm, Frontier Services Group, was one of the most active with forward operating bases in Xinjiang and Yunnan provinces of China. In Pakistan, a separate force was created in April 2015 for proving security to CPEC projects. In Zimbabwe, air defence equipment from China was deployed to protect the natural resources that had been secured in the country. The proliferation of Chinese defence equipment and support infrastructure will, by all indications, increase in these countries. Between 2008 and 2017, China exported some $ 14.4 billion worth of conventional weapons across the globe, making it the fifth largest arms supplier in the world – behind the USA, Russia, France, and Germany.[30] Media reports had emerged of joint production of military equipment planned in the industrial clusters coming up in Pakistan under the CPEC.[31] In April 2018, the Chinese Defence Minister, General Wei Fenghe, assured the visiting Pakistani Chief of Naval Staff, Admiral Zafar Mahmood Abbasi, that China will provide "strong security guarantees" for the joint building of the BRI.[32] In September 2018, reports surfaced of Chinese military presence in the Wakhan corridor of Afghanistan. It was denied by China and it clarified that it would provide training for Afghan troops in China.[33]

A greater stake in other nations also meant that the Chinese had to abdicate the stated rule of non-involvement in the internal affairs of other nations. The change of guard in Zimbabwe when Robert Mugabe stepped down in November 2017 was reported to have happened in consultation with the Chinese. In Cambodia's 2018 parliamentary elections, China supported Prime Minister Hun Sen and the Chinese envoy attended a political rally. In Nepal, China was reported to be behind the move of the Communist parties closing ranks to capture power in February 2018 and their subsequent merger in May that year. In Malaysia, the Chinese Ambassador visited the constituencies of ruling party candidates in the run-up to the 2018 elections.[34] Greater economic ties allowed China to impose punitive costs on some countries while rewarding friendly states with material rewards. Its use of economic coercion against Mongolia, Norway and South Korea are recent examples where it leveraged trade and tourism to assert itself.

Grand Strategy

When the BRI was announced, there was a certain ambiguity to it. Even the Vision published in 2015 had such an overarching umbrella that it could encompass everything that China did abroad. Commentators wrote about it as per their perceptions of what it could be. Some felt that it was a mere rebranding exercise to club together all the numerous Chinese investments across the world. The hawkish ones saw it as a rebranding to change the perception from the ominously worded "string of pearls" to the more benign "maritime silk road". Development economists conjectured on how the BRI could be used to plug development funding for the Millennium Development Goals promulgated under the auspices of the United Nations. Some saw it as an opportunity for developing nations to build up their infrastructure by collaborating with China. The focus was primarily on the hard infrastructure and financing. Databases sprang up from numerous think tanks listing Chinese infrastructure projects in different countries.

At the other end of the spectrum was the cynicism of those wary of Chinese intentions, a line of thinking that gained traction due to the lack of clarity on most aspects of the BRI. As the BRI was unrolled and all the resources of the Chinese state apparatus were employed for it, it gained a salience reserved only for vital national projects. On 18 October 2017, the BRI was included in the CPC Constitution. It was the clearest indication, if any more was required, that the BRI was at the apex of Chinese national plans. The ultimate aim of the Chinese state is the achievement of the 'Chinese Dream' – a national goal that was pronounced by President Xi Jinping and is closely associated with him. The Chinese dream seeks to achieve 'the great rejuvenation' of the Chinese nation. With the vast resources of the state and the gargantuan efforts put into it, the multiple layers of the BRI emerged and it became clear that the BRI is the Grand Strategy through which this dream was sought to be achieved.

At the highest layer, it is evident that China is creating parallel institutions to the 'Western' order. The BRICS and SCO are two of the multilateral forums that have a heavy Chinese imprint, with the SCO having a distinct security component. The AIIB and NDB are two of the financial institutions. Arbitration courts have been set up to settle disputes emanating from BRI projects, bypassing existing international channels of arbitration. These parallel institutions flow from the strategic level down to the lower levels. China has also managed to take control of several multilateral organisations including some that operate under the UN umbrella.

The corridors to be developed will primarily enhance the connectivity of foreign countries with China rather than among themselves. They will provide physical integration to enhance the supply chains and markets for China. The financing will provide China with influence and political leverage. The infrastructure development will provide projects for Chinese companies and employment of Chinese labour. The road, rail, telecom and IT infrastructure, power generation and transmission infrastructure – all serve to cement the space for Chinese technology, standards and companies across the world. Similarly, the soft infrastructure will establish Chinese standards and companies in other domains such as accounting, banking and payment gateways.

The physical and digital links will not just be a conduit for goods and services, they will also be channels for flow of ideas and culture (in a one-sided manner?). Surveillance technology, widely used in China, is now being exported to other countries in Africa and South America. The CPC has never hidden its contempt for democracy and its fragilities, preferring to label the political system in China as a Socialist democracy. It prefers to collaborate with authoritarian regimes that provide predictability rather than with democracies in which one carefully cultivated leadership gets replaced by another that may not be as friendly.

The digital links will also provide for expansion of the parallel cyber space created in China, the part of the Internet that resides beyond the Great Firewall. There will be a larger market and more users for the Chinese equivalents of social media and e-commerce giants (Baidu, WeChat and Alibaba in lieu of Google, Twitter and Amazon, for example). The fragmentation of the Internet, which is already upon us, will deepen. With a monopoly on the IT and telecom space, it is easier to collect user data that can be used in numerous ways.

The Chinese global navigation system BeiDou has already rolled out its global services. Several countries have started using its services. As China progresses in cutting-edge technologies such as Artificial Intelligence, its futuristic products such as autonomous vehicles will find ready markets in nations that have already adapted to its IT technology and standards.

The Confucius Institutes established around the world promote learning of Chinese language, history and culture. More people than ever before are getting acquainted with the Chinese language. More and more foreign students, many of whom are on scholarships, are studying in Chinese educational institutions. As the BRI progresses, Chinese language road signs, food and other cultural artefacts that seem alien now will become ubiquitous and, perhaps, more acceptable. This acceptability will facilitate Chinese nationals settling abroad for the furtherance of personal and national goals.

The security component of the BRI has already manifested itself in several ways. This will be more evident as Chinese influence spreads across the BRI. China has already become one of the major arms exporters in the world. As more nations acquire Chinese equipment, and set up the necessary infrastructure for life-cycle support of such equipment, it will also provide a possible support network for the PLA. As foreign militaries either exercise or get trained with the PLA, interoperability will be enhanced.

All in all, it can be imagined that this Grand Strategy uniquely combines geopolitical and economic aims in a grand manner that has rarely been observed on this scale. The scenario depicted above may appear too imaginative and prejudiced but all the elements of this Grand Strategy already exist and are playing out.

Initial Gains

The initial ascendancy of the BRI narrative within the Chinese establishment and the consequent research across the world on its contours became a self-reinforcing cycle for the BRI. The more importance BRI was given within China, the more the world focussed on it, which in turn convinced the Chinese to highlight it further. In the ambiguity of those initial days, the potential for economic prosperity drew both China's provincial governments as well as foreign governments to the BRI. The Chinese diplomatic corps approached national governments to sign up with the BRI. The silent diplomatic moves were helped by some high-profile events and financial pledges. As all projects – past, present and projected – were clubbed together, it became convenient to showcase completion of older projects as success stories of the BRI.

In this initial hubris, some hard questioning that was warranted did not happen. Even the USA was ambivalent and did not offer any significant pushback. Europe saw it primarily as an economic vision and no alarm bells rang on its strategic implications. Central and Eastern

European countries were particularly receptive and signed on with the BRI in large numbers. In May 2015, China and Russia signed an agreement pledging to find areas of cooperation between the Eurasian Economic Union (EEU) and China's BRI that would finally result in a free trade area.

Since past projects were also included under the rubric of the BRI, some of them were shown as its rewards. China had invested heavily in upstream petroleum facilities in Kazakhstan and Turkmenistan. The Kazakhstan-China oil pipeline has been in operation since 2005. Turkmenistan has three operational gas pipelines connecting it to Xinjiang, which the CNPC helped to construct between 2009 and 2013.[35] The Eurasian Land Bridge rail network has effectively operated since the 1990s.[36] These provided the 'low hanging fruit' to showcase the BRI. A train from Chongqing in China to Duisburg in Germany has been in operation since 2011 as part of the NELB.[37] New services of freight trains were opened between China and cities in Europe such as Warsaw, Duisburg, Madrid and Hamburg. The first cargo train from China to London completed its journey in January 2017. The first cargo train from China reached Amsterdam in March 2018.

China has long been a major investor in Central Asia's infrastructure building and natural resource extraction. During President Xi's tour to Central Asia in September 2013, contracts were signed with Kazakhstan ($ 30 billion), Uzbekistan ($ 15 billion), and Turkmenistan ($ 16 billion). Loans and aid were promised to Turkmenistan ($ 8 billion) and Tajikistan ($ 1 billion).[38] Deals were signed for Turkmenistan's gas reserves and Kazakhstan's oil deposits. Railway connectivity that was conceived before the advent of the BRI made progress. The Xian-Almaty international cargo train that commenced in November 2013 became one of the fastest modes for freight between China and the Central Asian Republics reducing the travel time of 26 days by road to only six.[39] In May 2015, a joint plan was announced for a rail line across Kazakhstan from Khorgos to Aktau, a Caspian Sea port. The Khorgos Gateway dry port, a key logistics hub, became operational in August 2015. On the other side of the Caspian, the Baku-Tbilisi-Kars rail (built by Azerbaijan, Georgia and Turkey) became operational in October 2017.

The first regular freight train from Yiwu in China arrived in Tehran in February 2016 after 14 days of travel.[40] Rail projects have progressed further westward towards Turkey and to the Iranian port of Bushehr.

In April 2015, China committed $ 46 billion to the CPEC over a period of 15 years of which about 76 per cent was for power projects and the rest for infrastructure, transport and communications. This became the flagship programme of the BRI. Projects were added on to it raising the pledged investment to $ 62 billion.

Misgivings

India did not join the BRI and was among the first countries to flag issues with the BRI. The CPEC runs through Gilgit-Baltistan, a region that is part of the Union Territory of Ladakh. A bilateral arrangement between China and Pakistan through this region was an obvious compromise on Indian sovereignty. India refused to climb onto the BRI bandwagon citing this infringement as also the fact that the BRI was a unilateral Chinese declaration rather than the result of a consultative process.

The spokesperson of the Ministry of External Affairs gave a detailed explanation on 13 May 2017 for the reasons why India had declined the invitation to attend the Belt and Road Forum.[41] "Connectivity initiatives must be based on universally recognized international norms, good governance, rule of law, openness, transparency and equality" and must "follow principles of financial responsibility to avoid projects that would create unsustainable debt burden for communities; balanced ecological and environmental protection and preservation standards; transparent assessment of project costs; and skill and technology transfer to help long term running and maintenance of the assets created by local communities". They "must be pursued in a manner that respects sovereignty and territorial integrity". "No country can accept a project that ignores its core concerns on sovereignty and territorial integrity". It was a position to which a lot of other nations aligned themselves with over the next two years. The misgivings kept rising and in that sense, 2018 was the watershed.

Apart from the fact that there was only a vision without any blueprint or coherent database of projects, discerning commentators pointed out certain basic economic truths. Maritime transport is cheaper than road and rail, and has unchallenged capacity. Even if the train journey is shorter, it can only cater for certain niche products that are not too bulky. Moreover, the differing standards of rail tracks across Eurasia presented a different set of challenges. There were reports of trains returning empty from Europe. The cost of rail transport was being subsidised by the

Chinese government under the BRI.[42] Similarly, pipelines cannot substitute for oil and gas tankers/carriers in either cost or capacity. For China's energy resources being sourced from West Asia and Africa, the 'Malacca dilemma' (and indeed every other maritime 'dilemma' along the sea route), if ever there was one, will continue to remain. The pipelines through Myanmar can provide only a minor fraction of the requirements. The pipelines through Pakistan, if they are envisaged, will face even greater technical challenges of pumping oil over high altitude passes.

In time, some other apprehensions of the BRI surfaced. It was the lack of transparency that was the foremost factor. All the projects were the result of bilateral negotiations. The terms and conditions were opaque and the tendering procedure as per global norms was not followed, with a majority of the contracts going to Chinese SOEs. The methodology for costing of the projects was questionable, with allegations of 'brass-plating'. Chinese labour and material from China were used with the benefits of employment not percolating down to the local population. A Grisons Peak report of 2015 observed that two-thirds of loans extended under the BRI have been tied to the involvement of Chinese companies.[43] The CSIS Reconnecting Asia Project estimated that of all the contractors participating in Chinese-funded transportation projects tracked by it, 89 per cent are Chinese companies, 7.6 per cent are local companies (companies headquartered in the same country where the project was being implemented), and 3.4 per cent are foreign companies (non-Chinese companies from a country other than the one where the project was planned). In comparison, out of the contractors participating in projects funded by the multilateral development banks, 29 per cent are Chinese, 40.8 per cent are local, and 30.2 per cent are foreign.[44]

The reallocation of markets and technology undertaken under the ambit of the BRI meant that low-technology like coal-fired power generation plants found its way to the recipient countries raising environmental concerns. In a report of January 2017, the global rating agency, Fitch, warned that BRI "projects might not be aimed at addressing the most pressing infrastructure needs and could fail to deliver expected returns".[45] Concerns over quality and corruption were also highlighted, some by political rivals during the election campaigns or after a change in government. Chinese investments have been linked to cases of corruption in Kyrgyzstan and Kazakhstan.[46] In Sri Lanka, Chinese firms involved in the development of Colombo and Hambantota ports were accused of illegally funnelling funds to the election campaign of Mahinda Rajapaksa.[47] In Bangladesh, the Chinese firm CHEC was blacklisted in 2018 for offering bribes to the country's communications secretary. Its parent company, CCCC, was debarred by the World Bank for eight years over fraud and corruption in a Philippines road project.[48]

'Debt Trap'

China has emerged as one of the world's largest providers of development finance. Between 2000 and 2014, it extended a total of $ 354 billion in loans, grants, and other resources to countries across the globe.[49] Its development finance differs from that of other countries. Over 75 per cent of China's worldwide financing between 2000 and 2014 did not meet the strict Official Development Assistance (ODA) standards set by the Organisation for Economic Co-operation and Development (OECD).[50] Rather, China's development finance is often categorised as Other Official Flows (OOF), which represent funding that is typically less concessional than ODA and is not necessarily designed to promote the economic development and welfare of recipient countries. They are akin to commercial loans that have to be repaid with interest. This means that China seeks economic returns on much of its aid financing. Development finance from other major economies, such as the USA, the EU, and Japan, typically conforms to OECD standards.

The landmark event that turned the tide of opinion against the BRI was the equity sale of Hambantota Port in December 2017. Under a $ 1.12 billion deal, Chinese firms now hold a majority stake in the port and a 99-year lease agreement to operate it. The dangers of the unsustainable loans taken by smaller nations became the central theme for discussions. In April 2018, the Managing Director of IMF, Christine Lagarde, advised Chinese policy makers against financing unsustainable projects in countries with heavy debt burdens. The IMF country reports highlighted the perilous state of economies like Djibouti. In March 2018, the Centre for Global Development released an authoritative study on the debt implications of the BRI. It indicated that 23 of the 68 countries participating in the BRI were at risk of debt distress. The eight countries at the highest risk (with their 2018 forecast of public debt as percentage of GDP) were identified as Tajikistan (56.8), Laos (70.3), Kyrgyzstan (65.5), Mongolia (89), Maldives (109), Montenegro (80.9), Djibouti (87.5) and Pakistan (67.6).[51] EXIM of China had provided $ 1.4 billion to Djibouti that was equivalent to 75 per cent of its GDP. Moody's analytic reports also brought out the rising levels of debt in many countries. Chinese lending to Sub Saharan African (SSA) governments rose nearly tenfold to more than $ 10 billion a year between 2012 and 2017, from less than $ 1 billion in 2001.[52] Much of the lending has focused on infrastructure projects, including the power, transport, and communication sectors. Angola, the Republic of the Congo, and Zambia were reported as among the most indebted to Chinese creditors. In Ghana, Angola, Zambia, and Nigeria, interest payments were absorbing more than 20 per cent of revenue. Zambia's external position was particularly fragile, given its very low foreign exchange reserves.

Hambantota was the first in a list of projects that were reported as unviable and pushing the recipient nations towards high debt. There were doubts about the viability of grandiose projects in thinly-populated regions that did not make economic sense; casinos and business districts in the South Pacific Islands being apt examples. The $ 6.7 billion railway China is funding in Laos is more than a third of the country's GDP.[53] The Matala Rajapaksha airport in Sri Lanka set up at a cost of $ 270 million earned the moniker of the 'emptiest airport in the world' and had to be shut down in June 2018 due to lack of flights. A highway being built in Montenegro to link the port of Bar to Serbia was expensive enough for a re-think after completion of the first 41 km of the 180 km planned.[54] The Standard Gauge Rail (SGR) from Mombasa to Nairobi in Kenya struggled to break even in operational costs. The Belgrade-Budapest rail line that was supposed to be the most high profile project of the BRI in Europe has run into problems too numerous to be chronicled here.[55] It is now projected to be ready by 2025. The government of Maldives elected in September 2018 was calculating its debt till months after the election.

It did not help matters that no details of Chinese loans were forthcoming, leading to considerable speculation regarding the conditions of the loans. This was particularly true for developing nations that lacked institutional transparency or sufficient accountability regulations. Chinese funding comprises a variety of credit arrangements ranging from fully commercial loans to interest-free loans, with some carrying sovereign guarantees meaning the recipient state was obliged to bridge outstanding debt liabilities. Whenever some of the details became public, there were surprises like sovereign guarantees on returns of investment in Pakistan and provision for taking over a facility in case of failure of repayment as was the case for an airport in Zambia. Smaller nations like Tonga openly appealed to China to restructure their debt to ease their burden. Debt relief provided by China has been considerable but it has been on a case-to-case basis where the quid pro quo is not always clear. The Paris Club is a grouping of creditor nations. China is not a member of the Paris Club and hence does not abide by its internationally acceptable standards of debt structuring.

As reports of debts emanated from across the globe – Venezuela in South America, Tonga in the South Pacific Islands, Pakistan and Sri Lanka in South Asia, and Zambia, Djibouti and Sierra Leone in Africa – the 'debt trap' narrative became a convenient route to broad-brush all commentary on the BRI. Some commentators alleged that China was deliberately pushing these countries towards unsustainable debts to take over their assets. Data from the Pacific Islands and Africa indicated that high debt levels were not necessarily due to loans from China but due to loans from other sources as well.

Sri Lanka's debt repayment problems were not solely due to Chinese loans since they comprised about 10 per cent of Sri Lanka's total foreign debt.[56] Of this debt, over 60 per cent was lent to Sri Lanka on concessional terms, typically at a fixed rate of 2 per cent (with other fees of 0.5 per cent) and average maturity of 15–20 years. The remaining 40 per cent was non-concessionary loans. Eighty per cent of such non-concessionary loans were from international capital markets. As a result of these high-interest borrowings, Sri Lanka faced foreign debt repayment of nearly $ 6 billion in 2019. Leasing the Hambantota Port was part of a strategy to find cash and stave off pressures on the available fund of reserves.

Venezuela's economy collapsed due to its internal mismanagement rather than any Chinese intervention. In fact, this has resulted in the single largest loss of Chinese capital estimated at $ 20 billion of the $ 62.2 billion lent by China to the Development Bank since 2007.[57]

Pushback

As the BRI narrative unravelled, the pushback against it started gaining momentum. French President Emmanuel Macron noted during his January 2018 visit to China that the Silk Road "cannot be one way" and that it was "never only Chinese". In January 2018, the Australian Minister for International Development, Concetta Fierravanti-Wells, criticised

Chinese projects as building "a road that does not go anywhere". In April 2018, twenty-seven of the 28 EU country ambassadors in China compiled a report criticising the SREB.[58] Hungary was the sole withholder.

The trend got stronger with change of governments in several countries that replaced those considered supportive to the Chinese. Chinese-funded projects got ensnared in the election campaigning with accusations of corruption. The new governments promised re-consideration of projects and even alleged corruption by the previous government. In Malaysia, Prime Minister Mahathir Mohamad cancelled the Trans-Sabah Gas pipeline (TSGP) and Multipurpose Gas pipeline projects. He also announced reconsideration of the $ 15.7 billion East Coast Rail Link, the single largest project in the BRI. The government commenced investigating links between the graft-stained 1MDB state investment fund of the previous government and Chinese funding. Myanmar renegotiated the Kyakpyu port and SEZ project to reduce the debt burden.

Even staunch ally Pakistan announced the cancellation of some power projects as part of the BRI and sought a change in the alignment of the CPEC. Bangladesh, whose economy has been booming lately, has been circumspect about taking Chinese loans. In 2016, it had turned down China's offer to develop a deep-sea port at Sonadia in favour of a Japanese proposal for a port at Matarbari, just 25 km away. In July 2018, the *Financial Times* quoted a RWR Advisory group report that 234 out of 1,674 Chinese-funded projects announced in 66 BRI countries since 2013 had encountered difficulties.[59]

Hit with the reality of the geopolitical implications of the BRI and the fact that nations required funding for building infrastructure, there were efforts to provide alternatives. Japan was the only other nation that was able to provide an alternative option. All the other endeavours, which we will look at in the later chapters, are still at a nascent stage. However, it became clear that an economic counter was necessary to balance the overwhelming implications of the BRI.

Internally within China, rare voices of discontent were heard against the BRI. In July 2018, Sun Wenguang, a retired professor of physics at Shandong University, wrote an open letter urging Xi Jinping to spend finances internally rather than on foreign projects. He felt that Chinese capital should not be employed abroad when it was needed to prevent the slowing down of the economy. On 24 July 2018, Xu Zhangrun, a law professor at Tsinghua University, published a lengthy online critique that, among other things, spoke against excessive international aid.

The biggest contest was not on the hard infrastructure but the soft one – technology to be more precise. China had long managed to procure high technology through various means that included foreign collaborations, takeover of foreign companies and IPR theft. Its Vision 2025 envisages propelling China towards self-sufficiency and leadership in the emerging fields of Artificial Intelligence, robotics, autonomous vehicles, etc. The USA and Europe finally took notice and initiated measures to prevent Chinese ascendancy in hi-tech sectors. In August 2018, the German government decided to stop the sale of a machine tool company, Leifeld Metal Spinning AG, to a Chinese company. The step is now being reinforced with proposed legislation seeking oversight on change in ownership in sensitive sectors. The USA has followed the same path and had even briefly banned transactions with the Chinese telecom giant, ZTE. In June 2018, Vietnam postponed legislation on setting up of SEZs after public protests over provisions that allowed land to be leased for 70 years. The Belgrade-Budapest rail line ran into objections of procedure and governance by the EU.

Recalibration

Apart from external criticism and alignment of nations against the BRI, and the internal criticism, a major cause for concern was the slowing down of the Chinese economy. The capacity of China to finance the BRI became doubtful. The Chinese economy had a dream run, post reform in 1979, due to its low cost production. This export-oriented economy got a severe jolt during the financial crisis of 2008. To boost the economy, China resorted to massive fiscal stimulus and investment in infrastructure. However, one of the after-effects was burgeoning internal debts. Between 2008 and 2018, China's gross debt exploded from 171 to 299 per cent of GDP.[60] China started balancing between the economically opposite steps of cleaning up its economy (shadow banking, etc.) while still resorting to investments to boost growth. However, growth inevitably tapered. On top of that, China and the USA got into a tariff war. The result was a decline in its foreign exchange reserves and its funding of BRI projects. As per a report of the Rhodium Group, China's overseas infrastructure lending has been declining since 2017.[61] Lending by CDB and EXIM of China dropped more drastically from a peak of $ 75 billion in 2016 to $ 4 billion in 2019.[62]

The public pronouncements on the BRI by Chinese government agencies and media also began to fall perceptibly. The boasting and self-congratulatory tone mellowed to a certain extent. It was apparent that the Chinese were aware of the headwinds and negative perceptions on the BRI, and were re-calibrating their steps to make it more acceptable. This change in direction was expected to be seen in the 2nd Belt and Road Forum.

Thirty-six Heads of State/Government attended the 2nd Belt and Road Forum held in Beijing in March 2019.[63] President Xi Jinping spoke about "extensive consultation", "green development", "sustainable development", adopting "widely accepted rules and standards", "people-centred approach", ensuring "commercial and fiscal sustainability of all projects" and "intellectual property protection".[64] He welcomed the participation of other multilateral and national financial institutions in the BRI. Release of documents on "Guiding Principles of Financing" and "Debt Sustainability Framework" was announced. The Joint Communiqué, also drafted on similar lines, spoke of "high quality, clean, resilient and sustainable infrastructure", "international anti-corruption cooperation" and "open, transparent and non-discriminatory public procurement procedures".[65]

Headline-grabbing news of the BRI receded but Chinese companies continue to progress. China has 27 firms among the top 100 global contractors, up from nine in 2000, whereas the USA has 7, down from 19.[66] While regular direct rail freight services from China to Europe did not exist earlier, by 2018 roughly 35 Chinese cities were connected with 34 European cities.[67] The BRI now has new narratives – "Health Silk Road" and "Green Silk Road".[68] The "Green Silk Road" is in line with President Xi Jinping's pledge that China's carbon dioxide emissions will peak before 2030 and reach net-zero emissions by 2060. The green initiatives of the BRI are now being highlighted.[69]

Conclusion

As one goes through the chronology of the BRI, it is clear that the Chinese establishment went about it by constructing, calibrating and re-constructing the narrative as it flowed along. The speeches that are universally described as those that launched the BRI were rather innocuous. The speech that mentioned the Maritime Silk Road spoke only of links to Southeast Asia. A Leading Small Group was formed over a year later and the first guideline, with vague mottos, was released over a year-and-half later.[70] The English names for the banners kept changing, the routes kept changing and fresh "Silk Roads" were added as per the flavour of the season. If there is any blueprint for the BRI, the world is not yet aware of it. Since no one is sure which projects constitute the BRI and what the finances are, the numerous databases built by public and private organisations across the world are merely indicative. Since these databases differ in content, any study done using them reaches different conclusions. There was a phase in which even the World Bank gave remarkably positive projections about the BRI in its reports.

The timelines of the BRI stretch till 2049. Hence, any conclusion on the success of this vision is premature. In the beginning, when the contours of the vision were not clear, it got favourable coverage since it was assumed to be an economic endeavour with investments in the infrastructure sector, which are badly needed, and would benefit the participating nations. However, as the scope and scale of the endeavour was unveiled, misgivings started to rise. The year 2018 proved to be a watershed due to the reversal in the tide for the BRI. It faced headwinds globally and other nations aligned to provide alternate provisions. Exacerbating the difficulty was the slowing of the Chinese economy and the consequent curb on financing of the BRI. By the end of the year, the Chinese leadership and media had distinctly lowered the rhetoric on it. The flow of investments had also come down. Funding for the BRI has been falling since 2017. Many nations that had taken loans are finding it difficult to repay and are requesting for re-negotiations for repayment.

It would be premature to assume that the BRI is a project with dwindling prospects. Nations across Africa and LAC are not unwilling to receive Chinese support. China has been evaluating the lessons learnt and re-calibrating its approach to present a repackaged BRI in a more acceptable form. In the post-COVID world, the BRI is expected to be more focussed and pared down. However, the BRI is clearly nowhere close in terms of finance disbursement and project execution to what was envisaged in its early years.

Meanwhile, history may repeat itself yet again in China. In 2020,

China unveiled an ambitious 15-year public transport plan, post the COVID pandemic, with the aim that it will enable doubling the size of its economy by 2035.[71]

NOTES

1. Christoph Nedopil, "Countries of the Belt and Road Initiative", IIGF Green BRI Centre, 2021 accessed from https://green-bri.org/countries-of-the-belt-and-road-initiative-bri/ on 27 March 2021.
2. Nadege Rolland, *China's Eurasian Century? Political and Strategic Implications of the Belt and Road Initiative* (USA: National Bureau of Asian Research, 2017), reprinted by New Delhi: Pentagon Press, 117.
3. Richard Javad Heydarian, "The 21st Century Silk Road – Perils and Opportunities of China's Belt and Road Initiative", *ADR Publications*, 2018, 18.
4. Rolland, *China's Eurasian Century?* 48.
5. Rolland, *China's Eurasian Century?* 48.
6. Rolland, *China's Eurasian Century?* 50.
7. Zheping Huang, "China's summit for its new silk road is missing 44 heads of state from the 65 involved", *Quartz*, 12 May 17.
8. National Development and Reform Commission (NDRC), et al., *Vision and Actions on Jointly Building Silk Road Economic Belt and 21st Century Maritime Silk Road*, 28 March 2015, 4.
9. NDRC, et. al., *Vision and Actions on Jointly Building Silk Road Economic Belt and 21st Century Maritime Silk Road*, 4.
10. John Hurley, et. al., "Examining the Debt implications of the Belt and Road Initiative from a Policy Perspective", *Centre for Global Development*, March 2018, 8.
11. Weidong Liu, Yajing Zhang and Wei Xiong, "Financing the Belt and Road Initiative", *Eurasian Geography and Economics*, 2020, DOI 10.1080/15387216.2020.1716822
12. This account of finance is from Liu, Zhang and Xiong, "Financing the Belt and Road Initiative".
13. Gregory Perdon, et al., "The New Silk Road – The $2 trn journey spanning 65 countries connecting 4 bn people", *Arbuthnot Latham Investment Management*, February 2019, 23.
14. Rolland, *China's Eurasian Century?* 58.
15. Jeff M. Smith, "China's Belt and Road Initiative: Strategic Implications and International Opposition", *The Heritage Foundation*, 9 August 2018, 3.
16. Liu, Zhang and Xiong, "Financing the Belt and Road Initiative".
17. Rolland, *China's Eurasian Century?* 89.
18. "China to establish court for OBOR disputes", *Asia Times*, 25 January 2018.
19. Rolland, *China's Eurasian Century?* 86.
20. Mifrah Haque, "China builds Digital Silk Road in Pakistan to Africa and Europe", *Nikkei Asia*, 29 January 2021.
21. Haque, "China builds Digital Silk Road in Pakistan to Africa and Europe".
22. NDRC, et al., *Vision and Actions on Jointly Building Silk Road Economic Belt and 21st Century Maritime Silk Road*, 10.
23. Bruno Macaes, *Belt and Road – A Chinese World Order* (Penguin Random House India, 2019), 75.

24. Smith, "China's Belt and Road Initiative", 5.
25. Gregory Perdon, et al., "The New Silk Road", 11.
26. British Geological Survey, *Risk List 2015*, accessed from http://nora.nerc.ac.uk/id/eprint/513472/1/Risk_List_2015_FINAL.pdf on 4 March 2019.
27. Raffaello Pantucci and Sarah Lain, "China's Eurasian Pivot – The Silk Road Economic Belt", *Whitehall Paper* 88, RUSI, 2017, 14.
28. *Ministry of Foreign Affairs*, People's Republic of China, "Xi Jinping: Let the Sense of Community of Common Destiny Take Deep Root in Neighbouring Countries", 25 October 2013.
29. The State Council Information Office, People's Republic of China, *China's Arctic Policy*, 26 January 2018.
30. China Power, "How dominant is China in the global arms trade?" accessed from https://chinapower.csis.org/china-global-arms-trade/ on 5 March 2019.
31. Maria Ari-Habib, "China's 'Belt and Road' Plan in Pakistan takes a military turn", *New York Times*, 19 December 2018.
32. Macaes, *Belt and Road*, 126.
33. Michael Martina, "Afghan troops to train in China Ambassador says", *Reuters*, 6 September 2018.
34. Murray Hiebert, Under Beijing's Shadow: Southeast Asia's China Challenge (CSIS:2020), 20.
35. Pantucci and Lain, "China's Eurasian Pivot", 34.
36. Rolland, *China's Eurasian Century?* 74.
37. *HKDTC Research*, "The Belt and Road Initiative", 21 January 2016.
38. Rolland, *China's Eurasian Century?* 82.
39. Rolland, *China's Eurasian Century?* 82.
40. Rolland, *China's Eurasian Century?* 84.
41. Ministry of External Affairs, Government of India, *Official Spokesperson's response to a query on participation of India in OBOR/BRI*, 13 May 2017.
42. Gregory Perdon, et al., "The New Silk Road", 39.
43. James Kynge, "Chinese Overseas Lending Dominated by One Belt, One Road Strategy", *Financial Times*, 18 June 2015.
44. Jonathan E. Hillman, "China's Belt and Road Initiative: Five Years later", *Centre for Strategic and International Studies*, 25 January 2018.
45. "Fitch – China's One Belt One Road initiative brings risks", *Reuters*, 26 January 2017.
46. Richard Ghiasy and Jiayi Zhou, *The Silk Road economic Belt: Considering security implications and EU-China cooperation prospects* (Stockholm: SIPRI, February 2017), 23.
47. Maria Abi-Habib, "How China got Sri Lanka to cough up a port", *New York Times*, 25 June 2018.
48. Smith, "China's Belt and Road Initiative", 13.
49. *China Power*, "Where is China targeting its development finance?" accessed from https://chinapower.csis.org/china-development-finance/ on 5 March 2019.
50. *China Power*, "Where is China targeting its development finance?"
51. John Hurley, et al., "Examining the Debt implications of the Belt and Road initiative from a Policy Perspective", 14.
52. *Moody's Investor Services*, "Chinese lending to Sub Saharan Africa can support growth, but brings risks", 14 Nov 2018.

53. John Hurley, et al., "Examining the Debt implications of the Belt and Road initiative from a Policy Perspective", 17.
54. John Hurley, et al., "Examining the Debt implications of the Belt and Road initiative from a Policy Perspective", 18.
55. Andreea Brinza, "China and the Budapest-Belgrade Railway saga", *The Diplomat* 28 April 2020.
56. Dushni Weerakoon and Sisira Jayasuriya, "Sri Lanka's debt problem isn't made in China", *East Asia Forum*, 28 February 2019.
57. Joy-Perez and Scissors, "Be wary of spending on the Belt and Road", 5.
58. Dana Heidi, et al., "EU Ambassadors band together against Silk Road", *Handelsblatt Today*, 17 April 2017.
59. James Kynge, "China's Belt and Road difficulties are proliferating across the world", *Financial Times*, 9 July 2018.
60. Macaes, *Belt and Road*, 153.
61. Mathew Mingey and Agatha Kratz, "China's Belt and road: Down but not out", *Rhodium Group*, 4 January 2021.
62. Jonathan Wheatley and James Kynge, "China curtails overseas lending in face of geopolitical backlash", *Financial Times*, 8 December 2020.
63. "Second Belt and Forum Top Level Attendees", *The Diplomat*, 27 April 2019.
64. *Ministry of Foreign Affairs*, PRC, "Working Together to Deliver a Brighter Future For Belt and Road Cooperation, Keynote Speech by H.E. Xi Jinping, President of the People's Republic of China, At the Opening Ceremony of the Second Belt and Road Forum for International Cooperation", 26 April 2019.
65. *Ministry of Foreign Affairs*, PRC, "Joint Communiqué of the Leaders' Roundtable of the 2nd Belt and Road Forum for International Cooperation", 27 April 2019.
66. Deborah Brautigam and Meg Rithmire, "The Chinese 'Debt Trap' Is a Myth", *The Atlantic*, 6 February 2021.
67. Jonathan E. Hillman, "The Rise of China-Europe Railways", *Centre for Strategic and International Studies*, 6 March 2018.
68. Ministry of Foreign Affairs of the People's Republic of China, *Opening Speech by State Councillor Wang Yi At the Meeting of the Advisory Council of The Belt and Road Forum for International Cooperation, 2020*, 18 December 2020.
69. Christian Shepard, "China pours money into green Belt and Road projects", *Financial Times*, 26 January 2021.
70. Jon Yuan Jiang, "China's Unfinished Road", *APAC News*, 11 March 2021.
71. Orange Wang, "China gets 15-year transport expansion plan as it seeks to double size of economy by 2035", *South China Morning Post*, 26 February 2021.

5

Maritime Component of the BRI

Introduction

The Maritime component of the BRI or 21st Century Maritime Silk Road (MSR) or the Road, in short, is generally understood as infrastructure and connectivity projects that seek to integrate sea routes between Asia, Europe and Africa. Infrastructure projects generally follow the standard combination of a 'port-park-city' model of development. It is also known as the Shekou model after the Chinese region, in Guangdong province, in which it was very successful.

This chapter will scan the horizon starting from the eastern coast of China to the coast of East Africa to provide an account of Chinese investments across the Indo-Pacific Region. The account includes more than just port-related infrastructure to provide a larger context to Chinese investments in the region. Port projects are not stand-alone events. The connectivity and infrastructure woven around them is also relevant.

The folklore is that President Xi Jinping announced the Maritime Silk Road in his speech to the Indonesian Parliament on 2 October 2013. Perusal of the text of the speech does not reflect such an announcement. "Southeast Asia has since ancient times been an important hub along the ancient Maritime Silk Road. China will strengthen maritime cooperation with ASEAN countries to make good use of the China ASEAN Maritime Cooperation Fund set up by the Chinese government and vigorously develop maritime partnership in a joint effort to build the Maritime Silk

Road of the 21st century" was what he said.[1] Initially mooted as an ASEAN-centric project in 2013, the MSR later expanded to include the Indian Ocean, the South Pacific and Arctic regions. It has now been extended to Latin America and the Caribbean (LAC) region.

The Road

The vision document for the BRI describes two routes for the 21st Century MSR.[2] The first one is from the coast of China to Europe, through the South China Sea and the Indian Ocean. The second one is from China's coast to the South Pacific. It mentions Fujian province as the core area for the MSR. A separate vision document for the MSR was released on 20 June 2017.[3] It spoke of a third "blue economic passage" envisioned from China's coast to Europe via the Arctic Ocean. It spoke of marine conservation, marine industry, maritime connectivity, maritime security and law enforcement, marine research, and developing mechanisms for cooperation. Apart from the announcement of a third route, the other distinguishing features were emphasis on environmental conservation, maritime security and governance structures. The first could be the result of criticism that ecological sustainability was not adequately catered for in the BRI, but the other two clearly indicated China's intention to participate in maritime security and set up regional governance structures. A policy document on "Asia Pacific Security Co-operation" released earlier in January 2017 was devoted primarily to security cooperation in the Indo-Pacific region.[4]

China's Arctic Policy was released on 26 January 2018 in which it described itself as a "Near Arctic State".[5] The document spoke of scientific exploration, environmental conservation, sustainable utilisation of resources, development of Arctic shipping routes and creating governance structures for the Arctic. A document released on 10 May 2017 by China's Leading Group for Promoting the Belt and Road welcomed the "participation of the Latin America and the Caribbean in construction of the Belt and Road".[6] In September 2017, Foreign Minister Wang Yi described the LAC region as a "natural extension of the Maritime Silk Road in history" to Foreign Ministers of the Community of Latin American and Caribbean States (CELAC).[7]

This, in effect, means that the MSR virtually covers the entire globe. Like, in the case of the Belt, the contours of the Road are not clear. It remains a nebulous concept invoking a loose structure of partnerships without any pre-determined scope of either projects or timelines. A few projects are indicated in the policy documents but there is no consolidated database of projects under the MSR banner. By July 2018, China had signed 38 bilateral and regional maritime agreements covering 47 countries.[8] It has been left to the wisdom of analysts to figure out what the MSR in its entirety is. Databases have been compiled by various organisations but they vary. Most maps continued to show Kolkata as part of the MSR although India had not joined the initiative. It is perhaps reflective of the efficacy of the Chinese narrative as also the fact that the world has accepted that there is a 'Road' on the high seas!

Under the Radar

In comparison to the avalanche of publications on the Belt, those on the Road were sparse. Unlike the Belt, there were no major 'achievements' that were publicised although the MSR label was used liberally for individual projects across the globe.

A major reason for this difference was that in moving westwards, China faced no major Great Power competition due to the absence of the USA in the Central Asian and Eastern European regions. Russia and China have worked out a tacit arrangement that allowed China to operate with relative freedom going west. Hence, the narrative of infrastructure and connectivity gained salience for Eurasia. However, moving seawards, China faced opposition primarily due to the overwhelming presence of the US Navy. The first chain of islands, the SCS and the straits of Indonesia are discussed more in terms of maritime contestation than flow of trade. Hence, for the Road, it is the military build-up and geopolitical implications that have gained prominence rather than infrastructure building.

Continental integration between Europe and Asia remains weak. Any nation seeking to strengthen physical integration gets the 'first mover advantage' of a clean slate to project itself as a pioneer with the flexibility to guide the narrative suitably. All the efforts in the past to integrate the land mass of Europe and Asia had failed. In the maritime domain, there were no such fresh attributes to be demonstrated. Although the routes and flow of maritime traffic have fluctuated as per the global demands of supply and demand, the fundamental economics of it remain unchanged. The Arctic region is the only maritime space where the fundamentals are changing and it offers a clean slate for the first mover. Hence, it is the sailing of merchant ships through this region that were invariably touted as 'achievements' akin to the trains that traverse through Eurasia. A similar argument is relevant for the announcements made about diving records achieved by underwater vehicles, and scientific expeditions to the Arctic.

Although the Road finds less mention than the Belt, China actually has a huge presence in the global maritime commercial space, something that the Chinese rarely boast about. China's shipping companies carry more cargo than those of any other nation. Seven of the top 10 container ports in the world are in China. Its SOEs own and operate ports and terminals across the world. China's shipbuilding industry is the largest in terms of tonnage.

By 2015, nearly two-thirds of the world's top 60 container ports had received some degree of Chinese investment. These ports handled about 67 per cent of global container volumes.[9] COSCO Shipping Ports and China Merchants Port Holdings bought stakes in cargo terminals across the world aided by easy access to finance, the biggest advantage of China's SOEs. In January 2017, COSCO secured a $ 26.1 billion pledge from the China Development Bank to support BRI. As on 30 September 2020, COSCO Shipping Ports operated and managed 360 berths at 36 ports worldwide, of which 206 were for containers, with a combined annual handling capacity of 115 million TEU.[10] China Merchants Port Holdings had a port network portfolio spanning 41 ports in 25 countries and regions.[11] Hutchison Ports, privately owned and based in Hong Kong, operated ports and terminals in 27 countries with a combined throughput of 86 million TEU in 2019.[12] In a statement on 26 July 2018, China's spokesperson of the Ministry of Transport said that Chinese companies are involved in construction and operation of 42 ports in 34 countries.[13]

Motivation

The motivations for the Road are the same as for the Belt and have similar implications. The integration of markets, redistribution of supply chain, access to energy and natural resources, consolidation of technical standards, and all the other factors have been listed in the previous chapter. In addition, the Road aims to develop the ocean economy. In

2017, the contribution of the Chinese ocean economy was 9.4 per cent of GDP, or more than $ 1.2 trillion.[14]

Maritime transport continues to be the undisputed mode of transport for world trade in terms of economy and capacity. Although the volume of cargo being transported by rail between China and Europe has been steadily increasing since 2016, it still remains marginal as a percentage of total trade. The share of rail transport in bilateral trade between China and the EU has increased from about 1 per cent in 2011 to about 4 per cent in 2020.[15] This is despite the fact that the number of train journeys in 2020 had increased seven fold since 2016.[16] Nearly 90 per cent of China's trade by volume and 60 per cent of trade by value is transported by sea.[17] China gets the majority of its energy resources and, increasingly, food over the seas. In 2018, approximately 70 per cent of its total oil needs came from imports, around 80 per cent of which had to be shipped through the choke points of Southeast Asia. Chinese companies have investments in agriculture and food-related acquisitions around the world. Africa and Latin America will be the major sources of food for China in future.

Owning and operating a network of logistical nodes across sub-continents would enable greater control of inbound and outbound freight. It will decrease the vulnerability of China's supply chains while providing it political and economic leverage vis a vis other nations. These gateways will provide Chinese vessels priority handling and lower docking fees, giving China's carriers and their shipping customers an advantage in the contest to deliver as much cargo as possible in the shortest time. Having dominance over the entire maritime spectrum – ship design and building, port operations, merchant fleet, scientific exploration, marine data, military and law enforcement – will provide adequate levers of power which could be leveraged to cement their competitive advantage. Since when COSCO acquired, upgraded and turned around the Greek port of Piraeus, China has been able to get Greek support in the European Union to block condemnations of China on issues such as human rights and jurisdictional issues in the South China Sea. As a complement to the Chinese purchase of Piraeus, Chinese banks provided loans to Greek shipping companies to build additional commercial vessels in Chinese shipyards.[18]

Greenfield projects provide easier access to natural resources and can alter the flow of maritime traffic. This is especially applicable to creation of supply lines with Africa. Africa was earlier seen as a source of natural commodities. However, the economic parameters of the continent are changing and the green shoots of an economic upsurge are emerging.[19] With a growing young population, it provides enormous business opportunities and a possible source of agricultural products for the world in the future. China is also attempting to shorten its maritime route to Europe. Hence, it has paid more attention to ports in southern Europe which are closer to China. Traditionally, it is the ports in Northern Europe that have dominated traffic but this may change. Of course, once the Arctic route opens, these ports will get another channel for traffic.

The Belt will connect with the Road at various 'gateway' ports. These will provide greater access to the sea to the interior provinces. It is claimed that they will even support a shorter route for transfer of oil and gas by pipelines, avoiding the choke points on maritime routes. However, this claim may not be correct since pipelines have limited capacity and cannot be laid and operated over high mountain passes.

Ideally, China would like to expand its maritime strategic space far beyond its enclosed adjacent waters but is constricted by opposing forces around it. However, the Road will provide it support in this endeavour to participate more actively in the global maritime order.

Even though the projects that constitute the MSR are not clear, a scan through the Indo-Pacific from East Asia to Africa will give an idea of the distribution of Chinese assets. In fact, if we start the scan from the western shores of the USA, China Shipping (North America) Holding Company Ltd., a subsidiary of China Shipping (Group) Company, has been operating in a terminal of the port of Los Angeles since 2005.

East Asia

China

China's vision documents have named Fujian province as the core of the MSR. The coastal regions and their SEZs are powerhouses for China's economy. The busiest ports in the world include Hong Kong, Yangshan (Shanghai), Yantian (Shenzen), Beilun (Ningbo), Xiamen, Qianwan (Quingdao), Qingdao, Ningo Anch, Xingang (Tianjin), Nasha (Guangzhou) and Dalian. The Big Bay Area Project integrating Guangdong-Hong Kong-Macao is one of the most ambitious endeavours in this region. The vision paper of BRI mentions them. From here, the MSR has four branches – Arctic, Latin America and Caribbean, Pacific Islands and Oceania and Indian Ocean.

Arctic

In recent decades, the Arctic region has witnessed a decline in the ice cover on the Arctic Ocean due to global warming. This has opened up opportunities to commercially utilise the three Arctic maritime routes (Northeast Passage, Northwest Passage and Transpolar Sea Route), exploit the natural resources of the region, and transform global shipping patterns. China has been exploring possibilities of opening up this route. In 2013, the first commercial Chinese-flagged ship, the 19,000-tonne cargo vessel *Yong Sheng* (Eternal Life), owned and operated by China Ocean Shipping Company (COSCO), sailed from Dalian to Rotterdam.[20] China has been augmenting its icebreaker fleet, undertaking scientific expeditions, setting up permanent scientific stations, investing in extraction of natural resources and becoming active in Arctic governance structures. Once fully open, the Arctic route will substantially reduce the distance between China and northern European ports.

Pacific Islands and Oceania

Australia

Australia has seen a dramatic reversal in its government's and the public's perception on China in recent years, particularly after disclosures of Chinese ingress into its political system, decision-making bodies and academia. In November 2015, the Northern Territory government leased the port of Darwin for 99 years to a subsidiary of Shandong Landbridge, a privately-owned Chinese company. Darwin has a major US Marines base and the USA complained that it had not been consulted. The port operator had been struggling financially to run it. The port of Newcastle was sold on a 98-year lease in 2014 and in June 2018, China Merchants Port Holding bought a 50 per cent stake in it. The port of Melbourne was sold to a foreign consortium in September 2016 that included the China Investment Corp.

Australia has not joined the BRI but the province of Victoria signed up to it providing a great case study of 'paradiplomacy'.[21] In January 2018, the Australian Minister for International Development, Concetta

Fierravanti-Wells, criticised Chinese projects and warned of the Pacific growing "full of useless buildings which nobody maintains, which are basically white elephants".

Pacific Islands

In April 2018, reports of a possible Chinese military presence at Vanuatu generated worldwide attention on the extent of Chinese interests in the South Pacific Islands. The story focused on upgrades to the Luganville wharf on the island of Espiritu Santo by the SOE Shanghai Construction Group, suggesting that the new facility could accommodate Chinese naval vessels.[22] This forced Australia and New Zealand to step up their economic and diplomatic efforts in the region. Australian officials questioned the value of Chinese infrastructure projects in the region and suggested that loans facilitating these activities had implications for the sovereignty of Pacific Island states. There was intense drama at the 49th Pacific Islands Forum (PIF) held in September 2018 at Yaren (Nauru) when the head of the Chinese delegation stormed out after a verbal exchange with the Chairman. More drama followed at the APEC Summit in November 2018 at Papua New Guinea when Chinese officials barged into the office of the Foreign Minister. When reports emerged of China planning to set up a naval base at Manus Island in Papua New Guinea, the USA and Australia got together to offer a development package to the island nation and possibly develop their own naval base at Manus Island. In fact, Papua New Guinea has the largest BRI projects among the island nations but there is considerable confusion on the nature and extent of Chinese financial assistance to it.[23]

The Pacific island countries are heavily dependent on foreign aid. Their inclusion in the MSR cannot possibly have any economic benefit. There is no major sea route or economy in the region. The geostrategic intent of China in having a presence in the Pacific Islands would be to break free from containment on its eastern seaboard. Many of China's larger infrastructure projects in the region raised concerns about unsustainable debt levels, political strings attached to Chinese aid, and, in some cases, the potential for China to use port and airport projects as a means of gaining military access to the region. The Prime Ministers of Tonga and Vanuatu publicly warned about Chinese investment and loans. The Vanuatu government did not have the funds to maintain the National

Convention Centre at Port Villa that never saw the surge of international conventions and seminars it was meant to.[24]

South East Asia

Despite maritime jurisdictional disputes, Chinese investments have been flowing into Southeast Asia and trade has been growing. While the ASEAN nations are interested in benefiting from economic engagement with China, most of them have misgivings about China's growing power. In Southeast Asia, the Belt is connected to the Road through the Mekong Basin region and the Malay Peninsula. A China-ASEAN FTA was signed in 2003 and became effective in 2010. In 2009, China became the largest trading partner of Southeast Asia. In 2012, it became the largest source of tourists. By 2016, an estimated 80,000 students from Southeast Asia were enrolled at universities in China, many on scholarships. Between 2013 and 2018, China invested $ 52.8 billion in the region, almost half of the amount invested by Japan. Corresponding figures from 2003 to 2017 are $ 123 billion by China and $ 220 billion by Japan.[25] BRI investments peaked in 2015 and dropped thereafter.[26]

The Philippines

The Philippines won a major ruling from the Tribunal of the Permanent Court of Arbitration in July 2016 regarding the South China Sea. However, President Rodrigo Duterte kept the issue on the backburner to explore possibilities of investment from China. His government was pushing an ambitious $ 180 billion "Build, Build, Build" plan. It planned 75 flagship projects that include six airports, nine rail routes, 32 roads, four sea ports, four power stations and 10 water resources projects.[27] Although China pledged as much as $ 26 billion in assistance, there was no major investment.[28] By late 2019, only three small schemes worth less than $ 200 million had been started.[29] Japan continued to be the largest investor with an investment of $ 600 million in 2017.

In January 2019, when the Hanjin Heavy Industries and Construction Philippines shipyard in Subic Bay filed for bankruptcy, two private Chinese firms expressed interest in taking over the shipyard.[30] This prompted a scramble in the government to take it over. The site of an erstwhile major US naval base in Chinese hands was an irony that was hard to miss.

Vietnam

China became Vietnam's largest trading partner in 2016 when bilateral trade touched $ 96 billion. China and Vietnam, of course, have a history of skirmishes over territorial issues. Not surprisingly, Vietnam has not been very enthusiastic about the Road. In June 2018, there were large-scale protests against a draft SEZ legislation that entailed a 99-year lease to Chinese investors.

Laos

Land-locked Laos is the poorest country in the region and completely dependent on China. As the largest lender and investor, China has poured more than US$ 12 billion into Laos, via 785 projects, ranging from special economic zones and industrial parks to large-scale infrastructure projects.[31] China is funding and building a 417-km single-track SGR from Boten to Vientiane. The $ 6.7 billion cost of this project is more than a third of the country's GDP. Despite its dependency on China, Lao officials negotiated for five years over issues of financing, land rights and other concerns.[32] Construction began in 2016 and is expected to be completed by December 2021. Originally, this line was envisaged as part of a link up to Singapore. However, Thailand is not too inclined to extend the line. This has cast a shadow on its economic viability. An estimate, made with the assumption that the railway would be up to Bangkok was that it would lose money in the first 11 years.[33]

Cambodia

Cambodia is another strong supporter of China in the region and is heavily dependent on it. China is the largest trading partner, the largest source of investment and aid, and the largest source of tourists. In 2018, Cambodia's external debt was $ 7.6 billion compared to its 2017 GDP estimated at $ 22.2 billion. Of this, $ 2.9 billion was owed to China.[34] The most intriguing project is one in which 36,000 hectares of land in the Koh Kong province and a fifth of the country's coastline is reportedly under a 99-year lease to the Union Development Group (UDG), a Chinese private company. The $ 3.8 billion project commenced in 2008 and consists of the Dara Sakor resort, a two-mile long runway and a deep water port capable of berthing four 20,000 tonne container ships.[35] In November 2018, rumours surfaced about the establishment becoming a Chinese base.[36]

In July 2019, there were reports, which were later denied by the Cambodian government, that there was a secret agreement to allow access to the Chinese military to the naval base at Ream near Sihanoukville for a period of 30 years.[37] The 190-acre naval base had two facilities built by the USA for the Cambodian Navy. These have apparently been demolished and will be replaced by two piers built by China – one for its own use and the other for the host.[38]

The unregulated development in Sihanoukville, where the country's only deep water port is located, due to Chinese private investment has been particularly controversial locally. Casino and hotels, mostly Chinese-owned, have sprung up to cater for Chinese tourists.

Thailand

Thailand is pushing for the $ 43 billion Eastern Economic Corridor (EEC) which aims to develop its eastern seaboard over a five-year period from 2017 to 2022. However, there are no major Chinese port investments.

In May 2014, Thailand pledged to complete a rail line from Bangkok to the Lao border to connect up with the line being built by the Chinese. After years of negotiations with the Chinese, the Thai government decided to allocate its own funds to build another line alongside the existing single line, rather than opting for a new and expensive Chinese rail line. Finally, in October 2020, "Contract 2.3" was signed between the State Railway of Thailand (SRT) and the China Railway International and the China Railway Design Corp. for construction of Phase 1 which will run from Bangkok to Nakhon Ratchasima. The next phase to reach Nong Khai on the border with Laos is still being examined.

The Kunming-Bangkok Expressway, completed in 2013, and increasing navigability of the middle Mekong River, engineered by China, is enabling Chinese products to flood northern Thailand.

Malaysia

Malaysian Prime Minister Najib Razak was a strong proponent of the BRI. His government had signed loan and investment agreements worth $ 30 billion with the Chinese. However, Mahathir Mohamad trounced him in the remarkable elections of May 2018 and became Prime Minister. During the election campaign, he had vowed to review all Chinese investments and followed up on his promise after becoming the Prime

Minister. In July 2018, he cancelled the Trans-Sabah Gas pipeline (TSGP) pipeline and Multi Product Pipeline (MPP) projects, and announced reconsideration of the $ 15.7 billion East Coast Rail Link (ECRL) being built by CCCC and financed by EXIM of China. Links between the graft-stained 1 Malaysia Development Berhad (1MDB) state investment fund of the previous government and Chinese projects also emerged.[39] In April 2019, the ECRL project was resumed after the cost was slashed by a third to $ 10.5 billion with a change in route.

The 688-km ECRL will act as a land bridge across Malaysia, an alternate route of sorts bypassing Malacca. It will start from Port Klang on the western coast and cross the Peninsula to reach Kuantan port on the eastern coast, and head north towards Thailand thereafter. It is now slated for completion in 2026.

The Kuantan port is jointly owned by IJM Corporation (a private company of Malaysia) and Beibu Gulf Holding of Hong Kong (a company owned by a SOE of China's Guangxi Zhuang Autonomous Region). The consortium is expanding the port, and two out of three phases of expansion have been completed.[40] The Malaysia-China Kuantan Industrial Park, launched in 2013, is jointly owned by a Malaysian-Chinese consortium.

The $ 7.2 billion Melaka Gateway project, located on the northern shores of the Malacca Strait, was being developed by KAJ Development Berhad (KAJD) of Malaysia and the Power China International Group Limited, a Chinese SOE. It was a mixed development project with three artificial islands and a fourth natural island. A deep sea port was to be constructed on the natural island of Pulua Panjong (with the Shenzhen Yantian Port Group Company and the Rizhao Port Group Company of China as additional partners). The other islands were to have facilities for tourism, free trade economic zones and maritime industrial areas. It was launched in 2014 and was expected to be completed by 2025. However, nothing happened beyond the initial reclamation. In November 2020, the provincial government of Melaka cancelled the project. The port project made no sense since two of Malaysia's largest ports, Port Klang and Port of Tanjung Pelepas, are nearby and not yet operating to full capacity. Port Klang is the main gateway port for the country, as it receives the bulk of Malaysia's imports and exports, and Port of Tanjung Pelepas accounts for the bulk of its trans-shipment.[41] Hutchison Ports operates Port Klang, in which has a 23.6 per cent stake.

Forest City is a $ 100 billion joint venture between the Chinese company, Country Garden, and Esplanade Danga, which is owned by the Sultan of Johor. It is Malaysia's largest residential property development. Reclamation is expected to create four artificial islands covering 20 square kilometres in the Johor Strait, which separates Malaysia from Singapore. It was launched in 2014, and 700,000 people were expected to live in the city on completion in 2035. The project was controversial since it is aimed at providing residence to foreigners, especially Chinese. Till July 2020, only one island was complete and one out of eight phases of development had been completed.[42]

Singapore

Singapore is the outlier amongst the countries in the region. It acts as a mediator and facilitator between China and the other nations by providing banking and legal support for projects. It is a financial and legal hub with a critical transhipment port. Thirty-three per cent of all outward investments related to the BRI flow through Singapore, while 85 per cent of inbound investments for the initiative make their way to China through Singapore.[43] COSCO Shipping Ports has 49 per cent stake in the COSCO-PSA terminal of Pasir Panjang port.

Indonesia

In May 2019, Indonesia proposed an ambitious plan of investing $ 412 billion in infrastructure over a five-year period ending 2024. President Joko Widodo had a vision to turn Indonesia into a Global Maritime Fulcrum. In 2018, Indonesia had offered Chinese companies a list of potential projects requiring $ 60 billion worth of investment. In 2019, its Investment Coordinating Board proposed 28 projects worth $ 91.1 billion for Chinese investment. Till 2019, the cumulative investment from China was $ 4.47 billion.[44] For port-related projects, although MoUs were signed, nothing fructified.

The $ 4.5 billion Jakarta-Bandung high speed rail project being built by China has seen several delays. In May 2017, financing was finalised with CBD largely providing the finance. Construction is held up primarily due to problems of land acquisition along the route.

Kra Canal

A long-pending idea is to bypass the 'choke points' in the south by building a canal through the Kra Isthmus in Thailand. This has been under consideration for a long time but has not fructified primarily due to two reasons – heavy financial requirement and cutting off of the southern part of Thailand that is plagued by Islamic insurgency. The canal will be around 135 km long and 25 metres deep, and is estimated to take 10 years to build. It was reported that this project was under consideration of the National Security Council of Thailand.[45] It is a mammoth project that is unlikely to be taken up although a Chinese company has expressed interest.[46] However, it will be a game changer if it ever comes through. According to the Thai Canal Association, it will reduce the transit by 1,200 kilometres compared to the route through the Straits of Malacca, saving two to three days of sailing time. It will save 2,800 kilometres and four to five days in comparison to the Sunda Strait. And ships will take five to six days less travelling 3,500 kilometres than vessels that go through the Lombok Strait.[47]

South Asia

South Asia has two of the most unviable projects of the MSR – Hambantota and Gwadar. This has led to speculation on the true intent of Chinese involvement in these ports. Gwadar and Kyaukpyu ports are the two 'gateway ports' that connect the Belt to the Road. They connect the Indian Ocean to the Xinjiang Uyghur Autonomous Region and Yunnan province of China.

The CPEC in Pakistan, the Trans-Himalayan Economic Corridor through Nepal, the CMEC through Myanmar, and Chinese investments in Sri Lanka and the Maldives raised anxiety levels in New Delhi.

Myanmar

In Myanmar, the focus of investments is the coastal town of Kyaukpyu in Rakhine province. In 2016, subsidiaries of China's CITIC group won contracts for the expansion of the deep-sea port and creation of a 4,200-acre industrial area in the accompanying SEZ. The port project was originally valued at $ 7.3 billion and the SEZ at $ 2.7 billion. Under the terms of the deal, CITIC will build and then run the project for 50 years with a potential extension for another 25 years.[48] An agreement of port ownership was signed in October 2017 after CITIC agreed to drop its stake from 85 per cent to 70. CITIC has a stake of 51 per cent in the SEZ. In September 2018, Myanmar scaled down the port project slashing the initial price tag to $ 1.3 billion from $ 7.3 billion to avoid excessive debt. This will fund the first stage in which one wharf capable of mooring two to three ships will be built. Additional investment will be made to expand the port if usage and profits are strong.[49]

Maday Island, off Kyaukpyu, is the terminus to a $ 1.5 billion oil pipeline and a parallel natural gas pipeline running to Kunming, the capital of China's south-western province of Yunnan. An agreement for the gas pipeline was signed in March 2009 and for the oil pipeline in June 2009. They were constructed by the China National Petroleum Corporation and Myanmar Oil and Gas Enterprise. The gas pipeline became operational in 2013 and can pump 12 billion cubic metres of gas annually to China. The oil pipeline became operational in April 2017, nearly three years after its completion, due to the Myanmar government's delay in signing some key documents.[50] It can carry 22 million barrels of oil per year, which is 6 per cent of China's oil imports in 2016.[51]

Kyaukpyu port is expected to provide closer access to the sea for Yunnan province, reducing the shipping distance by 1,200 km. A 1400-km rail line between Kunming and Kyaukphu is planned. The first 328 km between Kunming and Dali in China became operational in July 2018. The 336 km between Dali and Ruili (at the Myanmar border) is expected to be completed in 2022. The China Railway Erguan Engineering Corporation has completed surveying the 431-km line from Muse to Mandalay in Myanmar. An agreement has been signed for a survey of the line from Mandalay to Kyukpyu.

In December 2017, China and Myanmar agreed to establish a China-Myanmar Economic Corridor connecting Kyaukpyu to Kunming. A MoU providing the framework for projects in 12 sectors was signed on 9 September 2018.[52] Aung San Suu Kyi headed a 25-member steering committee that was appointed to oversee the implementation of joint venture projects with China. China had proposed 24 projects but Myanmar agreed to accelerate work on only nine of them. It included expressway projects between Kyaukpyu and Kunming, border trade zones in Kachin and Shan states opposite Yunnan, and an ambitious project for a "new city" adjacent to the old capital of Yangon that would cover an area twice the size of Singapore. The CCCC proposal for New Yangon is now being subjected to a 'Swiss Challenge' with the help of a foreign consultant.

Chinese investments in Myanmar have not had smooth sailing. In 2011, the Myitsone dam project was suspended and in 2012, there were violent protests over the Letpadaung copper mine forcing suspension of operations. Myanmar has also been sensitive to Indian interests. When the "string of pearls" narrative listed the Coco islands as one of the bases with Chinese assets, Myanmar invited the Indian Navy to visit the islands to ascertain the facts on the ground. In 2005, the Indian Chief of the Naval Staff stated that there was no Chinese facility on Coco Islands.[53] The country's 2008 Constitution forbids the deployment of foreign troops on its soil. However, the nation is highly dependent on China, especially during phases when it faces sanctions and isolation from the West.

Bangladesh

Bangladesh has witnessed an economic turnaround and the nation is expected to be a middle-income nation in 2021. It has been careful in accepting Chinese loans to avoid any debt servicing issues. In 2016, it turned down the Chinese proposal to develop Sonadia port and opted for the Japanese-funded Matabari port instead. In January 2018, Bangladesh scrapped the Dhaka-Sylhet Highway project and the contractor, CHEC, was blacklisted on charges of bribery.[54] Bangladesh formally joined the BRI during President Xi Jinping's visit in October 2016. The two countries signed a MoU for 27 projects totalling $ 22.5 billion. By July 2019, loan agreements for only seven projects totalling $ 5.4 billion had been signed and $ 981.36 million had been actually disbursed.[55]

The Karnaphuli tunnel will connect the existing port and city of Chattogram, west of the Karnaphuli River, to the industrial area east of the river. With the main tunnel under the Karnaphuli River of 3.5 km, the project will be cover 9 km and will cost $ 1.1 billion. It is being constructed by CCCC and is expected to be completed by 2022.

The Payra port is being constructed at an estimated total cost of $ 11-15 billion and has 19 components. It is planned to be completed by 2023. Two of the components are being built by the China Harbour Engineering

Company Limited and the China State Construction Engineering Corporation Limited.

The China Harbour Engineering Company Limited is setting up a SEZ on 783 acres of land in Anwara, close to Chattogram Port. It has a 70 per cent stake in the venture. The MoU was signed in June 2014 and progress has been slow. Other major Chinese investments include the rail-road bridge across the Padma River, digital connectivity and telecom projects, and power projects including coal-fired power plants at Pyra and Chattogram.

Sri Lanka

Since Hambantota Port became the cautionary tale of the BRI, it is worth recounting the chronology of events. The first feasibility study was conducted by the Canadian firm, SNC-Lavlin, in 2003. The second feasibility study was conducted by the Danish firm, Ramboll, in 2006. In 2007, EXIM of China agreed to fund the first phase of the project that would cater for transport of non-containerised cargo like oil, cars and grain, to start bringing in revenue. It provided a $ 307 million, 15-year commercial loan with a four-year grace period, at 6.3 per cent fixed interest.[56] The construction agreement was signed on 12 March 2007 between the Sri Lanka Port Authority (SLPA) and a consortium of the China Harbour Engineering Company (CHEC) and the Sino Hydro Corporation Limited.[57] Construction of the first phase was completed in 2010 and the port was opened. Instead of waiting for Phase 1 to generate revenue, President Mahinda Rajapaksha decided to go ahead with the second phase that would create facilities for container operations. In 2010, EXIM of China provided a loan of another $ 757 million at an interest rate of 2 per cent. The port was operated by SLPA and was losing money.

Around 2007, Sri Lanka was in the midst of a civil war. Tax revenues were low and there was no access to easy finance due to its low credit rating. China provided loans at commercial rates. In 2007, Sri Lanka issued its first international sovereign bond with an interest rate of 8.25 per cent to raise capital. In 2009, when the civil war ended, Sri Lanka took on more debt at commercial rates to build infrastructure and speed up economic growth. Economic growth picked up but so did the debt burden.

President Mahinda Rajapaksa had embarked on a series of ambitious projects in his home district, in addition to the port. This included an international airport, a cricket stadium and convention centre. They were all financed and built by Chinese entities.

The government changed in 2015. The steep payments on international sovereign bonds (8 to 12 per cent interest), comprising nearly 40 per cent of the country's external debt, created a financial crisis. Ninety-five per cent of the nation's revenue was being used to service its debt. By the end of 2016, Sri Lanka had an external debt of $ 46.4 billion that was 57 per cent of its GDP. About 10 per cent of this was owed to China.[58] In addition to loans from China, Sri Lanka owed debts to Japan, the World Bank and ADB that was larger but at lower rates. To generate cash, the Sri Lanka government decided to lease the port. In December 2016, after closed-door proceedings, a framework agreement was signed with CM Ports for an 80 per cent stake in the port with a 99-year lease on payment of $ 1.12 billion. In July 2017, a revised version was signed in which the stake of CM Ports was reduced to 70 per cent. Two entities were formed - Hambantota International Port Group (HIPG) and Hambantota International Port Group Services (HIPS). HIPG, with an 85 per cent stake held by CM Port, was mandated to run the port. HIGS, with CM Port holding 49.3 per cent stake, was mandated to oversee security. However, cross-holdings by CM Ports may mean that it has a majority stake in HIGS as well.[59] The agreement forbids the use of the port for military activities.[60] In March 2019, Sri Lanka announced the commencement of the construction of an oil refinery near the port.[61]

The Colombo port has five container terminals – Jaya Container Terminal, East Container Terminal, Unity Container Terminal, South Asia Gateway Terminal and Colombo International Container Terminal (CICT).[62] CM Port has an 85 per cent stake in CICT. It had invested $ 500 million to build the terminal and the joint venture has a 35-year concession to operate CICT. As part of the agreement with SLPA, it got a guarantee that container handling from Hambantota would be withheld till CICT reached a target volume. This contributed to the idleness of Hambantota Port in the first years of its operation.[63]

The other mega project is the $ 1.4 billion, 269-hectare (665 acres) Colombo Port City project being built by CHEC. Unlike other projects that have been financed by loans, this is a Foreign Direct Investment (FDI) by CHEC. The project commenced in 2015 and land has been reclaimed from the sea. The Sirisena government had suspended the project in 2015 but the suspension was lifted a year later. In August 2016, a tripartite agreement was signed (between Sri Lanka's Urban Development Authority, the Ministry of Megapolis and Western Development, and CHEC) in which the project was renamed the Colombo International Financial City and land ownership terms were modified. Earlier, land was to be provided to CHEC on a freehold basis but now 110 hectares is planned to be on 99-year lease.[64] The idea of the project is to offer favourable trade, investment, and tax policies to attract capital, the apocryphal next "Singapore" or "Dubai".

The Maldives

The Maldives took a decisive turn towards China under President Abdullah Yameen. It signed an FTA with China in December 2017. The biggest projects were an upgrade of the Velana International Airport ($ 421 million), China-Maldives Friendship Bridge ($ 210 million), construction of 11,000 apartments at Hulhumale ($ 547.9 million), and extension of electrical grid to Hulhumale ($ 180.9 million).[65] Chinese companies have reclaimed land to create tourist resorts. The island of Feydhoo Finolhu was leased to a Chinese enterprise for 50 years at a price of around $ 4 million.[66] By May 2020, it had been dramatically transformed into a beach resort with massive land reclamation.[67] Another island, the 7-km long Kalhufahalufushi, came even cheaper.[68]

The situation changed in 2018 with the election of President Ibrahim Solih. In 2018, the Maldivian Finance Minister had revealed that Chinese debts were $ 1.4 billion, about 38 per cent of the country's national debt of $ 3.7 billion and 78 per cent of its external debt of $ 1.8 billion.[69] In December 2018, New Delhi announced a $ 1.4 billion financial package for the Maldives during President Solih's visit.

Pakistan

The CPEC was supposed to be the flagship of the BRI. The committed amount for the CPEC were initially pegged at $ 46 billion and reached a peak of $ 72 billion. However, it is now clear that expenditure on CPEC will be capped closer to $ 25 billion with the completion of 38 projects. The first phase was primarily power projects and has been completed. The next phase was supposed to be SEZs but none are operational so far.

The Main Line 1 (ML1) railway line and the Gwadar Port and SEZ are the other important projects.

There is no progress on ML1 since Pakistan does not want to accumulate more debt and has asked for concessional loans that China is unwilling to provide. There are disagreements over the high insurance costs that Sinosure would charge on the ML1 loan and its currency as well.

Gwadar lies 400 km east of the Strait of Hormuz through which 40 per cent of China's imported oil transits. The Xinjiang region is 1,800 km away across the Karakoram mountain range. In August 2001, China committed itself to support the construction of a port at Gwadar. Construction commenced in March 2002, with CHEC as the principal contractor. EXIM of China provided finance consisting of $ 50 million in grants, $ 50 million in commercial credit and $ 98 million credit at concessional terms. Pakistan provided $ 50 million.[70] Phase 1 was completed in 2007.

The port is situated on the east bay of a hammer-shaped peninsula. The approach channel of 4.7 km was dredged to a depth of 14.5 metres. The 602 metre quay has three berths of 200 metre length, each capable of accommodating up to 50,000 DWT vessels with a 12.5 metre draught. The designed capacity is 137,000 TEU container cargo and 868,000 tons of general and bulk cargo per annum.[71] Continuous dredging is required to be undertaken to maintain sufficient depth for larger vessels.

In 2007, the Port of Singapore Authority (PSA) won a 40-year lease to build-operate-transfer the port. PSA was to build the second phase of the port with an investment of $ 550 million. In return, it was to get 91 per cent of the revenue of cargo operations and 85 per cent of free zone revenue. PSA failed to implement the second phase and the port struggled to generate business. In February 2013, PSA sold its entire equity to Chinese SOE China Overseas Port Holdings Company Ltd. (COPHC). Little is known about COPHC. It is not a mainstream SOE. It was registered in Hong Kong in 2012, ostensibly for Gwadar port. In November 2015, a 40-year lease of the port for COPHC was finalised, with the firm getting 91 per cent of its revenues. COPHC has revived the dysfunctional port infrastructure but, by all accounts, there is hardly any business. The port is mostly lying idle. In October 2016, 100 containers were shifted from Xinjiang to Gwadar traversing 3,115 km over 15 days for shipment from the port. That was the only instance of its use as a 'gateway port'.[72] A container service started by COSCO in March 2018 was stopped by May that year, restarted in 2020 but is irregular.[73] In January 2020, Gwadar was opened for use under the Afghanistan-Pakistan Transit Trade Agreement with a shipment of fertilisers delivered by a COSCO ship and transported to the Afghanistan border.

In 2015, COPHC also got a 43-year lease to develop a free trade and export processing zone over 2,281 acres. It is operated by the Gwadar Free Zone Company, a subsidiary of COPHC. The 60-acre Phase 1 was inaugurated in January 2018. Nothing much has happened about the expansion proposed in Phase 2 which includes expansion of the port as well. In 2019, Saudi Arabia pledged $ 10 billion to build a petrochemical refinery complex in the North Bay at Gwadar. However, there has been no progress thereafter.

Construction on the New Gwadar International Airport began in March 2019. It is financed by a $ 230 million grant by China and is being managed by the China Airport Construction Group. It is designed to be Pakistan's largest airport covering 18 square kilometres with a runway more than 12,000 feet (3,658 metres) long, capable of handling the largest military and commercial aircraft.

Chinese investment in Gwadar is estimated to be $ 1.62 billion till date.[74] There is very little commercial justification for Gwadar port. The region lacks basic infrastructure, and even water. There is no industry in the hinterland and connectivity is poor. Rail connectivity does not exist and road links are being built. Furthermore, there are issues of security as well. It is not surprising that commercial activity at Gwadar has been very limited and the port has seen very little vessel traffic in over a decade of operation. Almost all of Pakistan's maritime trade passes through the existing ports of Karachi and Qasim. Chinese firms are undertaking expansion in both of them.

Pakistan has a Special Security Division (SSD) consisting of around 15,000 armed personnel specifically to protect Chinese nationals and projects in Pakistan. In 2016, the Pakistan Navy established "Task Force 88" to provide security to the port of Gwadar.

Pakistan is in a precarious economic condition. In 2019, it received its thirteenth IMF bailout in the last 30 years with a loan of $ 6 billion. Its external debt in 2018 was $ 91.8 billion with a public debt-to-GDP ratio of 70 per cent. China has provided Pakistan $ 4.5 billion in commercial loans in fiscal year 2018-19. Saudi Arabia and the United Arab Emirates had also provided $ 3 billion each in commercial loan deposits at 3 per cent interest. They had also allowed deferment of $ 6 billion of oil payments for one year. Even then, the State Bank of Pakistan reserves stood at $ 8.2 billion, barely enough to cover two months of imports.

West Asia

The nations in West Asia have signed up to the BRI and China is involved in infrastructure projects in the region. Energy deals form a crucial part of the agreements. China's Arab Policy paper of 2016 describes a "1+2+3" cooperation pattern that includes energy cooperation; infrastructure construction and trade and investment facilitation; and new technology fields of nuclear energy, space and renewable energy.[75] These nations are also interested in creating massive commercial hubs to diversify their economies and deploying their sovereign wealth in foreign investments to reduce their dependency on the petroleum sector.

Iran

Iran is a key participant of the BRI and Chinese companies are involved in rail projects. The rail link from the Central Asian Republics comes to Iran and branches off in three directions. In 2016, China agreed to boost bilateral trade by more than 10 times to $ 600 billion over the next decade.[76] In 2017, the state-owned investment arm, CITIC Group, established a $ 10 billion credit line. In 2018, an OECD report stated that $ 25 billion worth of investment by Chinese SOEs (CNOOC, CNPC and Sino Hydro) in Iran is in "trouble".[77] China's investments in Iran peaked between 2014 and 2017 at $ 10.73 billion, and fell thereafter.[78] China sees Iran as an important source of energy. In 2020-21, there were multiple reports of a framework agreement according to which China will invest $ 400 billion in Iran over a period of 25 years in exchange for a regular supply of oil at a discounted price. However, the details of the agreement are still not clear. Iran plans to develop its largest commercial port and hub for its oil exports at Jask, which is east of the Strait of Hormuz.

Kuwait

Kuwait views the BRI as an important driver for its growth and has agreed with China to align it with the 'New Kuwait 2030' vision that seeks to transform Kuwait into a commercial and financial hub in the region. The flagship project is the development of Silk City and the five islands – Failaka, Warba, Boubyan, Miskan and Awha. China and Kuwait signed a deal in February 2019 to begin construction of Phase 1 of this project that will cost a whopping $ 86 billion. Part of it is the Mubarakal-Kabeer port with 24 berths that will be built by the CCCC. China and Kuwait are setting up a $ 10 billion investment fund.

Saudi Arabia

China is the largest consumer of oil while Saudi Arabia is one of the largest producers. Saudi Arabia and China signed deals worth $ 65 billion in March 2017. In 2017, an MoU was signed to develop a $ 20 billion Joint Investment Fund. Between 2005 and 2019, Chinese companies got $ 35 billion worth of construction contracts in Saudi Arabia.[79] The 'Saudi Plan 2030' adopted in 2016 seeks to diversify the economy away from its oil dependency, and Saudi Arabia has agreed to align it with the BRI. Apart from many energy agreements, MoUs have been signed with China's NDRC for infrastructure development but the details are not clear.

Qatar

Following a diplomatic rift with Bahrain, Saudi Arabia and UAE in 2014, Qatar started to shift its investments from developed to emerging markets. It has now invested billions in China, Japan, South Korea, ASEAN, India, and Russia. Qatar's sovereign wealth fund set up a $ 10 billion fund to invest in China. It has also invested heavily in Chinese companies and banks. It has a currency swap agreement with the People's Bank of China and in 2015, opened a centre for the settlement of transactions in renminbi, the first of its kind in the Middle East. Chinese firms are involved in infrastructure projects in Qatar, including those for the 2022 FIFA World Cup. Qatar was the first country to have 5G telecom services with Huawei as a partner.

Energy remains a crucial element in the relationship. Qatar supplies 20 per cent of China's natural gas requirement and is the second largest LNG supplier to China.

The $ 7.4 billion Hamad container port located 40 km south of Doha is the largest in Qatar and has been partly built by CHEC.

UAE

UAE and China signed an agreement to launch a \$ 10 bn strategic co-investment fund in December 2015. In September 2016, China's COSCO Shipping Ports was awarded a concession agreement to operate Container Terminal 2 at Abu Dhabi's Khalifa Port for 35 years with a 90 per cent stake in the terminal. Five Chinese companies have since pledged to invest \$ 300 million in the adjacent industrial zone. The Bank of China will provide financing to Chinese firms that establish operations there. The UAE handles 60 per cent of China's exports throughout the region.

Oman

The biggest Chinese-funded project in Oman is in Duqm. The China-Oman Industrial City spread over an area of around 12 sq km is located in the SEZ of Duqm. Oman Wanfang, a consortium of Chinese companies, is developing this industrial zone.

Africa

China hosted the Forum on China-Africa Cooperation (FOCAC) in Beijing on 3 September 2018 bringing together representatives from 53 African countries to discuss future cooperation. It pledged \$ 60 billion for development projects in Africa. This included \$ 15 billion in grants, interest-free loans and concessional loans, \$ 20 billion in credit lines, a \$ 10 billion special fund for development financing and a \$ 5 billion special fund for financing imports from Africa. Between 2000 and 2014, China funded 2,390 projects across Africa totalling \$ 121.6 billion and constituting 34.3 per cent of China's global development finance over that period.[80]

Djibouti

Djibouti is envisaged by Chinese companies as a major transhipment hub, and a gateway port for the economies in the Horn of Africa, most notably, Ethiopia. With an estimated \$ 15 billion investment in the development of Djibouti port and hinterland, China is the largest external commercial player in Djibouti.[81] In 2013, the China Merchants Port Holdings Company Ltd. (a subsidiary of the SOE China Merchants Group) bought 23.5 per cent equity of the Port de Djibouti SA (PDSA, the public port authority of the Djibouti government). This gives the Chinese company a stake in ownership and operations across facilities around the Gulf of Tadjoureh that includes the Doraleh Container

Terminal, Doraleh Multipurpose Port, Horizon Oil Terminal, Djibouti Old Harbour, Tadjoureh Port and Ghoubet Mineral Terminal.[82]

The Doraleh Container Terminal (DCT) opened in 2008 with a capacity of 1.5 million TEU. It was being managed by DP World under a 25-year concession granted in 2004. DP World held a 33 per cent stake in the joint venture with PDSA for the terminal. The USA relies on DCT to supply its Camp Lemmonier, the largest US military base in Africa. In February 2018, Djibouti terminated its joint venture with DP World, took over operations and transferred the port assets to a new public company. DP World sought litigation in London and Hong Kong. In August 2018, the London Court of International Arbitration ruled that DP World was the legal owner of the concession. In November 2018, it filed a lawsuit against CM Port in Hong Kong. In April 2019, a London Court awarded DP World $ 535 million for Djibouti's breach of contract.

The Doraleh Multipurpose Port is owned and operated by the joint venture. The $ 590-million project was financed by EXIM of China. Construction was undertaken by the China State Construction Engineering Corp. and the China Civil Engineering Construction Corp. between 2013 and 2017. The port became operational in 2017. The total capacity for non-containerised cargo is 8.8 MTPA.[83] Although it has a designed capacity of 220,000 TEU for container cargo, it moved only 49,000 TEU in 2018.[84] Construction of the Tadjoureh Port commenced in 2012 and was completed in 2017. It was to export potash from northern Ethiopia via rail from Semera. However, the rail connection never happened and the port was lying idle.[85] The Ghoubet mineral terminal was built by China Harbour Engineering Corporation between 2013 and 2017, with $ 64 million in preferential loans from EXIM of China. It was meant to export 5 MTPA of processed salt from Djibouti's Lake Assal. CCCC established the Djibouti Salt Investment Company Ltd. and has exclusive rights for 50 years to develop the local salt and bromine resources.[86] In 2018, all these bulk terminals handled only 4.4 MTPA against an installed capacity of 20 MTPA.[87]

Adjacent to the Doraleh Multipurpose Port is the Djibouti International Free Trade Zone. It was established in March 2015 with an agreement between the China Merchants Group and the Djibouti Ports and Free Zone Authority. In January 2017, China's Dalian Port Corporation began construction of the initial phase over an area of 2.4 square km that would cost $ 370 million. The complete project envisages investment of $ 3.5 billion to develop 48 square km.[88] However, the project seems to have halted in the initial phase with no major industries coming up on site.

EXIM of China has provided 95 per cent of the $ 340 million for the water pipeline for transporting groundwater pumped from wells in Ethiopia to towns in Djibouti 320 km away.[89] The pipeline started operating in June 2017.

In February 2014, China and Djibouti signed a "Security and Defence Partnership Agreement" that allowed PLA to have a military facility in Djibouti. China was provided a ten-year lease at $ 20 million per year, with the option to extend it by another 10 years.[90] Construction began in February 2016 and the facility was formally opened in July 2017. It was initially described as a logistics facility for anti-piracy operations. However, its true nature is more than that. The base has facilities to store fuel, weapons and equipment. It also has maintenance and repair facilities. It is estimated to have a capacity to house 10,000 personnel. There is a heliport with hangars and a 400-metre runway. In May 2018, construction of a 330-metre long dedicated naval pier was commenced and it is now complete. The pier is capable of accommodating China's aircraft carrier. The Doraleh Multipurpose Port located next to the base provides adequate berth space for the biggest ships of the PLA Navy.[91] One of the six berths is reserved for use by it.[92]

Eritrea

In 2016, CHEC had completed a $ 400-million project to expand Massawa port with a 70,000-tonne bulk cargo terminal and a 50,000-tonne multipurpose terminal. There are plans to modernise the port in Assab. Landlocked Ethiopia's access to Assab and Massawa ports was cut off in 1998, forcing Addis Ababa to turn to Djibouti for sea access.

Ethiopia

The ports in Djibouti handled 90 per cent of Ethiopia's trade. The 576-km Addis Ababa-Djibouti railway was built between 2011 and 2016 by the China Railway Group (CRG) and the China Civil Engineering Construction Corporation (CCECC). EXIM of China provided 70 per cent of the $ 3.4 billion for the Ethiopian section of the railway. Capital for 85 per cent of the $ 578 million for the Djibouti section was provided by China's banks. It started commercial operations in January 2018 as

Africa's first fully electrified cross-border railway. It has run into financial and operational difficulties that include lower than expected use, electrical power outages and cattle collisions.[93] Sinosure, China's state-owned insurer, was forced to write off $ 1 bn in losses on the project. The railway's prospects have dimmed further with the signing of a peace deal in July 2018 between Ethiopia and Eritrea, which gives Ethiopia access to the Eritrean ports of Assab and Massawa. Ethiopia is also trying to get access to the Berbera Port of Somaliland operated by DP World where Ethiopia took a 19 per cent stake in a 30-year concession.

The profitability of the port and SEZ infrastructure constructed in Djibouti is dependant to a large degree on its use by Ethiopia. However, if Ethiopia diversifies its trade routes, it will jeopardise the economic viability of these investments.

Kenya

There is a race between Kenya and Tanzania to establish themselves as the trade gateway for the Great Lakes countries of Rwanda, Burundi and Uganda. They have both laid rail lines from their largest ports to these countries.

The Lamu Port will be the largest deep-sea port in East Africa when completed. Thirty-two berths are planned to be constructed. In August 2014, the Kenya Ports Authority awarded the contract for construction of the first three berths to CCCC. Construction commenced in 2016. The first berth was completed in 2018 and the other two completed by December 2020. The port is expected to commence operations in 2021.

The China Roads and Bridges Corporation (CRBC) and CCCC have constructed the $ 3.2 billion, 479-km Mombasa-Nairobi SGR. The rail line is losing money and has failed to achieve its goal of cutting congestion on the parallel highway by shifting freight from trucks to trains.[94] In December 2018, a report by Auditor-General Edward Ouko was leaked. The auditors found that the Kenya Port Authority's assets were committed as collateral for the loan provided for the SGR.[95] However, authorities in Kenya have allayed these fears.[96]

Tanzania

The $ 10 billion Bagamayo port and SEZ project was financially backed by the China Merchants Holdings International (CMHI) and Oman's State

General Reserve Fund. The port, being built 75 km north of Dar-es-Salaam, was to become Tanzania's biggest. The agreement was signed in 2013. Phase I of the project commenced in 2015 and was to take three years. The whole project including roads, railways and the economic zone was expected to take 10 years to complete with the Chinese firm handling much of the construction work. However, after a change of government in October 2015, there have been multiple hiccups. Construction was suspended by Tanzania in January 2016, revived in 2018, and suspended again in 2019. In July 2019, the President of Tanzania, John Magufuli, accused the promoters of "exploitative and awkward terms" for financing the project.[97]

In July 2017, President Magufuli had officially launched the project to upgrade Dar-es-Salaam port to more than double its capacity. The $ 421 million upgrade involves improving the existing seven berths, addition of a new berth, dredging of the main channel and improvement of inter-modal infrastructure. The project is being financed by the World Bank and construction is being undertaken by CHEC.

Cobalt is an essential material to produce lithium-ion batteries. About 54 per cent of the global cobalt supply comes from the Democratic Republic of Congo (followed by Argentina). Chinese imports in 2017 were valued at $ 1.2 billion (India was at $ 3.2 million).[98] The mines are located in the southern part of Congo (Katanga) near Tanzania.

Mauritius

President Xi Jinping visited Mauritius in July 2018. In 2016, China wrote off $ 17 million worth of debt and provided $ 730 million in grants and interest-free loans to construct a sports complex. Yihai Investment Ltd. has secured a $ 315 million contract for a 200,000 square metre real estate development. China financed the Bagatelle Dam, which was built by a subsidiary of the China Three Gorges Corporation. Beijing has offered loans and support in the construction of a new airport terminal, roads and hospitals.

So What?

Having scanned the entire Indo-Pacific for an overview of Chinese investments in the maritime sector, the question arises as to why it is a matter of concern. After all, the top two largest shipping companies in the world are AP Moller-Maersk of Denmark and the Swiss-Italian owned

Mediterranean Shipping Company. PSA International of Singapore is the world leader in container terminal operations. It is a subsidiary of Temasek Holdings owned by the government of Singapore. The third largest is Dubai Ports World that is owned by the government of Dubai. If these global giants do not arouse suspicion, why should it be any different for Chinese investments?

There are several reasons for Chinese investments being perceived differently. The first is that the Chinese SOEs have access to easy finance from Chinese banks and can outpace other companies in the acquisition of assets. Due to state backing, they have the staying power to buy assets that may not be profitable and can be sustained for long periods before the assets turn profitable. These companies can, for all practical purposes, be considered as operators of the state with CPC members represented in the management. Hence, all acquisitions by these companies may not be with purely commercial intent. In addition, the separation between public and private enterprises in China can be rather blurred. The fusion between the government, public and private entities in China is suspected to be more seamless than in other nations. Maritime trade and shipping cannot be divorced from the maritime security environment in the region. The PLA Navy has undertaken a doctrinal shift to secure national interests in the "far seas". It is expanding its range and duration of deployments, and augmenting its expeditionary capabilities. It is now undergoing one of the fastest naval expansions in history. Grey zone warfare with the use of the Coast Guard and fishermen militia, creeping assertion, and reclamation and militarisation of maritime features in the South China Sea have all added to the misgivings about China's intentions.

There are two primary concerns about Chinese investments – one is commercial and the other is military. The commercial concern is that China is gaining dominance in all sectors of maritime business and is getting into a position where it can manipulate the flow of maritime trade. The fear is that if this were to happen, China can use it for coercion in the same manner that it has used economic power for coercion in the recent past. The military concern is that ports acquired around the world will be used to support military assets for China's growing security interests. They can potentially be used for espionage and other non-commercial activities. The 2013 Science of Military Strategy by the PLA Academy of Military Science advocates the setting up of overseas strategic branch (strong) points in the Indian and Pacific oceans "in order to provide support for overseas military activities, or to serve as forward bases for the disposition of overseas military strengths, to bring about political and military influences on the relevant regions".[99] Chinese sources make it a point to distinguish these overseas points from military bases. They seek to describe them as facilities for supporting the benign overseas presence of the PLA Navy in contrast to the military facilities of the USA that is ostensibly for offensive purposes.

These two issues will be explored in Chapter 8 where we look at the implications of Chinese presence and influence.

Conclusion

One can conclude several things from this journey from the shores of China to the shores of Africa. The first is that there is no coherent Chinese plan that can be said to constitute the Maritime Component of the BRI. It has been left to the rest of the world to figure out what the projects of the MSR are. The port and port-related investments are by provincial SOEs, central SOEs and private companies. There is no reason to get alarmed over every Chinese investment or project. Many of them are purely commercial with the company having won an open tender. The only ones to watch out for are those that either do not make commercial sense or progress in an opaque manner. Closed-door bilateral deals, opacity in terms of finance, opacity in the process of award of contract to a firm, corruption, negligence about financial viability of the project, and negligence of environmental norms are some of issues that should ring alarm bells. Secondly, the dynamics of Chinese investment varies from nation to nation even when they are of the same region. Hence, broad-brushed descriptions do not hold true. In Southeast Asia, for example, the quantum of Chinese investment in infrastructure varies between Thailand and Vietnam on one side and Laos and Cambodia on the other. Of course, certain characteristics keep popping up. Thirdly, the Chinese tried to replicate the Shekou model of port-park-city abroad while completely neglecting to acknowledge that the factors that enabled Shekou to prosper did not exist in foreign locations like Gwadar or Djibouti. It is no surprise that these locations have failed to become like "Dubai" or "Singapore" as they were planned to be. Fourthly, Chinese prowess in planning is vastly overestimated. Neither Gwadar nor Kyaukpyu are anywhere close to becoming Indian Ocean 'gateways' for China's inner provinces. As the chronology of Gwadar and Hambantota shows, it was the keenness of the host nation rather than China's prescience that was initially responsible for setting up of the port. Of course, it has to be acknowledged that Chinese SOEs have massive staying power and seem to be capable of persisting in a country for decades despite not having highly profitable ventures. Lastly, it has to be noted that projects tend to be dynamic in nature and their status changes continuously. Many reports tend to add up all (initially estimated) project costs and end with an exaggerated picture. They do not take into account projects and investments that did not fructify beyond the initial offer or projects that have got cancelled. For example, the Chinese offers for Chattogram and Sonadia ports never materialised. Melaka Gateway and Bagamoyo port projects stand cancelled as of now. A 2017 report by Grisons Park estimated that Chinese companies had plans to invest $ 20.1 billion in nine overseas ports by July that year. The *Financial Times* reported that it was much higher than the $ 9.97 billion invested in overseas ports estimated for 2016.[100] However, many of the investments mentioned in the reports never fructified. In addition, the terms and conditions keep on changing, sometimes as a response to public outrage. In Sri Lanka's Colombo International Financial City project, the land that was planned to be given on freehold was converted into a lease arrangement. The Hambantota port holding structure too changed between the Framework Agreement of December 2016 and the final agreement in July 2017.

Chinese investments are tracked keenly by strategic analysts since the key issue continues to be the lack of transparency in many of the dealings by Chinese entities, especially SOEs. It is often not clear why certain investments have been undertaken and what the long-term strategy, either commercial or political, is.

NOTES

1. President Xi Jinping, *Speech to Parliament of Indonesia*, 3 October 2013 accessed from http://www.asean-china-center.org/english/2013-10/03/c_133062675.htm on 21 February 2019.
2. NDRC, et al., People's Republic of China, *Visions and Actions on Jointly Building Silk Road Economic Belt and 21st Century Maritime Silk Road*, 28 March 2015, 4.
3. NDRC and SAO, People's Republic of China, *Vision for Maritime Cooperation under the Belt and Road Initiative*, 20 June 2017.
4. State Council Information Office, People's Republic of China, *China's Policy on Asia-Pacific Security Cooperation*, January 2017.

5. State Council Information Office, People's Republic of China, *China's Arctic Policy*, January 2018.
6. Leading Group for Promoting the Belt and Road, *Building One Belt One Road Together: Philosophy, Practice and China's Contribution*, 10 May 2017, accessed from http://www.xinhuanet.com/politics/2017-05/10/c_1120951928.htm on 22 February 2019.
7. Ministry of Foreign Affairs, People's Republic of China, *Wang Yi Meets with Quartet of CELAC Foreign Ministers*, 22 September 2017, accessed from https://www.fmprc.gov.cn/mfa_eng/zxxx_662805/t1496940.shtml on 22 February 2019.
8. "China invests in 42 overseas ports under Belt and Road project", *Hellenic Shipping News*, 30 July 2018.
9. James Cynge, et al., "How China rules the waves", *Financial Times*, 12 January 2017.
10. Accessed from https://ports.coscoshipping.com/en/AboutCSP/Corporate Profile/ Overview/ on 25 February 2021.
11. Accessed from http://www.cmport.com.hk/EN/about/Profile.aspx?from=2 on 25 February 2021.
12. Accessed from https://hutchisonports.com/about-us/company-profile/ on 25 February 2021.
13. H.E. Haralambides, "China's Belt & Road Initiative: Connecting maritime transport flows for trade-driven prosperity, multilateralism and global peace", *OECD International Transport Forum*, 15-16 April 2019, accessed from https://www.itf-oecd.org/sites/default/files/docs/china-belt-road-haralambides.pdf on 26 February 2021.
14. Richard Ghiasy, et al., *The 21st Century Maritime Silk Road – Security Implications and ways forward for the European Union*, (SIPRI: 2018), 3.
15. Yingzhi Zhang, "Alternate transport mode: China-EU trade on rail", *IHS Markit*, 17 March 2021.
16. Thomas Hale, "China embraces rail to transport goods to Europe", *Financial Times*, 28 March 2021.
17. Richard Ghiasy, et al., *The 21st Century Maritime Silk Road*, 5.
18. John Lee, "China's Trojan Ports", *The American Interest*, 29 November 2018.
19. Acha Leke et al., "Africa's overlooked business revolution", *Mckinsey Quarterly*, November 2018.
20. Camilla T.N. Sorensen and Ektarina Klimenko, "Emerging Chinese-Russian Cooperation in the Arctic", *SIPRI Policy Paper* No. 47, June 2017, 33.
21. Paradiplomacy refers to diplomatic relations between agencies other than the central government of two nations.
22. Greame Smith and Terence Wesley-Smith, *The China Alternative: Changing regional order in the Pacific Islands* (ANU Press: 2021), 4-5.
23. Sarah O. Dowd, "Bridging the Belt and Road Initiative in Papua New Guinea" in *The China Alternative: Changing regional order in the Pacific Islands*, Eds. Greame Smith and Terence Wesley-Smith (ANU Press: 2021), 397-425.
24. Loop Pacific, "Vanuatu PM calls for scrutiny of projects funded by China", 19 February 2019, accessed from http://www.loopvanuatu.com/vanuatu-news/vanuatu-pm-calls-scrutiny-projects-funded-china-82609 on 24 February 2019.
25. Murray Hiebert, *Under Beijing's Shadow: Southeast Asia's China Challenge* (CSIS: 2020), 34.

26. Hiebert, *Under Beijing's Shadow*, 38.
27. Richard Javad Heydarian, *The 21st Century Silk Road – Perils and Opportunities of China's Belt and Road Initiative* (ADR Publications: 2018), 35.
28. Heydarian, *The 21st Century Silk Road*, 35.
29. Hiebert, *Under Beijing's Shadow*, 14.
30. Nyshka Chandran, "A bankruptcy in the Philippines sparks concerns of Chinese firms taking over a former naval US base", *CNBC*, 25 January 2019.
31. Maria Siow, "If Laos fell into a Chinese debt trap, would it make a noise?" *South China Morning Post*, 20 February 2021.
32. Hiebert, *Under Beijing's Shadow*, 16.
33. Hiebert, *Under Beijing's Shadow*, 181.
34. Hiebert, *Under Beijing's Shadow*, 159.
35. Hiebert, *Under Beijing's Shadow*, 40.
36. Prashanth Parameswaran, "What's in the China-Cambodia Military Base hype?" *The Diplomat*, 24 November 2018.
37. Jeremy Page, Gordon Lubold and Rob Taylor, "Deal for Naval Outpost in Cambodia Furthers China's Quest for Military Network", *Wall Street Journal*, 22 July 2019.
38. Hiebert, *Under Beijing's Shadow*, 145.
39. Hiebert, *Under Beijing's Shadow*, 337-339.
40. Francis Hutchinson and Tham Siew Yean, "The BRI in Malaysia's Port Sector: Drivers of Success and Failure", *Economics Working Paper* No. 2020-10, *ISEAS-Yusof Ishak Institute*, November 2020, 12.
41. Hutchinson and Yean, "The BRI in Malaysia's Port Sector:" 12.
42. P. Prem Kumar, "Coronavirus slows China-funded $100bn city in Malaysia", *Nikkei Asia*, 7 July 2020.
43. Richard Ghiasy, et al., *The 21st Century Maritime Silk* Road, 17.
44. Tirta Nugraha Mursitama and Yi Ying, "Indonesia's perception and strategy toward China's OBOR", *The Chinese Economy*, DOI 10.1080/10971475. 2020.1809816
45. Amitabh Revi and Prateek Suri, "A 341 year old idea whose time has come?", *SNI Wire*, 8 November 2018.
46. Bruno Macaes, *Belt and Road – A Chinese World Order* (Penguin Random House India: 2019), 65.
47. Revi and Suri, "A 341 year old idea whose time has come?"
48. Gregory B. Poling, "Kyaukpyu – Connecting China to the Indian Ocean" in *China's Maritime Silk Road - Strategic and economic Implications for the Indo-Pacific* (CSIS: March 2018), 5.
49. Yuichi Nikita, "Myanmar cuts cost of China funded port project by 80%", *Nikkei Asian Review*, 28 September 2018.
50. Ruosui Zhang, "To suspend or not to suspend: A cost benefit analysis of three Chinese mega-projects in Myanmar", *The Pacific Review*, DOI: 10.1080/09512748. 2020.1776757, 2 and 17.
51. Poling, "Kyaukpyu – Connecting China to the Indian Ocean", 5.
52. Nikita, "Myanmar cuts cost of China funded port project by 80%".
53. Andrew Selth, "Burma, China and the Myth of Military Bases", *Asian Security*, Vol. 3, No. 3, 2007, 279-307, DOI: 10.1080/14799850701568929
54. "Bangladesh cancels Chinese road construction project on corruption charges", *ANI*, 24 January 2018.

55. Rejaul Karim Byron and Jagaran Chakma, "Chinese funded projects: Red tape holds back progress", *The Daily Star*, 19 October 2019.
56. Deborah Brautigam, "A critical look at Chinese 'debt-trap diplomacy': the rise of a meme", *Area Development and Policy*, Vol. 5, No. 1, 2020, 1-14, DOI 10.1080/23792949.2019.1689828
57. Hong Zhang, Beyond "Debt-Trap Diplomacy": The Dissemination of PRC State Capitalism, *China Brief*, Vol. 19, Issue. 1, The Jamestone Foundation, 5 January 2019.
58. Brautigam, "A critical look at Chinese 'debt-trap' diplomacy".
59. Devirupa Mitra, "Despite Security Assurances, Chinese Consolidation of Sri Lankan Ports Remains a Worry for India", *The Wire*, 30 July 2017.
60. Nirupama Subramanian, "Geopolitics, home stress in Colombo's new Hambantota deal", *Indian Express*, 28 July 2017.
61. AFP, Sri Lanka starts work on $4 billion refinery, *Livemint*, 25 March 2019.
62. Website of Sri Lanka Ports Authority (SLPA) accessed from https://www.slpa.lk/port-colombo/terminals on 21 March 2021.
63. Zhang, "Beyond "Debt-Trap Diplomacy".
64. Ranga Sirilal and Shihar Aneez, "Sri Lanka blocks sale of freehold land in $1.4 billion Chinese deal", *Reuters*, 12 August 2016.
65. Simon Mundy and Kathrin Hille, "The Maldives counts the cost of its debts to China", *Financial Times*, 11 February 2019.
66. Dipanjan Roy Chaudhury, "Chinese company bags Maldivian Island on 50-year lease", *The Economic Times*, 30 December 2016.
67. Saikiran Kannan, "How China has expanded its influence in the Arabian Sea", *India Today*, 15 May 2020.
68. Brahma Chellaney, "Beijing loses a battle in the Maldives - but the fight for influence goes on", *Nikkei Asia*, 25 September 2018.
69. Amitabh P. Revi, "India, Maldives Building Physical, Financial Bridges", *StratNews Global*, 13 August 2020.
70. Peter A. Dutton, Isaac B. Kardon and Conor M. Kennedy, "Gwadar: China's potential strategic strongpoint in Pakistan", *China Maritime Report* No. 7, China Maritime Studies Institute, April 2020, 12-13.
71. Dutton, Kardon and Kennedy, "Gwadar: China's potential strategic strongpoint in Pakistan", 12-13.
72. Dutton, Kardon and Kennedy, "Gwadar: China's potential strategic strongpoint in Pakistan", 3.
73. Dutton, Kardon and Kennedy, "Gwadar: China's potential strategic strongpoint in Pakistan", 17.
74. Dutton, Kardon and Kennedy, "Gwadar: China's potential strategic strongpoint in Pakistan", 9.
75. Ministry of Foreign Affairs of the People's Republic of China, "China's Arab Policy Paper", 13 January 2016.
76. "China, Iran expected to sign 25-year accord, Iranian state media says", *Reuters*, 26 March 2021.
77. OECD, "China's Belt and Road Initiative in the trade, investment and financial landscape", *OECD Business and Finance Outlook*, 2018, 29.
78. Jeremy Garlick and Radka Havlova, "The dragon dithers: assessing the cautious implementation of China's Belt and Road Initiative in Iran", *Eurasian Geography and Economics*, 2020, DOI 10.1080/15387216.2020.1822197

79. Jonathan Fulton, "China-Saudi Arabia relations through the '1+2+3' cooperation pattern", *Asian Journal of Middle Eastern and Islamic Studies*, DOI 10.1080/25765949.2020.1841991
80. Data from https://chinapower.csis.org/china-development-finance/ accessed on 5 March 2019.
81. Peter A. Dutton, Isaac B. Kardon and Conor M. Kennedy, "Djibouti: China's first overseas strategic strongpoint", *China Maritime Report* No. 6, China Maritime Studies Institute, April 2020, 5.
82. Dutton, Kardon and Kennedy, "Djibouti: China's first overseas strategic strongpoint", 11.
83. Ibid.
84. Ibid.
85. Dutton, Kardon and Kennedy, "Djibouti: China's first overseas strategic strongpoint", 12.
86. Ibid.
87. Ibid.
88. Dutton, Kardon and Kennedy, "Djibouti: China's first overseas strategic strongpoint", 15.
89. Dutton, Kardon and Kennedy, "Djibouti: China's first overseas strategic strongpoint", 20.
90. Dutton, Kardon and Kennedy, "Djibouti: China's first overseas strategic strongpoint", 28.
91. The description of the PLA Navy military facility is from Dutton, Kardon and Kennedy, "Djibouti: China's first overseas strategic strongpoint", 29-31.
92. Erica Downs, Jeffrey Becker and Patrick deGategno, *China's Military Support Facility in Djibouti: The Economic and Security Dimensions of China's First Overseas Base* (Arlington, VA: Centre for Naval Analyses, 2017), 26.
93. David Pilling and Emily Feng, "Chinese Investments in Africa go off the rails", *Financial Times*, 6 December 2018.
94. Pilling and Feng, "Chinese Investments in Africa go off the rails".
95. George Omondi, "Mombasa Port at Risk as audit finds it was used to secure SGR loan", *The East African*, 20 December 2018.
96. N. Jiraini Muchira, "Kenya: China Cannot Seize Port of Mombasa if Debt Default Occurs", *The Maritime Executive*, 16 March 2021.
97. Shem Oirere, "Tanzania Suspends $10B Bagamoyo Port Project", *Engineering News-Record (ENR)*, 25 June 2019.
98. Macaes, *Belt and Road*, 81.
99. Academy of Military Science, "The Science of Military Strategy" (as translated by *In their own words: Foreign Military Thought*, China Aerospace Studies Institute, USA in), 2015, 253.
100. James Kynge, "Chinese purchases of overseas ports top $20bn in past year", *Financial Times*, 16 July 2017.

6

Other Infrastructure Initiatives

Introduction

The most quoted report on infrastructure needs in Asia is a study published by the Asian Development Bank (ADB) in February 2017.[1] It calculated that Asia will need to invest $ 26 trillion from 2016 to 2030, or $ 1.7 trillion per year, if the region is to maintain its growth momentum, eradicate poverty, and respond to climate change. This was the "climate-adjusted estimate" that caters for changes in climate annually. Without climate change mitigation and adaptation costs, $ 22.6 trillion will be needed, or $ 1.5 trillion per year. If it is estimated that the BRI, over a 20-year period, will see an investment of $ 8 trillion, it amounts to less than 1.5 per cent of GDP per annum for the BRI countries. These levels are modest compared to the ADB report for Asia that projected the need for 5.1 per cent of the region's GDP needs to be spent on infrastructure.[2] The World Bank report on South Asia also suggests that a 7.5 per cent GDP growth would result in increased demand for infrastructure services that in turn would require investment amounting to about 5 per cent of GDP. These estimates illustrate that the BRI, by itself, will fall short in catering for the infrastructure needs of the participating nations.

Assistance for infrastructure and connectivity enhancement was one of the many arrows in the quiver for spreading national influence in foreign lands. In fact, it was part of a basket that included economic aid, food assistance, technical training and assistance, and all such benign measures. They were packaged as a foil for the politically potent issues like trade and security cooperation that form the core of bilateral relationships between nations. However, the announcements of the BRI changed that perception. Infrastructure development was once again perceived as a pivot in geopolitics. When the sheer ambition of the BRI, and possible spread of Chinese influence that it implied, dawned on the rest of the world, there were moves to counter it. Infrastructure and connectivity or their proxy terms like "economic prosperity" moved up from the lower paragraphs in bilateral and multilateral joint statements.

It is not as if the requirement of infrastructure was not thought of earlier or plans for connectivity enhancement did not exist. The realisation was always there and numerous bilateral and multilateral platforms have been engaged in infrastructure development for decades. The major difference is that now it is perceived more through the prism of geopolitics. Moreover, the perception that economic prosperity and heft is the first step to move up the ladder in global standing has deepened. Infrastructure and connectivity are perceived as critical requirements to progress economic growth. It is also politically expedient for leaders to portray all infrastructure projects as symbols of progress and achievements of their regime to their people.

Although there have been numerous international initiatives in infrastructure sectors in the past, they have often stagnated or failed due to lack of either financial backing or political will. Sometimes, political turmoil in a region has nixed optimistic visions. One of the reasons for the landmass of Europe and Asia having been considered as separate is that there was hardly any connectivity between the two ends of this super-continent. Of course, the post-World War II ideological divide and the Iron Curtain were primarily responsible for it. Despite that, numerous attempts were made to improve connectivity but none fructified. The Belt is the latest initiative that tries to overcome this historical impediment. A similar initiative is playing out between the coasts of Africa. Geographies are dissolving and nations have again begun considering ambitious possibilities that were rejected earlier.

This chapter will scan the infrastructure and connectivity initiatives in recent years in the Indo-Pacific region.

Japan

Overseas Development Aid (ODA) was a major tool employed by Japan in the post World War II years to enhance its credibility and its commitment to international economic prosperity. With its technological innovations and quality, Japanese industry progressed and the economy grew. This provided Japan with adequate capital to enhance its reputation as a responsible nation and for its industry to invest in viable economies. It has been working in collaboration with the ADB in which it is a founding member, one of the two largest shareholders and the largest contributor. Much of the work on infrastructure in Central Asia in the 1990s was undertaken by ADB. Its Greater Mekong Sub-region (GMS) program, launched in 1992, aimed to construct a network of roads, ports, railways, industrial zones and power transmission grids in the Mekong region. It has spent billions of dollars on two economic corridors – a North-South one connecting China to the Mekong nations and an East-West one connecting Myanmar to Vietnam. Japan's outward FDI has also been significant. Between 2013 and 2018, Japan's investment in Southeast Asia was $ 102.3 billion, nearly twice as much as the $ 52.8 billion the region received from China. A BMI Research report of 2018 showed that Japan's infrastructure investment since 2000, completed and ongoing, totalled about $ 230 billion, while that of China reached about $ 155 billion.[3]

The Japanese ODA was augmented after the revision of the Development Cooperation Charter in 2015. It was tailored to cater for Japan's more proactive foreign policy and greater defence options. On 21 January 2015, Prime Minister Shinzo Abe announced the "Partnership for Quality Infrastructure" initiative. It was committed to providing, along with the ADB, about $ 110 billion over the next five years for development of "quality infrastructure" in Asia in collaboration with other countries and international organisations. The following year, on 23 May, he announced the "Expanded Partnership for Quality Infrastructure" in which the financial commitment was increased to $ 200 billion globally over the next five years. "Quality" was the key distinguishing factor of the Japanese initiative when compared to the BRI. The emphasis on "quality" was to contrast it with China's quantity and speed of execution. The implications were of higher standards in accounting, procurement practices, environmental sustainability and safety. The terms and conditions of loans were in accordance with the repayment capability of the recipient nations.

The main institutions that have a pivotal role are the Ministry of Foreign Affairs (MOFA), Japan International Cooperation Agency (JICA), Ministry of Economy Trade and Industry (METI), Japan Bank for International Cooperation (JBIC) and Japan External Trade Organisation (JETRO). MOFA is responsible for the development assistance policy and corresponding diplomatic effort. JICA implements the policy and manages Japan's bilateral aid. More than half of the financial assistance is provided in Asia with India and Bangladesh being the top two recipients. METI designs the investment and export support policy. JETRO implements METI's directions. JBIC provides financing to support activities of Japanese firms abroad.

The Japan Infrastructure Initiative is a joint venture of Mitsubishi UFJ Lease & Finance (47.55%), Hitachi Capital (47.55%), and Bank of Tokyo-Mitsubishi UFJ (4.9%). It aims to invest $ 878 million into Japanese-directed infrastructure projects, such as railways and power plants, throughout Asia, Europe, and the USA. The Japan Overseas Infrastructure Investment Corporation (JOIN) is another public-private infrastructure investment fund for Japanese companies.

Japan is financing and building infrastructure all across the Indo-Pacific up to Africa. Japan is the only credible competitor to the BRI as of now. It prefers to keep a low profile and does not actively promote its projects. In this way it generates goodwill among the recipient nations without creating any alarm. It is perceived as benign and the spread of its influence is not a cause of concern to nations. The data on Japan's international assistance and investments is freely available. The terms of the loans can be accessed. This transparency ensures that Japan's projects are not tracked and dissected, the way Chinese ones are, to comprehend the possible political or security intent.

Port-related projects funded by Japan under its "Free and Open Indian-Pacific Policy" include Nacala port in Mozambique ($ 320 million), Mombasa port project in Kenya ($ 400 million), Toamasina port in Madagascar ($ 400 million), Matarbari port and power station in Bangladesh ($ 3.7 billion), Yangon Container Terminal in Myanmar ($ 200 million), and Dawei port and SEZ in Myanmar ($ 800 million). Japan has set up SEZs in the Philippines, Indonesia, Myanmar, Vietnam and Bangladesh.

India is the largest recipient of Japanese ODA since 2003 and it is providing technical and financial assistance to some of the largest infrastructure projects in India. Japan is providing a loan of $ 12 billion to cover the project cost of $ 15 billion for the Mumbai-Ahmedabad High Speed Rail (MAHSR) project, incorporating Japanese *Shinkansen* technology. The Mumbai-Delhi Dedicated Freight Corridor (DFC) that consists of a double line electric rail track of 1,490 km is being progressed with Japanese assistance. The Delhi-Mumbai Industrial Corridor (DMIC) envisages the setting up of industrial zones and cities along the DFC. Part of the estimated $ 90 billion cost of the project is being financed through Japanese funding. The other major infrastructure projects being undertaken with Japanese assistance include the Chennai-Bengaluru Industrial Corridor (CBIC), metro rail projects and development of Japan Industrial Townships (JITs).

There is special emphasis on the development of India's northeast region and increasing connectivity between India and Southeast Asia. JICA is supporting construction of highways in Northeast India.[4] The India-Japan North East Forum was launched on 5 December 2017 to identify specific projects for economic modernisation of India's Northeast region.[5]

Collaborative projects between Japan and India in Sri Lanka, Myanmar, Bangladesh and Kenya have also been envisaged.[6] Japan has substantial investments in South Asia, with the exception of Pakistan. Japan has been providing Bangladesh soft loans of around $ 2 billion since 2012 and is its largest bilateral donor. In Myanmar, other than the 2,342-hectare Thilawa SEZ outside Yangon, Japan's private industry is involved in the $ 1.7 billion Paluzawa coal mine and power plant, and the $ 3.5-billion Myeik coal-fired power plant. Japan has committed to rescue the troubled Dawei Special Economic Zone (SEZ). This ambitious $ 8 billion project ran into trouble and the Thai company developing it pulled out in 2013. Situated on the coast of the Andaman Sea, it was to be linked by road to the Gulf of Thailand.

Collaboration with Africa is through the five-yearly Tokyo International Conference on African Development (TICAD) that was launched in 1993. In 2016, PM Shinzo Abe pledged $ 30 billion in public and private support for infrastructure projects in Africa.

Unlike India, Japan has not rejected participation in the BRI. On one hand, India-Japan joint statements routinely mention all the factors that the Indian MEA statement of 13 May 2017 had flagged with regard to the BRI. On the other hand, Japan does engage with China on joint projects from time to time. In December 2017, PM Abe, while addressing Chinese and Japanese executives, mentioned the possibility of working together with China on BRI projects. In May 2018, China, Japan and Malaysia agreed to pursue collaboration in the Eastern Economic Corridor SEZ of Thailand. During the October 2018 visit of PM Abe to China, the two nations agreed to progress business collaboration in third countries.

Asia-Africa Growth Corridor

India and Japan institutionalised a dialogue on Africa in 2010. In November 2016, during Prime Minister Narendra Modi's visit to Japan, the idea of the two countries promoting a trade corridor with Africa fructified.[7] The vision document of the Asia-Africa Growth Corridor (AAGC) was unveiled on the occasion of the 52nd Annual Meeting of the Africa Development Bank held at Gandhinagar on 22-26 May 2017. The document was prepared by Research and Information System for Developing Countries (RIS), Economic Research Institute for ASEAN and East Asia (ERIA) and Institute of Developing Economies – Japan External Trade Organisation (IDE-JETRO).

Both India and Japan have platforms for cooperation with Africa. India Africa Summit is held once in three years. Three summits have been held so far (2008: New Delhi, 2011: Addis Ababa and 2015: New Delhi). Japan has the Tokyo International Conference on African Development (TICAD) that is held every five years. Five summits have been held since 1993. Collaboration between India and Japan has its complementarities. Japan has the capital and technology to offer to African nations. India has historical linkages with them. The linkages have been maintained in modern times due to the common cause against colonialism, South-South cooperation, and multilateral efforts involving developing nations. The Indian diaspora resides in many of the African nations. Hence, there is a synergy between the linkages of India and the capital from Japan. Moreover, to cater for the expanding market of Africa,

Japanese industry will find it convenient to manufacture in India and export to Africa. Japanese industry is more used to the Indian environment and impediments to manufacturing are lower in India than in Africa.

The Vision Document lists the pillars of the AAGC as "Development and cooperation projects, Quality infrastructure and institutional connectivity, Enhancing capacities and skills, and People-to-People partnerships".[8] The vision of being "aligned with development priorities", quality infrastructure" and "harmony with local environment" gave a subtle contrast to the prevailing views on the BRI. The Geographical Simulation Model developed by IDE/ERIA was to be used to estimate the impact of proposed connectivity projects and evolve a plan for the AAGC. A Research Support Unit (RSU) comprising of RIS, ERIA and IDE-JETRO was set up in RIS, New Delhi, to conduct the preparation study and submit its report in 2018.

Till now, the only progress has been that formation of a "Platform for Japan-India Business Cooperation in Asia-Africa Region" for business houses and a MoU for support of business projects in Third World countries that has been signed between Nippon Export and Investment Insurance (NEXI) and Export Credit Guarantee Corporation of India (ECGC).[9]

Whenever the economic corridors and projects get finalised, it will be safe to assume that they will connect Japanese SEZs and industrial zones in India, Bangladesh and Myanmar to the Japanese-funded ports in Mozambique and Kenya.

ASEAN Connectivity 2025

On 6 September 2016, leaders of ASEAN adopted the Master Plan on ASEAN Connectivity 2025 (MPAC 2025) in Vientiane. The MPAC 2025, which succeeded the Master Plan on ASEAN Connectivity 2010, focuses on five strategic areas – sustainable infrastructure, digital innovation, seamless logistics, regulatory excellence and people mobility. It estimated a requirement of at least $ 110 billion investment every year to support future growth. Forty priority projects were identified. The financing of the projects is through Public-Private Partnership. The ASEAN Connectivity Coordinating Committee monitors and reports the status of implementation of the Master Plan on ASEAN Connectivity to the

ASEAN Summit. Supporting finance is the major issue. Of the 125 projects in 19 sectors identified in the earlier Master Plan of 2010, only 39 could be completed by end May 2016.

USA

Post World War II, the USA contributed crucially to the development of Europe, Japan and South Korea. The end of the Cold War and fall of the Iron Curtain gave the USA another opportunity to employ its enormous resources to do something similar in Eastern Europe and Central Asian nations. However, exercising this option was not a priority. It therefore only worked towards ensuring access to new markets for its industry. State-funded infrastructure development abroad as a tool to rejuvenate the economy had probably been forgotten. It was a job to be done by private industry propelled by market forces. The USA meanwhile concentrated on advancing the boundaries of NATO and pursuing military interventions to secure its interests around the world. There was also economic facilitation provided to China. The assumption in the USA probably was that as China increases its participation in the international system and reaps the benefits of the market-based economy, its political system would also change. It was an assumption that proved to be completely wrong.

Interestingly, it was the USA that first mentioned an initiative called "New Silk Road". It was mentioned by Secretary of State Hillary Clinton in July 2011 in a speech in Chennai. The context was about providing connectivity with Afghanistan. Nothing was heard about it thereafter. Some analysts believe that China formed a study group in 2011 to look at the possibility of a "New Silk Road" buoyed by this announcement. During the India-US Strategic Dialogue of 2013, the US Secretary of State referred to the potential of an Indo-Pacific Economic Corridor (IPEC) between the economies of South Asia and Southeast Asia to transform trade, development and investment. These two terms, not heard for years after they were initially mentioned, resurfaced in May 2017 when it was reported that the US State Department had made budgetary requests for supporting two initiatives – the New Silk Road (NSR) focused on Afghanistan and its neighbours, and the Indo-Pacific Economic Corridor linking South Asia with Southeast Asia.

In October 2017, the US Overseas Private Investment Corporation

(OPIC) signed a MoU with the Japan Bank of International Cooperation and the Nippon Export and Investment Insurance to offer "high quality" infrastructure investment alternatives in the Indo-Pacific Region.[10] In May 2018, OPIC signed a MoU with the Association of European Development Finance Institutions to promote collaboration on sustainable investments in developing nations.

On 30 July 2018, while addressing the Indo-Pacific Business Forum, US Secretary of State Pompeo announced a $ 113 million initiative to support foundational areas of the future – digital economy, energy and infrastructure. Of this, $ 30 million was for infrastructure. The relatively small amount drew sniggers but more commitments were planned.

The most significant step was the Better Utilisation of Investments Leading to Development (BUILD) Act passed on 5 October 2018 to reform and strengthen US development aid capabilities. It created the US International Development Finance Corporation (USIDFC). It will facilitate the participation of private sector capital and skills in the economic development of countries with low and lower-middle-income in order to complement US assistance and foreign policy objectives. The new agency has a spending cap of $ 60 billion, more than double the previous cap of $ 29 billion that OPIC had. However, it still offers a private sector, market-based solution. In a transition plan, the functions of all existing government agencies such as OPIC and the US Agency for International Development (USAID) were to be rejigged.

On 31 December 2018, US President Donald Trump signed the Asia Reassurance Initiative Act (ARIA) into law. This Act states that "it is imperative that the United States continue to play a leading role in the Indo-Pacific region by defending peace and security; advancing economic prosperity; and promoting respect for fundamental human rights".[11] Among the diplomatic strategies is "to work with and encourage Indo-Pacific countries to pursue high-quality and transparent infrastructure projects". It authorises $ 1.5 billion every year from 2019 to 2023 to further the US strategy in the Indo-Pacific Region and to support its allies. Of course, infrastructure development forms a small part of the many security and economic aspects that this Act covers.

On 4 November 2019, the USA released another policy document on "Free and Open Indo-Pacific".[12] It read almost like an election manifesto listing all the achievements of the USA in the Indo-Pacific region. It was a long list – over $ 1.9 trillion of two-way trade in 2018; $ 2 trillion of foreign assistance since World War II; commitment of $ 29 million for energy development in the Mekong Region (with Japan); $ 3.8 billion provided in assistance to Mekong region countries in the last 10 years; $ 350 million annually for the Pacific Island nations and an additional $ 100 million in 2019; $ 23 million to the Papua New Guinea Electrification Partnership (PEP) with Australia, Japan, and New Zealand; $ 23 million foreign assistance for the Maldives; $ 2.9 billion support through various agencies for private investment in the region; partnership with ADB to mobilise $ 7 billion for energy projects in Asia; $ 2.3 billion assistance through the US Millennium Challenge Corporation (MCC) to Indo-Pacific nations since 2004; and so on.

A plethora of institutions has been set up. The Blue Dot Network seeks to be a conglomeration that will certify a project as adhering to international standards. Asia EDGE (Enhancing Development and Growth through Energy) seeks to support private sector investments in the energy sector. However, USA is yet to gain the perception that it is enhancing infrastructure in a significant manner in the Indo-Pacific region.

Australia

In November 2018, the Australian government announced the establishment of the Australian Infrastructure Financing Facility for countries in the Pacific Region with a fund of $ 2 billion. The facility became operational on 1 July 2019. An additional $ 1 billion was provided to Export Finance and Insurance Corporation (EFIC), the government's export credit agency. Australia has also stepped up its aid to the Pacific Island nations.

European Union

Infrastructure connectivity has been on the agenda of the EU since the 1990s with the launch of the Transport Corridor Europe Caucasus Asia (TRACECA) programme in 1993. The EU established a Central Asia strategy in 2007, which was updated in 2015, with the goal of stable, secure and sustainable development of the region.

On 19 September 2018, the EU presented its strategy on connecting Asia and Europe.[13] It described the "European Way" as "sustainable, comprehensive and rule-based connectivity". It spoke of transport, digital and energy connectivity. It also dwelt on bilateral, regional and international partnerships and highlighted the need for funding infrastructure development. In September 2019, the EU and Japan signed the "EU-Japan Partnership on Sustainable Connectivity and Quality Infrastructure". The partnership is backed by a 60 billion euro ($ 65.48 billion) EU Guarantee Fund. The joint statement is heavy on normative elements. Similar norms are stated in the India-EU Roadmap to 2025.

Multilateral Efforts

In September 2015, India, Japan and the USA agreed on the formation of an expert group to identify collaborative efforts that can help strengthen regional connectivity at a meeting of the India-Japan-USA trilateral dialogue.[14] This group, known as the Trilateral Infrastructure Working Group, met in February 2018. The ARIA provides the possibility of financing any arrangement that the Australia-India-Japan-USA Quadrilateral may decide.

In November 2018, Australia, Japan and the USA signed a trilateral partnership to invest in projects in the Indo-Pacific. In April 2019, the trilateral partners undertook a joint mission to Papua New Guinea to identify projects. An LNG project was identified but not heard about thereafter.[15] In October 2020, the three nations agreed to finance $ 30 million to provide an undersea fibre-optic cable connection to Palau.[16] The three nations, along with New Zealand, are working on a program to provide electricity to 70 per cent of the population in Papua New Guinea by 2030.

Thailand proposed a regional fund with its neighbours to back infrastructure and other development projects in Thailand, Cambodia, Laos, Myanmar and Vietnam. This proposal was under the aegis of the Ayeyawady-Chao Phraya-Mekong Economic Cooperation Strategy (ACMECS), a regional organization initiated by Thailand in 2003. The proposed fund was initially to become operational in 2019 and utilised for projects under the ACMECS 2019-2023 Master Plan.[17]

The United Nations Economic and Social Commission for Asia and the Pacific (ESCAP) has been promoting connectivity in the region. One major initiative was the Asian Land Transport Infrastructure Development (ALTID) project that comprises the Asian Highway

Network and Trans-Asian Railway. The Asian Highway Network is a 141,000-km network of roads running across 32 countries.

National Initiatives

The Indo-Pacific region has some of the fastest-growing economies in the world. Infrastructure development is not only an immediate requirement to progress economic prosperity but also an effective political message of progress for the national leadership. Hence, almost every nation in the region has embarked on an ambitious programme of infrastructure development. Starting from East Asia in 2017, South Korea announced a New Northern Policy and a New Southern Policy. The New Northern Policy is focused on infrastructure and connectivity through North Korea, Russia, Belarus, Ukraine, Mongolia, China, and the five Central Asian countries. The New Southern Policy aims to bolster economic cooperation with Southeast Asia and South Asia. The Philippines has 'Build, Build, Build', Indonesia has 'Global Maritime Fulcrum', Thailand has Eastern Economic Corridor and so on.

Conclusion

There are numerous national, bilateral and regional initiatives aimed at enhancing infrastructure. Some mechanisms under the aegis of the World Bank and the Asian Development Bank have been operating for decades. A lot of the achievements touted in the BRI are riding on existing infrastructure created by regional and multilateral organisations.

Outside of the multilateral financial institutions, Japan is still the only credible alternative to China in infrastructure funding in the Indo-Pacific region. All other initiatives are either in a nascent stage or too limited in scope. The US effort is different in that it seeks to channelise private capital. However, it is clear that the funding is inadequate. If that be the case, infrastructure and connectivity will maintain the pivotal position in geopolitics that it has gained.

NOTES

1. Asian Development Bank, "Meeting Asia's Infrastructure Needs", February 2017.
2. John Hurley, et al., "Examining the Debt implications of the Belt and Road initiative from a Policy Perspective", *Centre for Global Development*, March 2018, 5.
3. Siegfried Alegado, "Japan still beating China in southeast Asia infrastructure race", *Bloomberg*, 9 February 2018.

4. "Cooperation with India not in disputed area: Japan to China", *Mint*, 18 November 2014; "Japan funds to improve NE roads", *The Telegraph*, 18 April 2016; Press Information Bureau, "Highway Projects in North Eastern Region", 3 March 2016.
5. Ministry of External Affairs, "Launch of India-Japan Act East Forum", 5 December 2017.
6. Press Information Bureau, "India-Japan Fact Sheets", 29 October 2018.
7. Ministry of External Affairs, "India Japan Joint Statement during the visit of Prime Minister to Japan", 11 November 2011.
8. RIS et al., "Asia Africa Growth Corridor – Partnership for Sustainable and Innovative Development", May 2017.
9. Ministry of External Affairs, "India-Japan Vision Statement", 29 October 2018.
10. Jeff M. Smith, "China's Belt and Road Initiative: Strategic Implications and International Opposition", *The Heritage Foundation*, 9 August 2018, 21.
11. US Congress, S.2736-115th Congress (2017-2018), accessed from https://www.congress.gov/bill/115th-congress/senate-bill/2736/text on 25 February 2019.
12. Department of State (USA), "A Free and Open Indo-Pacific: Advancing a shared vision", 4 November 2019.
13. European Commission, "Connecting Europe and Asia – Building Blocks for a New Strategy", 19 September 2018.
14. Embassy of India in Washington, "Inaugural US-India-Japan Trilateral Ministerial Dialogue", 29 September 2015.
15. Grant Wyeth, "Australia Japan US start down their own Indo-Pacific Road in LNG", *The Diplomat*, 26 June 2019.
16. Jason Scott, "Australia Joins U.S., Japan to Fund $30 Million Undersea Cable in South Pacific", 20 October 2020.
17. Yukako Ono, "Thailand plans regional infrastructure fund to reduce Chinese dependence", *Nikkei Asian Review*, 4 June 2018.

7

Indian Initiatives

Introduction

India's growing economy and expanding sphere of interests have led it to take up a slew of initiatives to enhance infrastructure and connectivity. There has been a manifold increase in India's spending on its infrastructure over the last two decades. Infrastructure development in foreign nations has become an element in Indian foreign policy engagement.

India's efforts in infrastructure development and connectivity can be evaluated at three levels – national, regional and multilateral. One way to consider it would be in expanding concentric circles starting from India itself, to its immediate neighbourhood and beyond.

Internal Infrastructure

Foremost in infrastructure development by India has to be the development of infrastructure within India itself. The World Economic Forum reports suggest that India will be the largest consumer market and third-largest economy in the world by 2030, just 9 years from now. Considering the poor state of Indian infrastructure, it is obvious that the infrastructure within India itself needs to be upgraded to cater for this predicted economic growth and large market. India has launched the National Infrastructure Pipeline (NIP) to create infrastructure from 2020 to 2025. The Government of India's Economic Survey of 2019-20 estimated that India needs to spend about $ 1.4 trillion (Rs. 100 lakh crore) on infrastructure development if it desires to achieve the target of becoming a $ 5 trillion economy by 2024-25.[1] This has been derived from the report of the Task Force on NIP that projected a requirement of Rs. 111 lakh crore of infrastructure investment for the period from 2020 to 2025.[2] To give some context to this number, the total investment on infrastructure in FY 2018 and FY 2019 was around Rs. 10 lakh crore each year.[3] The augmentation of infrastructure within India in the next two decades will be among the most massive in the world. The process has commenced and the list is already quite long, but some deserve mention.

The National Rail Plan of India seeks to develop capacity by 2030 to cater for demand up to 2050.[4] The Western Dedicated Freight Corridor (DFC) will be a 1,504 km double line electric rail track from Jawaharlal Nehru Port (near Mumbai) to Dadri (Uttar Pradesh). It will allow freight trains, stacked to two-container height, to run at 100 kilometres per hour from the western ports to North India. Similarly, there will be an Eastern DFC of 1,856 km that will be between Ludhiana (Punjab) and Dankuni (West Bengal). The projects are estimated to cost around $ 13 billion and will be completed by June 2022.[5] In 2006, the Dedicated Freight Corridor Corporation of India Limited (DFCCIL) was set up to implement the project. Funding is from multiple sources that include the World Bank, Indian Railways, JICA and Public Private Partnerships (PPP). The four other DFCs in the planning stage are North-South (Delhi-Tamil Nadu), East-West (West Bengal-Maharashtra), East-South (West Bengal-Andhra Pradesh) and South-South (Tamil Nadu-Goa). Construction of these DFCs will continue in phases till 2051.[6]

The 508-km Mumbai-Ahmadabad High Speed Rail is the first HSR project in India. It is being constructed as per Japanese standards and with Japanese assistance. The project is expected to be completed by 2023. However, it is facing delays primarily on account of land acquisition and will cost upwards of $ 13 billion.[7] The National High-Speed Rail Corporation Limited (NHSRCL) was set up on 12 February 2016 to finance, construct, maintain and manage the HSR Corridor in India. Twelve more HSR routes totalling 7,500 km are planned to be built in phases by 2051.[8] The most difficult new rail line is the 345-kilometre Jammu-Baramula railway line that will establish rail connectivity with the Kashmir Valley. The line includes the world's tallest rail bridge being built at a height of 359 metres over the Chenab River and the 11.2-km Pir Panjal (Katra-Qazigund) tunnel that was inaugurated in June 2013. The

125-km Jiribam-Imphal rail line is another challenging project expected to be completed by March 2021. The line has 52 tunnels, 149 bridges and the world's tallest pier bridge.[9] Other challenging rail lines of strategic importance for which surveys are being undertaken include Bilashpur-Manali-Leh (498 km), Tawang-Tenga-Missamari (170 km), North Lakhimpur-Silapathar (249 km), and Pasighat-Tezu-Parsuram Kund-Rupai (227 km). In September 2018, India decided to have complete electrification of rail tracks by 2022 so as to reduce pollution, dependence on fossil fuels and costs.

The National Industrial Corridor Development Programme has an ambitious aim to develop new industrial cities along five industrial corridors. The industrial corridors are Delhi Mumbai Industrial Corridor (DMIC), Amritsar Kolkata Industrial Corridor (AKIC), Chennai Bengaluru Industrial Corridor (CBIC) with extension to Kochi via Coimbatore, East Coast Economic Corridor (ECEC) with Visakhapatnam Chennai Industrial Corridor (VCIC) as Phase 1, and Bengaluru Mumbai Industrial Corridor (BMIC). The National Industrial Corridor Development Corporation (NICDC) is mandated to undertake development of the industrial corridors. The DMIC is being created along the Western DFC. Twenty-four cities are planned to be built and eight are being constructed now under Phase 1. The total cost is estimated at over $ 100 billion and will be completed in four phases by 2040, making it one of the largest infrastructure projects worldwide.[10]

India has already embarked on massive road construction, and it has now been combined under the Bharatmala Pariyogna. Phase 1 was approved in 2018 for construction of 34,800 km by 2022.[11] The road projects include major works like the 9.2 km Chenani-Nashri tunnel between Jammu and Srinagar, and the 9.2 km Atal Tunnel under Rohtang Pass. Rail and road construction has significantly picked up in recent times in India's Northeast region. The best indication of this is the number of bridges constructed recently or under construction across the Brahmaputra River – the 9.15-km Dhola-Sadia bridge (over the Lohit River), the 4.9-km Bogibeel Rail-Road bridge, the 9-km Majuli-Jorhat bridge and the 19-km Dhubri-Phulbari bridge. Of course, all the road construction is not for economic or social reasons alone. The Border Roads Organisation (BRO) constructs roads in India's border areas. For the five-year period from 2018-19 to 2022-23, the plan is for construction and improvement of 272 roads of 14,545 km length. Of these, 61 roads of length 3,324 km have been identified as strategic.[12] By March 2021, 59 roads with a total length of 3,205 km had been constructed.

Air connectivity is being progressed by setting up new airports and modernising existing ones. The commercial air network is being expanded and flights are being cross-subsidised under a regional air connectivity scheme called UDAN to expand the profile of air travellers.

India has 14,500 km of navigable waterways that can be developed. As per a Rail India Technical and Economic Service (RITES) report of 2014, one litre of fuel moves 24 tonne km on road, 95 tonne km on rail and 215 tonne km on Inland Water Transport.[13] The National Waterways Act of 2016 has notified 111 National Waterways. A study was conducted by RITES on setting up an Integrated National Waterways Transportation Grid. As per the study, an investment of Rs. 22,763 crore is required to set it up by 2023. However, implementation is fraught with challenges since channel draught is not uniform and some of the rivers are seasonal. The continuous maintenance and dredging that is required is capital intensive.[14] The Jal Marg Vikas Project was taken up in 2017 for augmentation of National Waterway 1 between Varanasi and Haldia. In October 2018, the Inland Waterways Authority of India (IWAI) transported container cargo from Kolkata to Varanasi on the Ganga River. In February 2019, Maersk, the world's largest container ship operator started operations on the same route. By March 2021, there were 16 operational National Waterways in the country. Twenty-three will be operational by 2030.[15] The transportation of cargo on National Waterways increased from 6.59 million tonnes in 2014-15 to 72.31 million tonnes in 2018-19. It has grown at a Compound Annual Growth Rate of 19 per cent over the last five years.[16] Development of 36 more waterways was found to be technically and economically feasible and will be undertaken. Five major ports have been directed to take up development of National Waterways in their vicinity.[17]

Finance for the projects is being sourced from multiple sources. In the Union Budget of 2021, the Government of India announced the launch of an asset monetisation programme. Capital will be raised by monetising existing operational assets. Infrastructure Investment Trusts (InvITs) also provide the same function of using operating assets to raise capital for the private sector. In 2020, India had seven InvITs, of which two were publicly listed.[18] Road construction in India was substantially financed by charging a road cess on the sale of petroleum products. In March 2021, the Union Cabinet approved the setting up of a Development Finance Institution (DFI) for long-term funding of infrastructure development. With a capital infusion of Rs. 20,000 crore from the government, the professionally-managed institution is expected to raise Rs. 3 lakh crore from the market in the coming years.[19] Apart from internal resources, finance is being provided by multilateral financial institutions. India is also the largest recipient of Japanese assistance since 2003. The National Investment and Infrastructure Fund (NIIF), set up in 2015, is India's first Sovereign Wealth Fund with a commitment of $ 3 billion from the Government of India. It is an investment vehicle for funding commercially viable greenfield, brownfield and stalled projects in the infrastructure sector. Presently, it manages around $ 4.4 billion across three funds, each with a distinctive investment strategy. Its first agreement was with the Abu Dhabi Investment Authority that committed to invest $ 1 billion in October 2017. Qatar has also evinced interest in the fund. As one of the fastest growing economies in the world today, there are several countries that are interested in investing in India, especially the oil-rich countries with large sovereign funds.

In addition to the hard infrastructure, 'soft' infrastructure for integration is also being developed. The Goods and Services Tax regime follows a single tax and enables unimpeded movement of cargo within India.

Sagarmala and Maritime Vision 2030

Moving outwards from the mainland, we come to the coastline and ports of India. The Sagarmala project aims to reduce logistics cost for export-import and domestic trade, and provide "port-led development". It has five components – modernisation of existing ports and development of new ports; enhancement of port connectivity to the hinterland; development of industrial clusters near ports and coastal areas; sustainable development of coastal communities; and impetus to transport cargo by coastal shipping and inland waterways. The National Perspective Plan (NPP) of the project was released on 14 April 2016, and the Final Report giving details about the proposed development was released in November 2016. The NPP and the Final Report list all the constraints and inefficiencies of freight transfer in India and provide details of the proposed solutions. Some of these constraints and inefficiencies will be covered later in Chapter Nine.

The Sagarmala project is much more than merely port modernisation. The origin and destination of all key commodities have been analysed to arrive at the optimum route for them. They include petroleum products, coal, iron ore, steel, cement, fertilizers, and, of course, containers. Ports are proposed to be modified or created to cater to this flow of commodities. The first step will be to address infrastructural and operational challenges of Indian ports. Turnaround Time (TAT) at major ports was approximately four days in 2014-15, whereas the global average benchmark was 1-2 days. Only some private sector ports in India had a turnaround time of around 2 days. The connectivity between the hinterland and ports is sought to be improved. Last mile connectivity to the ports is one of the major constraints in the smooth movement of cargo resulting in a lot of "idle time" during its transit. The movement of freight is also sought to be shifted from rail and road to National Waterways and coastal shipping to reduce costs and improve efficiency. Although water-borne transport is much safer, cheaper and cleaner, compared to other modes of transportation, it accounts for less than 6 per cent of India's modal split. The modal mix of transport (road, rail, and water) for each commodity is sought to be optimised for the lowest cost and highest efficiency. The distances between manufacturing centres and ports are large. This adds to the exporting cost. Industrial clusters are sought to be created in the coastal regions so that goods need not travel long distances. These industrial clusters would be located optimally to benefit from the planned industrial corridors mentioned earlier. Sustainable development in coastal regions, including development in island territories, is also part of Sagarmala. Coastal community development is also given importance by focussing on skill development and job creation; studying the social and environmental impact of projects; and encouraging sustainable fishing practices.

The port modernisation projects aim to improve the efficiency and enhance capacity of existing ports. Capacity will be enhanced in 12 existing major ports. The draught at Ennore (Kamarajar Port) and Paradip will be increased from 16 m to 18 m. New port locations that are proposed include Sagar in West Bengal, Paradip Outer Harbour in Odisha, Enayam in Tamil Nadu and Vadhavan in Maharashtra. Enayam, with a natural deep draught of 20 m, was proposed to be a transhipment port. The connectivity projects will augment coastal shipping and inland waterways; provide last-mile connectivity to ports and set up seven multimodal hubs or inland 'dry' ports. The coastline has been segregated into 14 Coastal Economic Zones (CEZs) for development of industrial clusters in each. The industrial clusters will be of 12 major industries that are being divided in three themes of energy (refinery and petrochemical complex), bulk material (like steel and cement) and manufacturing (electronics, food processing, apparel, leather, footwear and furniture).

More than 574 projects at a cost of $ 82 billion (Rs. 6 lakh crore) have been identified for implementation during 2015 to 2035. As of 30 September 2019, a total of 121 projects (costing Rs. 30,228 crore) had been completed.[20] Fifty-eight projects involving a cost of Rs. 49,950 crore have been identified as part of NIP for infrastructure augmentation and development at major ports up to FY 2025.[21]

The Maritime India Vision 2030 (MIV 2030) was released on 2 March 2021 and can be considered as an extension of the Sagarmala Plan to the broader sector. Unlike the Sagarmala documents that are at levels of project execution till 2035, the Maritime Vision is a policy level document providing goals to be achieved by 2030. It is a ten-year blueprint to overhaul the maritime sector in India. The vision outlines more than 150 initiatives across 10 themes. It envisages a total investment of Rs. 3-3.5 lakh crore in ports, shipping and waterways. Of these, Rs. 1 to 1.25 lakh crore will be into port infrastructure. Like the Sagarmala documents, the MIV 2030 too undertook origin-destination analysis across commodities and (eight) regional clusters to develop traffic projections, and finalise the infrastructure enhancements required. As per this forecast, the 12 major ports need to augment capacity by 423 MTPA in 10 years with an investment of over Rs. 33,500 crore. The four regional clusters of West Bengal-Odisha, Gujarat, South Andhra Pradesh-North Tamil Nadu, and North Maharashtra are considered high-potential clusters for the next decade. In line with the global trend of mega-ports, three mega-ports with a total capacity of than 300 MTPA can be developed at Vadhavan-JNPT Cluster (Gujarat), Paradip Port (Odisha), and Kandla (Gujarat). Ennore (Tamil Nadu) can also be considered after one or two years.

At present, approximately 75 per cent of India's transhipment cargo is handled by ports outside India, including Colombo, Singapore and

Klang. This increases the cost of transport of goods for India. Therefore, there are plans to increase the transhipment capacity so that Indian ports handle more than 75 per cent of India's transhipment requirements by 2030. This will be done by commissioning of Vizhinjam port, development of additional transhipment hubs at Kanyakumari and Campbell Bay, and increasing capacity of existing ports like Kochi.

Automation of ports, seamless movement of cargo and paperless transactions are considered essential to become a top player in global maritime trade. Digital Enterprise Business Solutions will be implemented to simplify and digitise processes across major ports by 2021. Additionally, more than 50 'smart' interventions have been identified to transform major ports into 'smart ports'. Average vessel turnaround time for container vessels will be reduced from the present 25 hours to below 20 hours. Average container dwell time will be reduced from the present 55 hours to less than 40 hours. A National Logistics Portal (NLP)–Marine will be implemented to have 100 per cent paperless processes for marine logistics. Freight transport will be shifted from rail and road to coastal shipping and inland waterways.

Existing shipping legislation is being amended to strengthen the institutional framework. The Major Port Authorities Act 2021 provides autonomy for the major ports to function independently. The Indian Ports Association will be restructured. A regulator will be provided through the Indian Ports Bill. An Indian Maritime Centre will be set up to drive a unified approach to maritime policy across different sub sectors and focus on building an integrated Indian maritime ecosystem. It will have domain experts as part of working groups, and will be supported by a secretariat for day-to-day operations. A Maritime Development Fund is recommended for providing easy finance to the maritime sector.

There is also an ambitious aim to transform India into a major shipbuilding, ship repair and recycling nation. The gross tonnage of ships built in India is sought to be increased from the current 27,000 tons to 500,000 tons by 2030. The aim is to be in the top ten globally in shipbuilding and repair, and the number one in ship recycling.

The total number of passengers availing cruise travel will be increased from the present 468,000 to more than 150,000. Dedicated cruise terminals will be created at 12 selected ports to promote cruise tourism around five selected themes – pilgrim, heritage, ayurvedic and wellness, island tourism and regional international circuit (India, Sri Lanka, Myanmar and Thailand). The new national and international routes for Roll On-Roll Off Cargo (Ro-Ro), Roll On-Roll Off Cargo and Passenger (Ro-Pax) and ferry services identified by the Ministry of Shipping include Visakhapatnam to Chattogram (Bangladesh), Paradip to Chattogram (Bangladesh), Kolkata to Chattogram (Bangladesh), Karaikal to Jaffna (Sri Lanka), Kochi to Seychelles, Kochi to Madagascar, along India's coastline and on the Brahmaputra.

Maritime institutions for training and development will be raised to global standards to enable increasing India's share of seafarers from the 12 per cent at present to over 20 per cent.

Twenty-three National Waterways will be made operational and cargo movement through them will be increased from the present 73 MTPA to over 200 MTPA. An Eastern Waterways Connectivity Transport Grid will be developed between National Waterway 1 (Ganga-Bhagirathi-Hooghly system), National Waterway 2 (Brahmaputra) and neighbouring countries for enhancing regional connectivity and reducing the cost of transportation with Bangladesh, Nepal, Bhutan and Myanmar. A Bay of Bengal Initiative for Multi-Sectoral Technical and Economic Cooperation (BIMSTEC) centre is planned to be established in India.

Till date, India has not manufactured cargo containers and has relied on foreign supplies, primarily Chinese. It is estimated that India will require 60,000 new containers between 2021 and 2026. Orders have been placed on two public sector companies, Braithwaite and Bharat Heavy Electricals Limited, to manufacture 1,000 containers each.[22] The Sagarmala Development Company Ltd. has signed an agreement with the Dubai-based Transworld Group to build a cargo container manufacturing facility in Gujarat with an investment of about Rs. 200 crore.[23]

Development of Island Territories

Development of the island territories, especially those of the Andaman and Nicobar Islands, has acquired urgency due to commercial and security reasons.

In June 2017, the government constituted the Island Development Agency (IDA) with the Home Minister as the Chairman and the Lieutenant Governor of the Andaman Nicobar Islands as the executive head.[24] The agency includes the Cabinet Secretary, CEO of NITI Aayog and Secretaries of many relevant ministries.[25] Since its formation, the agency has drawn up a focused, result-oriented plan to develop the island chains.

"Holistic development of islands" has been taken up as a priority project by the NITI Aayog. In the first phase, development projects have been identified in five islands of Andaman and Nicobar, and five islands in Lakshadweep. In the second phase, contracts are being awarded for identification of development projects in 12 islands of Andaman and Nicobar, and five islands in Lakshadweep.[26]

A major project is the proposal for a transhipment terminal at Campbell Bay in Great Nicobar.[27] Campbell Bay is less than 100 nautical miles from the western edge of Malacca Strait. On 10 August 2020, Prime Minister Narendra Modi announced that India is considering investing Rs. 10,000 crore for building the transhipment port while inaugurating the first undersea cable to provide high-speed Internet services to the islands. The 2,312-km cable was laid at a cost of Rs. 1,224 crore. Physical connectivity through air and water is being improved with the islands.

Runways of four existing airfields at Diglipur, Port Blair, Car Nicobar and Campbell are being extended from around 1,000 metres (3,000 feet) to around 3,200 metres (10,000 feet).[28] The Indian Navy has three air bases – INS Utkrosh at Port Blair, INS Baaz at Campbell Bay and INS Kohassa at Shibpur. The Indian Air Force has a base at Car Nicobar.

In Lakshadweep, the identified projects include construction of Minicoy Airport, extension of airstrip at Kavaratti from the existing 1,000 metres to 3,200 metres, modernisation of the existing jetty at Kavarati and three tourism projects (Suheli, Minicoy and Kadamat). In addition to INS Dweeprakshak at Kavaratti, the naval facilities at Minicoy Islands are being upgraded.

The Sagarmala Project Report examined several project options for the Andaman and Nicobar Islands.[29] It ruled out setting up of a Free Trade and Warehousing Zone in the Andamans, and a transhipment hub and bunkering facilities in Great Nicobar. It came to the conclusion that setting up facilities for cruise tourism in Great Nicobar was the only feasible option.

Neighbourhood First

Though South Asia occupies only 3.4 per cent of the world's land surface area, it is home to 24 per cent of the world population. In terms of economic growth over the past decade, South Asia has collectively been one the fastest-growing in the world. However, it is also the least integrated region in the world, with intra-regional trade amounting to 5 per cent of the region's total trade. A World Bank study of September 2014 estimated that between $ 1.7 trillion and $ 2.5 trillion was needed to be invested in South Asia to close its infrastructure gap.[30] An ADB paper of September 2018 estimated that South Asia needs to invest approximately nine per cent of its total GDP on infrastructure development over the next 15 years to sustain economic growth and enable regional integration.[31] It is more than twice more expensive to export or import a container in South Asia than it is in East Asia.[32] However, South Asia, if integrated, can be an economic powerhouse with its enormous market, young population, low labour costs, access to the sea and performing economies of India and Bangladesh.

A recalcitrant neighbour in the west has completed cut off India's land connectivity towards Central Asia. However, under its "Neighbourhood First" policy, India has tried to carry the focus on connectivity beyond its borders in all other directions. India is today devoting more resources and assigning greater priority to building connectivity, contacts and cooperation in the immediate neighbourhood. This is manifest in projects in sectors ranging from transport to power generation and transmission. The "Neighbourhood First" policy was launched in 2014. The Indian policy of "Neighbourhood First", in addition to being "committed to developing friendly and mutually beneficial relations with all its neighbours", is "based on a *consultative, non-reciprocal and outcome-oriented approach*, which focuses on delivering benefits like greater connectivity, improved infrastructure, stronger development cooperation in various sectors and areas, security and broader people-to-people contacts".[33] It is a "*generous, non-reciprocal policy* towards our neighbours".[34] Since 2014, a considerable amount of work has been initiated by India to improve regional connectivity across multiple sectors. While this may have broken decades of stupor, it has also exposed India's capacity and execution challenges.

Between 2014 and 2018, India's assistance to six neighbouring countries amounted to over Rs. 21,100 crore. Approximately half this amount was dedicated towards infrastructure projects.[35] A Concessional Financing Scheme has been instituted since 2015 to support Indian entities bidding for infrastructure projects abroad through EXIM of India.[36]

An exhaustive account of all the projects will be too long but we can have a look at some of the work underway beginning with the rail links, some of which are being revived after decades.

The first passenger rail service between India and Bangladesh started in 2008 when the Maitree Express between Dhaka and Kolkata was inaugurated. In 2017, the Bandhan Express was started between Kolkata and Khulna. In fact, Bangladesh is the only neighbouring country having passenger rail services with India right now. The 7.5 km Haldibari-Chilahati railway track was part of the broad gauge main route from Kolkata to Siliguri in undivided India. Trains from Bangladesh to Darjeeling, via Siliguri, operated till 1965. In December 2020, the Prime Ministers of India and Bangladesh inaugurated the newly rebuilt rail line from Haldibari to Chilahati.[37] In March 2021, the third passenger train connecting Dhaka with New Jalpaiguri was inaugurated on this route. The other four operational rail links between India and Bangladesh are Petrapole (India)-Benapole (Bangladesh), Gede (India)-Darshana (Bangladesh), Singhabad (India)-Rohanpur (Bangladesh), and Radhikapur (India)-Birol (Bangladesh). The Agartala (India)-Akhaura (Bangladesh) rail link is expected to be completed by September 2021.[38] The track will open a trade route from Tripura to Chattogram port. The Agartala-Kolkata distance can also be reduced from 1,700 km to 400 km. The rail link from Karimganj/Mahisasan in India to Shahbazpur in Bangladesh is being revived. The first cross-border container train from India reached Bangladesh in July 2020. India is assisting Bangladesh in 17 railway projects with a commitment of $ 2.44 billion. India has offered lines of credit for these projects at a rate of interest of 1 per cent a year, with repayment over 20 years with a moratorium for five years. Nine projects had been completed by July 2020.[39]

The only rail link between India and Nepal is the 10-km Raxaul (India)-Birjung (Nepal) line. Although about 110 freight trains run on this line every month, passenger service has not commenced.[40] A MoU for development of five rail lines between India and Nepal was signed in 2010. The 68.72-km Jayanagar-Janakpur-Bardibas-Bijalpura and the

18.6-km Jogbani-Biratnagar lines are under construction. India's Konkan Railway Corporation Limited will prepare a Detailed Project Report (DPR) for a possible rail line to connect Kathmandu with Raxaul.[41] Incidentally, both India and China will be undertaking rail projects in Nepal. However, the two nations use different rail standards. Chinese rail tracks are 1,435 mm wide standard gauge while the Indian ones are 1,676 mm wide broad gauge.

Road links are also being improved. Passenger bus services exist with Nepal, Bhutan, and Bangladesh, and are planned with Myanmar. Integrated Check Posts (ICPs) are being set up to facilitate trade along the borders. They are operated by The Land Ports Authority of India. Six ICPs are operational, one is under development and 13 more are planned.[42] In March 2021, the 1.9-km Maitri Setu over the Feni River was inaugurated. This will provide road connectivity between Tripura and Chattogram port which is just 80 km from the Indian ICP at Sabroom.

The internal waterways of India and Bangladesh are planned to be used to provide connectivity to Nepal, Bhutan and India's Northeast region. With Nepal, one route will be over the Gandak River from Bagha (Nepal) to Gaighat (Bihar), over a distance of 300 km, where it meets the Ganga. Nepal will also be permitted to operate vessels on three routes of India's inland waterways. Goods can reach Tripura through ports and internal waterways of Bangladesh. In September 2020, 50 metric tonnes of cement was transported on the Gumati River from Daudkandi in Bangladesh to Sonamura in India in the first trial run. In July 2019, a ship of IWAI transported 70 tonnes of cargo from Dhubri in Assam to Narayanganj in Bangladesh over the Brahmaputra. The cargo had been originally transported 160 km over land from Phuentsholing in Bhutan to Dhubri.

India and Bangladesh have a protocol on Inland Water Transit and Trade since 1972. Under this Protocol, inland vessels of both the countries can ply on the designated protocol route and dock at ports of call in each country, notified for loading/unloading of cargo. It was last renewed on 6 June 2015 with the provision of automatic renewal thereafter. The two countries have agreed to make arrangements for the use of their waterways for passage of goods and commerce. The routes and ports of call earlier agreed upon were increased in May 2020.[43] There are now 10 protocol routes, 11 ports of call each and two extended ports of call each.

In July 2020, container cargo from Kolkata reached Agartala through Bangladesh's Chattogram port. In FY 2019-20, 3.5 million metric tonnes of cargo was transported between India and Bangladesh on the protocol routes.[44]

India and Bangladesh also signed a Coastal Shipping Agreement on 6 June 2015 to allow shipping companies of the two nations to operate vessels directly between ports of the two nations. This allows for cargo to be shipped directly between the two nations, resulting in significant savings in time and costs. As per the agreement, sea transport between India and Bangladesh is considered coastal shipping, making it eligible for 40 per cent concession on vessel-related charges. Coastal shipping commenced in March 2016, when the container vessel MV *Harbour 1* sailed from Chattogram Port in Bangladesh to Krishnapatnam Port in India to pick up cotton.

On 6 June 2015, a MoU was also signed for the use of Chittagong (now Chattogram) and Mongla ports for movement of goods to and from India. On 25 October 2018, the agreement for the use of Chattogram and Mongla ports for movement of goods to and from India was signed.

In March 2016, Agartala got India's third Internet gateway, after Mumbai and Chennai. The gateway is plugged into the network at Akhaura check post. Internet traffic travels through undersea cables. Bangladesh allowed for the cable to be laid to the landing station at Cox Bazar.

Power grids are another avenue of connectivity. India has proposed the creation of a common electrical grid for South Asia. In 2018-19, around 3,000 MW of power was traded in the South Asia region among India, Bhutan, Bangladesh, Nepal, Pakistan, Sri Lanka and Myanmar. India imported around 1,200 MW power from Bhutan, and exported 1,200 MW to Bangladesh, 450 MW to Nepal and 3 MW to Myanmar.[45] In March 2019, the Central Electricity Regulatory Commission notified regulations for the sale and purchase of power between entities in India and neighbouring nations. India is setting up power plants in Bhutan and Bangladesh.

In September 2019, the first cross-border oil pipeline in the region became operational between Motihari (India) and Amlekhgunj (Nepal). The 69-km pipeline with a capacity of 2 million metric tonnes per annum was first proposed in 1996.

In May 2017, India launched the South Asia Satellite that was completely funded by it. The satellite is being jointly used by Afghanistan, Bangladesh, Bhutan, India, the Maldives, Nepal and Sri Lanka for communications, broadcasting and Internet services.[46]

A SAARC currency swap facility is being provided by the Reserve Bank of India since November 2012. The framework, revised in 2019, provides a total corpus of $ 2 billion. This corpus is available for SAARC nations to overcome short-term foreign exchange liquidity requirements.

India and Myanmar have finalised but not yet signed a coastal shipping agreement. However, direct bulk cargo shipping from India to Myanmar does take place. In October 2014, the Shipping Corporation of India launched a direct container shipping line between Chennai-Krishnapatnam (India) and Yangon (Myanmar).

The Kaladan Multi-Modal Transit Transport Project aims to provide an alternative route for goods between Kolkata and Mizoram. The agreement was signed in 2008 and construction began in 2010 but there have been cost and time overruns. The estimated cost of Rs. 536 crore in 2008 has now ballooned to Rs. 3,200 crore. Freight ships can sail around 540 km from Kolkata (and Haldia) to Sitwe in Myanmar. An integrated port and Inland Waterway Terminal (IWT) has been constructed by India at Sitwe. Thereafter, cargo will be shifted to barges that will move up the Kaladan river till Paletwa, 158 km away. Seven barges (of 300 tonne capacity each) have been supplied by India in 2017, and the transhipment terminal has been constructed at Paletwa. Thereafter, the cargo will move by road to Zorinpui on the Indian border, 110 km away, and 87 km further on to Lawngtai in Mizoram to reach National Highway 54. The construction of the road from Paletwa to Zorinpui is in progress. The project is expected to be completed by 2023.

Myanmar is India's gateway to Southeast Asia by land. The improvement of the road network in Northeast India and key infrastructure projects in Myanmar will provide India connectivity with Southeast Asia. The Rhi-Tiddim (around 80 km) and Rhi-Falam (around 151 km) roads connect Mizoram with Myanmar's Chin state. The trilateral highway will link India's Northeast through Myanmar to Thailand. Once operational, there will be a 1,360-km long road link from Moreh (Manipur) to Mae Sot (Thailand), making it one of the first sub-regional connectivity projects that will link South Asia to Southeast Asia. It is proposed to be extended till Vietnam. The Tamu–Kalewa–Kalemyo road, or the India–Myanmar Friendship Road, was inaugurated in 2001. In 2012, India agreed to repave the existing highway and upgrade the bridges along the road. The construction of the bridges in the Tamu–Kalewa section (150 km) of the highway and upgrading the Kalewa–Yagyi section (120 km) is being undertaken by India, and is likely to be completed by May 2021. Along with the efforts to enhance connectivity with Cambodia, Myanmar, Laos and Vietnam (CMLV), India is contributing in the development of industrial clusters along this route. These clusters are expected to become viable and benefits by using the connectivity backbone of the roads planned. Budgetary allocations are provided for CMLV annually in the Union Budget.

Connectivity efforts between Indonesia and the Andaman and Nicobar Islands are a significant recent development. Since the islands are close to Indonesia, direct trade between them is being encouraged.[47] In May 2018, a task force was set up to enhance connectivity and to promote trade, tourism and people-to-people contacts. In December 2018, an Indonesian cargo vessel from Port Malahayati in Aceh, laden with 150 tonnes of commercial goods, docked at Port Blair marking the first step in an effort to forge business connectivity between the two regions.[48] The first meeting of the India-Indonesia Business Forum (IIBF) was held at Port Blair in November 2018 to facilitate commercial and people-to-people linkages with Aceh and North Sumatra Province of Indonesia. A Joint Task Force has also been set up to undertake projects for port-related infrastructure in and around Sabang (Aceh).

There are plans to augment air connectivity, including extension of the UDAN scheme, between India's Northeast and adjoining foreign airports.

India has traditionally supported certain critical sectors in Sri Lanka. The Colombo port primarily services India as a transhipment port. The petroleum product distribution within Sri Lanka is undertaken by Indian Government-owned oil marketing companies. India has extended nearly $ 1.2 billion towards the development of the railway sector. The Jaffna airport is now reconnected with a direct flight to India. India is contemplating development of the deep water port in Trincomalee, including its bunkering facilities. However, there has been no progress primarily due to doubts on economic viability. India is also providing affordable housing in the northern region of Sri Lanka that was ravaged by the civil war.

Relations with the Maldives have fluctuated depending on the ruling dispensation there. Since the Presidential elections of September 2018 and taking over of the new government in the Maldives in July 2018, it has received financial assistance exceeding $ 2 billion in the form of budgetary support, grants, currency swap agreements and concessional Lines of Credit. In March 2019, a Line of Credit of $ 800 million was offered to finance projects that include a port at Gulhifahu, development of airports at Hanimaadhoo and Addu Gan, roads and drainage systems in Addu City, water and sanitation infrastructure on 34 islands (spanning 14 atolls), a cancer hospital in Hulhumalé, and a cricket stadium in Hulhumalé. In August 2020, it was a $ 500 million package that included a grant of $ 100 million and a $ 400 million line of credit to support the Greater Male Connectivity Project (GMCP).[49] The GMCP will connect Malé and three neighbouring islands of Villingili, Gulhifahu and Thilafushi with a bridge and causeway link of 6.7 km. In August 2020, India also provided a loan of $ 250 million, with soft repayment terms, to provide budgetary support to the Maldivian economy hit by the COVID-19 pandemic. Other projects include construction of a National College of Policing and Law Enforcement Studies in Addu City, road development projects, and construction of 2,000 social housing units in Hulhumalé. High Impact Community Development Projects (HICDP) and Small Grants Projects are being undertaken in addition. In July 2020, India handed over $ 5.6 million to fund nine HICDPs that include three fish processing plants that will enable the catch by Maldivian fishermen to be processed within the country itself.[50] In March 2019, India began disbursing $ 7 million cash grants for 18 small projects.[51] A line of credit of $ 40 million was offered for enhancement of sports infrastructure. A line of credit of $ 50 million was provided for defence projects. In February 2021, India and Maldives signed an agreement to develop, support and maintain a Maldives National Defence Force Coast Guard Harbour at Sifvaru (Uthuru Thilafalhu atoll) near Malé.[52] In September 2020, the Shipping Corporation of India launched a cargo ferry service between Tuticorin and Kochi in India, and Kulhudhuffushi and Malé in the Maldives.[53]

The Indian Ocean Region

The Chabahar port in Iran is seen by India as a gateway for access to Afghanistan and Central Asia. It is 950 km from the Milak border crossing of Afghanistan and about 768 nautical miles from Mumbai. Chabahar currently has two port complexes – Shahid Kalantari (traffic port) and Shahid Beheshti (future regional hub port). The port's capacity is eight million tonnes per annum and is expected to rise to 20 million tonnes.[54] Iran has planned a free trade zone around the port. A gas pipeline extending to 200 km has already been built and a second airport is planned.

In May 2016, India signed a trilateral transit agreement with Afghanistan and Iran to enable passage of Indian goods to Afghanistan via Iran. India committed itself to invest $ 500 million for port development and related infrastructure. The first phase, consisting of two berths at the Shahid Besheshti port terminal, was inaugurated by the President of Iran in December 2017. It was built by India with an investment of $ 85 million. India will expend $ 23 million on annual revenue expenditure on a 10-year lease.[55] The first consignment of wheat from India to Afghanistan via Chabahar was flagged off from Kandla on 29 October 2017. During the visit of the President of Iran to India in February 2018, an agreement was signed with Iran giving the India Ports Global Private Limited (IPGPL) operational rights of Chabahar's Shahid Besheshti port terminal for 18 months. India has subsequently taken over the logistics and cargo handling services of the port. Commercial operations at the port began on 30 December 2018. Officials from India, Iran and Afghanistan also opened an office of the India Ports Global Chabahar Free Zone (IPGCFZ). On 27 January 2019, India formally established shipping lines with the port. It was decided that every two weeks Indian ships will go from three Indian ports – Mumbai, Kandla and Mundra.[56] On 24 February 2019, the first trade convoy to carry cargo from Afghanistan to India via Chabahar was flagged off from the border city of Zaranj by President Ashraf Ghani.

The port links up through the Iranian road network to the Afghan border town of Zaranj from where India has built a 218-km road to Delaram at a cost of over Rs. 600 crore. It was handed over to Afghanistan in 2009 and links up with the Garland highway connecting major Afghan cities. In February 2018, a MoU was signed for India to finance a $ 1.6

billion, 500 km rail line from Chabahar to Zahedan, an Iranian city near the Afghan border.

A Tripartite Agreement between India, Iran, and Uzbekistan has been signed for the use of Chabahar port and a working group met for the first time in December 2020. Other Central Asian Republics have also evinced interest. A "Chabahar Day" event on 4 March 2021 had the attendance of Ministers from Afghanistan, Iran, Uzbekistan, Russia, Kazakhstan, and Armenia.

However, there are several factors that inhibit optimism. The geopolitical environment ensures that the India-Iran partnership will never be without complexities. Iranian hesitation in awarding India the deal to develop the Farzad-B gas field is one example. The presence of a Pakistani Minister during the inauguration of the Chabahar Terminal and later suggestions that 'others' can join the endeavour could have hardly inspired confidence in India. China continues to be the largest foreign investor in Iran. Iran is becoming a crucial link in the BRI to West Asia and the Mediterranean. Continuing sanctions of the USA also create impediments in doing business with Iran.

In a bid to reduce dependency on the Suez Canal for transporting cargo to Europe, India is collaborating with Iran and Russia to create the multi-modal International North-South Transport Corridor (INSTC). The agreement for it was signed in 2000. Goods would travel by sea from the ports of Mumbai and Kandla in India to Bandar Abbas in Iran. Thereafter, they would be transferred by rail to St. Petersburg through Volvograd and Moscow. The original route was across the Caspian Sea. However, with rail links in Eurasia improving, the route is now through Baku (west coast of Caspian Sea). A route through Aktau (east coast of Caspian Sea) is also being explored. Dry runs have been undertaken thrice – once in 2002 and twice in 2014. The new route is expected to be 30 per cent cheaper and reduce transport time by 10-12 days.

India was admitted to the Ashgabat Agreement on 3 February 2018. This agreement was instituted in April 2011 to establish an international multi-modal transport and transit corridor between Central Asia and the Persian Gulf. Accession to the Ashgabat Agreement would enable India to utilise the existing transport and transit corridor to facilitate trade and commercial interactions with the Eurasian region. Further, it would synchronise with India's efforts to implement the INSTC for enhanced connectivity.[57]

The other region of interest in the Indian Ocean is the South Western Indian Ocean.

In Mauritius, India has assisted in the construction of Metro Express (light rail system), the Supreme Court, a hospital, social housing, the Civil Service College and a jetty for the National Coast Guard at Port Louis. North Agalega is a Mauritian island located in the south-western Indian Ocean about 1,122 kilometres north of Mauritius. India is upgrading the existing airstrip and jetty on the island as per an agreement signed in March 2015. Construction of a new runway and jetties, along with associated facilities, are expected to improve connectivity, facilitate economic development of the island as well as enhance maritime security cooperation.[58]

A similar project was planned in the Assumption Island near the northern entrance to the Mozambique Channel. It involved the development of an airstrip, jetty, and housing infrastructure for the Seychelles Coast Guard. As explained by the Indian Ministry of External Affairs, the aim of the project was "to assist Seychelles secure the vast EEZ, including near Mozambique Channel, located over a thousand kilometres from the main island of Mahe". However, this project has not taken off, despite the original agreement of 2015 being reworked in January 2018, due to the internal political debate within Seychelles. It was opposed by the then opposition leader, Wavel Ramakalawan, who has now been elected the President of Seychelles.

Regional, Minilateral and Multilateral Organisations

To proceed with integration of the region without the recalcitrant western neighbour, India has used the regional platforms of BIMSTEC and BBIN to progress connectivity. In the 17th BIMSTEC Ministerial Meeting held on 1 April 2021, an ambitious Master Plan for Transport Connectivity was finalised. It is expected to be adopted at the next Summit Meeting later in the year. The BIMSTEC Coastal Shipping Agreement is also expected to be finalised soon.

The South Asia Sub-regional Economic Cooperation (SASEC) was set up in 2001 through ADB. It brings together Bangladesh, Bhutan, India, the Maldives, Myanmar, Nepal, and Sri Lanka. As of October 2018, SASEC countries had implemented 50 regional projects worth over $ 11 billion in the energy, transport, trade facilitation, economic corridor development, and information and communications technology (ICT) sectors. The Asian Development Bank (ADB) serves as the Secretariat for the SASEC member-countries. It has provided $ 6.35 billion in loans and grants, while member-countries have contributed about $ 4.7 billion worth of investments.

The Forum for India-Pacific Islands Cooperation (FIPIC) was established in 2014 with India and 14 Pacific Island nations as members. The Forum was launched in Suva, Fiji, in November 2014 during Prime Minister Narendra Modi's visit. The 2nd Summit was held on 21-22 August 2015 at Jaipur. Since climate change is the most critical issue for these islands, India has always sought to convey the importance it accords to this issue. In Jaipur, the PM proposed the establishment of an Institute for Sustainable Coastal and Ocean Research in the region and a network of marine biology research stations in various island nations. India has offered to establish a 'Space Technology Applications Centre' in any one of the island countries for the entire region and provide support for training in space applications. India has also offered the setting up of an early warning system and incident response system against natural disasters using space technology. The other initiatives by India include providing Lines of Credit for infrastructure and industry, scholarships for education, skill development, providing expertise in agriculture and food processing, providing training for personnel including diplomats, supporting democratic institutions, setting up of Information Technology (IT) centres and developing IT infrastructure.

India's collective engagement with Africa is through the India-Africa Forum Summit. It was established in 2008 and three summits have been held, the last being in New Delhi in 2015. Numerous infrastructure projects have been completed using finance under lines of credit. These include the Parliament building of Gambia, the Presidential Palace in Ghana, the Kosti power project in Sudan, Grand Katende Hydro-electric project in Congo and the Nyaborongo Power Project in Rwanda. A total of 211 lines of credit amounting to $ 12.85 billion have been extended to the African countries in various infrastructure projects.[59]

Since infrastructure development has acquired greater geopolitical salience in recent years, India has also aligned with like-minded nations for joint collaboration. India and Japan have already agreed to progress projects jointly in third countries such as Sri Lanka. The AAGC is another joint endeavour that was planned but not yet fructified. The European Union has invited India to collaborate with it to enhance Europe-Asia connectivity. The India-Japan-USA Trilateral has a working group on infrastructure but there have been no announcements.

The Coalition for Disaster Resilient Infrastructure (CDRI) and International Solar Alliance (ISA) are two multi-stakeholder platforms being advocated by India in its goals to control climate change and shift to renewable energy.

In June 2017, India became the 71st country to ratify the TIR Convention under the auspices of the United Nations that enables faster international movement of goods.

SAGAR

The concept of Security and Growth for All, or SAGAR, was first laid out by Prime Minister Narendra Modi during his speech on the occasion of the commissioning of the Coast Ship *Barracuda* in Mauritius on 12 March 2015.[60] The vision was described by the PM as "rooted in advancing cooperation" and "to use our capabilities for the benefit of all in our common maritime home". The first element is security provided by India. India will ensure security of its territory, work towards a secure Indian Ocean Region and rescue mariners in distress. The second element is economic and security cooperation with "friends in the region especially our maritime neighbours and island states". India will "build their maritime security capacities and their economic strength". The third element is "collective action and cooperation" to "advance peace and security in our maritime region". India "supports efforts to strengthen our regional mechanisms for maritime cooperation". The fourth element is to "seek a more integrated and cooperative future in the region that enhances the prospects for sustainable development for all". This includes "greater collaboration in trade, tourism and investment; infrastructure development; marine science and technology; sustainable fisheries; protection of marine environment; and, overall development of Ocean or Blue Economy". The fifth element is based on the premise that "those who live in this region have the primary responsibility for peace, stability and prosperity in the Indian Ocean". However, "there are other nations around the world, with strong interests and stakes in the region". India is "deeply engaged with them" "to seek a climate of trust and transparency; respect for international maritime rules and norms by all countries; sensitivity to each other's interests; peaceful resolution of maritime issues; and increase in maritime cooperation".

The EAM, in a speech in August 2018, elaborated on three elements of SAGAR[61] – projects to promote hinterland linkages and strengthen regional connectivity; linking South Asia to South East Asia (Act East) and to the Gulf (Think West); and playing an active and constructive role in strengthening regional maritime security.

In his famous keynote address at the Shangri-La Dialogue in Singapore on 1 June 2018, the Prime Minister had said that "Sagar stands for Security and Growth for All in the Region and, that is the creed we follow to our East now even more vigorously through our Act East Policy". This was probably the moment when India announced that the "Region" in SAGAR was now the Indo-Pacific Region and not merely the Indian Ocean Region that it was called earlier.

In summary, SAGAR can be said to be the Indian vision for the Indo-Pacific Region that has the elements of Security, Capacity building, Collective action, Sustainable development, Maritime engagement, and Regional connectivity.

Indo-Pacific Oceans Initiative (IPOI)

The vision of SAGAR is sought to be implemented through the architecture proposed in the Indo-Pacific Oceans Initiative (IPOI). The IPOI was introduced in the speech of the Prime Minister of India at the East Asia Summit (EAS) at Bangkok on 4 November 2019. IPOI seeks cooperation in seven sectors (or 'pillars') – Maritime security; maritime ecology; maritime resources; capacity building and resource sharing; disaster risk reduction and management; science, technology and academic cooperation; trade, connectivity and maritime transport. As is evident from this list, the IPOI seeks to act on the entire spectrum of challenges in the maritime domain. It seeks to widen the scope of the Indo-Pacific narrative beyond traditional security and geopolitical challenges to include economic, development and environmental challenges in the maritime domain. The proposed architecture is open, cooperative and inclusive. Any two or more nations can start collaborating in a particular sector. Other nations can join in at any point if they perceive value in the collaboration. Hence, it will be a loose mechanism that is expected to evolve over time since collaborations that have relevance and value will gain more participants. There is no immediate plan to provide supporting structures for the initiative. Structures can be built, if partner nations desire, once the initiative gains traction.

The IPOI is probably the optimum response that India can offer. India need not, and cannot, match the Chinese funding of infrastructure development given its capacity constraints. India seeks to provide the nations in the region, especially the smaller ones, assistance in sectors that matter most to them in terms of economic prosperity, sustainable development, protection from natural calamities, measures to stall climate change, and security of national assets. Having taken its time to finalise its vision of the Indo-Pacific, India is keen to provide "visible efforts to create a safe, secure and stable maritime domain" in the region.[62] These efforts, rather than remaining obsessed merely on traditional security, will be broad-based to make them more acceptable and relevant to all. To emphasise inclusivity, and probably keep it simple, these efforts are sought to be progressed through existing regional and multilateral organisations rather than seeking to create new structures. Conscious effort has been made by India to emphasise commonality with existing initiatives of such organisations.

External Aid

The main instruments of India's development assistance include Lines of Credit (LOC), Grant assistance, Small Development Projects (SDP), Technical Consultancy, and Disaster Relief and Humanitarian aid. Capacity building and training programmes are provided to 161 nations under the Indian Technical and Economic Cooperation Programme (ITEC). Grant assistance projects are concentrated primarily in India's neighbourhood in Afghanistan, Bangladesh, Bhutan, Nepal, the Maldives, Myanmar, Sri Lanka, Mauritius and in some African countries. India's external aid programme, though modest, has been augmented gradually to fund projects in India's immediate neighbourhood and other developing nations. In the last 15 years, India has granted $ 40 billion of aid to foreign nations.[63]

Lines of Credit on concessional terms form an important component of India's development cooperation policy. They are extended through the EXIM Bank of India. The Lines of Credit of EXIM of India already cover 65 countries and is being expanded to 75. India has lent its expertise in 650 projects in these 65 countries. More than 300 LOCs worth $ 30.66 billion have been extended. Of the total LOCs of $ 30.66 billion, $ 15.90 billion have been extended to Asian countries, with the largest value of commitments having been made in India's immediate neighbourhood. LOCs worth $ 7.862 billion have been extended to Bangladesh, $ 2.02 billion to Sri Lanka, $ 1.65 billion to Nepal, $ 964.80 to Mauritius, $ 840 million to the Maldives, $ 538.90 million to Myanmar and $ 128 million to Seychelles. A total of 98 connectivity projects for $ 6.93 billion have been taken up under LOCs in five countries in India's neighbourhood, of which 44 projects have already been completed.

Conclusion

The Indian effort in connectivity and infrastructure enhancement can be considered by beginning from India and moving outward from it. Within India, the development of infrastructure has been picking up pace over the last two decades and promises to continue over the next two as well. Some of the biggest infrastructure projects in the world are underway in India right now. The effort includes rail, road, air, inland waterways and coastal shipping. Indian ports are being upgraded and at least four mega ports are planned. Industrial clusters are being set up near the ports. Efforts are on to create infrastructure on island territories and use it in a sustainable manner.

Connectivity within the immediate neighbourhood is guided by a policy of assistance through mutual consultation and without expecting reciprocal benefits. These efforts cover road, rail, air, water, and electricity supply grids. The idea is that free flow of goods will benefit the region and bring economic prosperity. These initiatives have gathered pace particularly after 2014. Although they have resulted in opening up of routes closed for decades, they have also exposed the limitations of capacity of the Indian state.

Indian efforts at connectivity and infrastructure development cover a large number of countries that include the CMLV region, Afghanistan, Iran, Mauritius, Seychelles and Africa. The Indian Development

Assistance Programme has been increasing in scope and volume over the years.

The Indian story in infrastructure development and connectivity has just started. The augmentation of infrastructure within India will boost its economic growth and create the largest consumer market in the world. When connectivity (both hard and soft) is provided to its neighbours, they will also benefit from this market. When linkages with Southeast Asia and Africa improve, India will be in a position to create supply chains and develop industrial clusters for its benefit.

NOTES

1. Ministry of Finance, Government of India, "Economic Survey 2019-20", Vol. 2, 232.
2. Department of Economic Affairs, Government of India, "Report of the Task Force on National Infrastructure Pipeline", Vol. I, April 2020, 32.
3. Department of Economic Affairs, "Report of the Task Force on National Infrastructure Pipeline", 26.
4. Ministry of Railways, GoI, "National Rail Plan", December 2020.
5. Data from the website of Dedicated Freight Corridor Corporation of India Limited, https://dfccil.com/Home/ProgressStatusImage accessed on 5 March 2021.
6. Ministry of Railways, GoI, "National Rail Plan", December 2020.
7. Ashok Upadhyay, "Can India get its first bullet train by 2023?" *India Today*, 22 December 2020.
8. Ministry of Railways, GoI, "National Rail Plan", December 2020.
9. Prerna Katiyar, "How poor rail connectivity is acting as a hindrance to India's Act East policy", *The Economic Times*, 20 October 2019.
10. Data from website of NICDC, https://www.nicdc.in/ accessed on 5 March 2021.
11. Data accessed from https://morth.nic.in/bharatmala-phase-i on 5 March 2021.
12. Manjeet Negi, "India building 61 strategic roads along Pakistan, China borders", *India Today*, 15 July 2019.
13. Press Information Bureau (PIB), "Operational National Waterways in the Country", 27 December 2018.
14. Debasish Mallick, "Inland waterways – positive impact on economy", *ORF*, 20 January 2020.
15. Press Information Bureau (PIB), "PM inaugurates Maritime India Summit 2021", 2 March 2021.
16. Ministry of Ports, Shipping and Waterways, GoI, *Maritime India Vision 2030* (2021), 168.
17. Press Information Bureau (PIB), "Shri Mandaviya Says, Cargo Transport on National Waterways Rose from 6.59 Mt in 2014-15 to 72.31 in 2018-19", 18 July 2019.
18. Prerna Mehndiratta and Sandeep Kumar Mohanty, "InvITs in India and the way forward", *Mint*, 21 September 2020.
19. ENS Economic Service, "DFI to raise Rs. 3 lakh cr for infra spend; Rs. 20K cr to be infused", *The Indian Express*, 17 March 2021.
20. Data from Sagarmala website, http://sagarmala.gov.in/projects/projects-under-sagarmala accessed on 6 March 2021.

21. Press Information Bureau (PIB), "Infrastructure of Ports", 19 March 2020.
22. Avishek G. Dastikar, "To reduce China role, India takes first steps to make cargo containers", *Indian Express*, 5 March 2021.
23. "In a First, India to Foray into Cargo Container Manufacturing to Steer Clear of Chinese Dependence: Report", *News 18*, 5 March 2021.
24. Nitin Gokhale, "Andaman as springboard for India's Act East Policy", *SNI Wire*, 22 October 2018.
25. Press information Bureau (PIB), "Shri Amit Shah chairs Meeting of the Island Development Agency focusing on 'Green Development in the Islands to reach a new Height", 13 January 2020.
26. PIB, "Shri Amit Shah chairs Meeting of the Island Development Agency".
27. Gokhale, "Andaman as springboard for India's Act East Policy".
28. Gokhale, "Andaman as springboard for India's Act East Policy".
29. Ministry of Shipping, "Final Report for Sagarmala", Vol. VI, 1-12.
30. Luis Andres, Dan Biller, and Matias Herrera Dappe, "Infrastructure Gap in South Asia: Infrastructure Needs, Prioritization, and Financing", *Policy Research Working Paper* No. 7032, *World Bank Group*, September 2014.
31. Shikha Jha and Rosa Mia Arao, "Infrastructure Financing in South Asia," *South Asia Working Papers* (59), Asian Development Bank, September 2018, 1.
32. Mathew Funaiole and Jonathan Hillman, "China's Maritime Silk Road Initiative – Economic Drivers and Challenges", in *China's Maritime Silk Road - Strategic and economic Implications for the Indo-Pacific*, CSIS, March 2018, 21.
33. Ministry of External Affairs, "Rajya Sabha Question No. 3692. Neighbourhood First Policy", 25 July 2019.
34. Ministry of External Affairs, "Transcript of Press Conference by External Affairs Minister on 100 days of Government (September 17, 2019)", 18 September 2019.
35. Constantino Xavier and Riya Sinha, "Land comes in the way of Modi govt's Neighbourhood First and Act East, study shows", *The Print*, 31 August 2020.
36. Press Information Bureau (PIB), "Cabinet approves Extension of Concessional Financing Scheme (CFS) to support Indian Entities bidding for strategically important infrastructure projects abroad", 1 August 2018.
37. Debasis Sarkar, "New Indo-Bangla Rail service to facilitate trans-border trade and commerce", *The Economic Times*, 26 February 2021.
38. PTI, "India Bangladesh Rail Link: Amit Shah assures Tripura of developing Integrated Check Post", *Mint*, 7 January 2021.
39. Shreya Nandi and Elizabeth Roche, "India hands over to Bangladesh 10 railway locomotives in a bid to bolster 'neighbourhood first' policy", *Mint*, 27 July 2020.
40. Prerna Katiyar, "How poor rail connectivity is acting as a hindrance to India's Act East policy", *The Economic Times*, 20 October 2019.
41. IANS, "Nepal agrees to fast-track rail connection from Kathmandu to India", *Business Standard*, 9 December 2020.
42. Data from website of The Land Ports Authority of India, http://www.lpai.gov.in/content/innerpage/next-phase.php accessed on 8 March 2021.
43. Press Information Bureau (PIB), "Second Addendum on Protocol on Inland Water Transit and Trade between India and Bangladesh, 2020", 20 May 2020.
44. Dipanjan Roy Chaudhury, "Delhi Dhaka to open new trade connectivity route via inland waterways from Sep 3", *The Economic Times*, 26 August 2020.

45. Sudheer Singh, "CERC notifies cross border power trade regulations", *Economic Times*, 19 March 2021.
46. K.V. Venkatasubramanian, "South Asian Satellite to boost regional communication", *Press Information Bureau* (PIB), 7 May 2017.
47. Ministry of External Affairs, "Shared Vision of India-Indonesia Maritime Cooperation in the Indo-Pacific", 30 May 2018.
48. Rezaul H. Laskar, "Indonesian Ship brings cargo to Port Blair", *Hindustan Times*, 5 January 2019.
49. Ministry of External Affairs, "Meeting between External Affairs Minister and Foreign Minister of Maldives", 13 August 2020.
50. Parul Chandra, "Eye On China, India Steps Up Financial Aid To Maldives", *StratNews Global*, 29 July 2020.
51. Chandra, "Eye On China, India Steps Up Financial Aid To Maldives".
52. Ministry of External Affairs, "Joint Press Statement on Official Visit of External Affairs Minister of India to the Maldives", 21 February 2021.
53. Rezaul H. Laskar, "India, Maldives launch cargo ferry service connecting Tuticorin and Cochin with Male", *Hindustan Times*, 21 September 2020.
54. Harsh V. Pant, India-Iran Cooperation at Chabahar Port - Choppy waters, *China's Maritime Silk Road - Strategic and economic Implications for the Indo-Pacific*, CSIS, March 2018, 17.
55. Harsh V. Pant, India-Iran Cooperation at Chabahar Port - Choppy waters, *China's Maritime Silk Road - Strategic and economic Implications for the Indo-Pacific*, CSIS, March 2018, 17.
56. Siddhant Sibal, Afghanistan all set to get connected to India via Chabahar, WION, 23 February 2019.
57. P. Stobdan, "Significance of India joining the Ashgabat Agreement", *IDSA*, 12 February 2018.
58. Samuel Bashfield, "Agalega: A glimpse of India's remote island military base", *The Interpreter*, Lowy Institute, 2 March 2021.
59. Ministry of External Affairs, "Question No. 1557, Infrastructure Development In African Countries", 10 February 2021.
60. Ministry of External Affairs, "Prime Minister's remarks at the commissioning of Offshore Patrol Vessel (OPV) in Mauritius", 12 March 2015.
61. Ministry of External Affairs, "Remarks by External Affairs Minister at the 3rd Indian Ocean Conference, Vietnam", 27 August 2018.
62. Ministry of External Affairs (MEA), GoI, "Prime Minister's Speech at the East Asia Summit (4 November 2019)", 4 November 2019.
63. Shoumojit Banerjee, "Need to reset trade ties with China, says Foreign Secretary Shringla", *The Hindu*, 28 February 2021.

PART III

THE FUTURE

8

Attack Warning Red

Introduction

The first part of the book created the background. It looked at the space described as the Indo-Pacific, provided a snapshot of the maritime history of the region, and brought out the inextricable linkages between technology, infrastructure and geopolitics. The second part described the infrastructure creation and connectivity enhancement activities of the various actors in the Indo-Pacific Region – China, Japan, the USA, European Union, ASEAN, Australia and India. The third part is perhaps the most ambitious. It seeks to explore the geopolitical implications of these developments for India, and if that is not enough, seeks to further list out what India could do to mitigate the threats emanating from them. So, the first part dealt with the past, the second with the present, and this part delves into the future.

The rise of China is undoubtedly the primary phenomenon debated across the Indo-Pacific. There is no dearth of literature dwelling on the implications and challenges for India emanating from the rise of China and its increasing presence in the Indian Ocean. This chapter seeks to explain it in a simple and straightforward manner at the risk of making it too simplistic. It will focus on the immediate Indian Ocean Region rather than the whole Indo-Pacific Region.

Geopolitical equations play out over the long term, but the direction of their flow is often predictable. A "dark swan" or "wild rhino" event may disrupt the flow but seldom stops or reverses it. If we are considering a geopolitical play that, for convenience, can be assumed to have started from the beginning of this century and is expected to run for the next three decades, breathless commentary hardly does justice to it. To use a cricketing analogy, this is a test match rather than a T20 match. It can also be described as an extended marathon ('ultra marathon' being the contemporary term).

Great Power Competition Arrives Home

Global geopolitics and the structural changes underway in the world order are beyond the scope of this book. However, it is important to recollect the settings as a backdrop before we proceed further. We are at that cusp in history where the incumbent global power is being challenged by a rising power. The global financial crisis of 2008 convinced China that 'Western' institutions had got weakened and that it had a strategic window to elevate itself in the world order. Since 2009, there have been growing signs of Chinese assertion – an assertive foreign policy; reclamation and militarisation of maritime structures in the South China Sea; massive military modernisation, expansion and reformation; setting up of parallel multilateral organisations; taking control and undermining of existing multilateral organisations; rise in internal authoritarianism; an overtly ambitious BRI; coercive economic measures; dividing regional organisations like ASEAN and EU; and ambitions to be the world leader in a range of technologies. It is quite clear that China seeks a bipolar global order, in which it will share space with the USA, and a unipolar Asia in which it will be the dominant power. It has disdain for democratic governance and is keen to convince the world that its political model is the one best suited to bring about prosperity. This global outlook creates a structural incompatibility with a democratic India that seeks to provide security and prosperity to its citizens amidst political freedom, and seeks a multi-polar Asia and a multi-polar world.

Many nations across the globe have significantly reassessed their outlook on China in recent times. The ill-founded hope in the US establishment that China will imbibe political openness when it benefits economically from a globalised world has been severely jolted. Having comprehended that the economic and technological gains of China make it a serious challenger to its hegemony, there is bipartisan consensus within the USA to take a hard line against China. Along with tit for tat tariffs that threatened to spiral out of control into a trade war, there have been attempts to curb access to technology to Chinese companies. Europe, especially Western Europe, is yet to shake off its ambivalent attitude that is founded on the belief that its ties with China would economically benefit it enough to out-weigh other issues. The EU Strategic Outlook of March 2019 described China as a partner, competitor and systemic rival. Meanwhile, Australia underwent a veritable about-turn in its China outlook after revelations of Chinese influence across its media, political setup and educational institutions were made public.

The China-India relationship is a 'complex' one. Along with unsettled borders, there are several causes of concern for India – prevention of India's entry into the Nuclear Suppliers Group (NSG), opposition to India's entry into the UN Security Council (UNSC) as a Permanent Member, supporting Pakistan to tie down India on its western border, a massive trade deficit, and supply chain dependencies across a range of sectors, to name only a few. Although both sides have expressed the desire to "not let differences become disputes", the hope that competition and cooperation can coexist is getting increasingly difficult to accept. Historically, India has preferred the 'middle path' and steered clear of great power rivalry. However, that skill may now be tested to its limit. To add to the difficulties, Russia, one of India's most reliable partners and a major supplier of military equipment, has developed close ties with China. Russia and China have conducted joint naval exercises with Iran and South Africa in the Indian Ocean Region. Russia has commenced supplying military equipment to Pakistan and conducting joint military exercises with it. The Russian Foreign Minister has been unequivocally clear about Russia's views on the Indo-Pacific and the "Quad".

In this century, the Indian Ocean Region has never been as crowded as either the Eastern Pacific or the South China Sea. However, there is a perceptible change underway. While the security dynamics in East Asia and the South China Sea will not ease in the near term, the Indian Ocean too will witness an increased presence of regional and extra-regional players. Apart from China, there will be others. The increase in trade between Asia and Europe, coupled with China, Japan and South Korea sourcing their energy needs from West Asia, has made the security of sea lanes in the Indian Ocean critical for many nations. France considers itself a resident power and already has a presence in the region. The United Kingdom seeks to maintain a Carrier Battle Group with logistics provisions at Duqm in Oman. Japan is progressively increasing the presence of JMSDF, as well as promoting cooperation with its Coast Guard. It has signed a mutual logistics support agreement with India that will support its operations in the region. On 11 November 2020, Russia announced an agreement with Sudan to set up a naval base at Port Sudan. India has adequate primacy at the moment to project itself as the 'First Responder' and 'Preferred Partner' in the region. However, this benefit acquired due to the relatively low density of regional and extra-regional navies in the region will diminish with time. Unlike in the past, when India was not in favour of extra-regional navies having a presence in the Indian Ocean, it recognises "that there are other nations around the world, with strong interests and stakes in the region".[1] India will need to negotiate with greater international maritime presence in its immediate neighbourhood. The task will become harder if it seeks to enlarge its strategic theatre into the larger Indo-Pacific Region.

With this backdrop in mind, we can return to looking at the infrastructure play around India's neighbourhood.

The Pitfalls in Infrastructure Development Abroad

Infrastructure development projects tend to be messy. They tend to soak up capital, extend over a long term and present unforeseen challenges despite the best of planning. It is not unusual to have cost and time overruns in such projects. At the end of it, despite the most extensive feasibility studies and detailed project reports, the project may finally turn out to be unviable due to wrong assumptions or, simply, changed circumstances. Even the best of nations with formidable reputations in quality have their share of failed infrastructure projects. When infrastructure development is undertaken abroad, it presents another set of problems. To get a sense of the difficulties, let us have a look at the myriad problems that India has faced in recent times.

As we have seen in Chapter Seven, India has been forced to up the ante to enhance connectivity abroad and work out new avenues of access. However, India faces two major issues – limited capacity and slow speed of execution. The slow speed of execution is not always India's doing.

The Chabahar port project got slowed down due to US sanctions against Iran. Exemptions had to be sought from the US Administration to enable procurement of port equipment. When the first phase of the

Shahid Beheshti Port was inaugurated by Iranian President Hassan Rouhani in December 2017, the invitees included Pakistan's Minister for Ports and Shipping, Hasil Khan Bizenjo. The Iranian Foreign Minister, Javad Zarif, on his visit to Pakistan in March 2018, invited Pakistan and China to participate in Chabahar and also suggested that Iran could join the CPEC.[2] Pakistan's Foreign Office spokesman confirmed it and described Chabahar and Gwadar as "sister ports".[3] During another visit to Pakistan in May 2019, the Iranian Foreign Minister proposed that the Chabahar port could be connected to Gwadar port by rail.[4] Afghanistan has benefitted immensely from the port and has praised India for it. However, India and Iran's interests do not exactly align in Afghanistan. More worrying for India is the increased Chinese presence and investment in Iran, including the reported signing of a 25-year security and economic agreement. Iran provides the sole access route for India to Afghanistan and Central Asia. However, the geopolitical play in the region makes this access tenuous and casts a shadow on India's eagerness to fund it.

In Myanmar, the maritime and internal waterway part of the Kaladan Multimodal project has been completed. The delay in road construction is due to several reasons – difficult terrain; presence of hostile insurgent groups and the usual problems in contracting government projects.[5] Recent reports suggest that insurgent groups may have received resources from a 'third' country.

The project to develop facilities in the Assumption Islands in the Seychelles has failed to move ahead due to political opposition to it in Seychelles. The facilities were meant to help the Seychelles' Coast Guard to patrol its Exclusive Economic Zone (EEZ). Discussions started 10 years ago when piracy in the region was at its peak and Seychelles was searching for partners for getting assistance. The agreement of 2015 to set up a joint facility was not opposed by any political party. However, somewhere along the way, the narrative shifted to the setting up of a "foreign base" and loss of sovereignty.[6] The project has not recovered despite multiple efforts.

In Nepal, Indian road and rail building efforts have been delayed due to litigation and delays in land acquisition.[7]

These additional pitfalls of infrastructure projects in foreign countries can seriously hurt national reputation when things go wrong. There is always the danger of getting caught in the internal political and social dynamics of the host nation. The goodwill that it sought to be generated by building infrastructure can get tarnished due to a plethora of reasons, some of which may not be foreseen – cost and time overruns; financial problems in the host economy; associated environmental degradation; displacement of local populations; charges of favouritism; and hostile political opposition, to name only a few. The reputational costs of not living up to promises can sometimes be worse than not making any promise at all. Hence, to avoid these pitfalls, nations avoid undertaking infrastructure development and financing abroad directly on their own. The financing is usually routed through multilateral financial institutions that have transparent procedures and conditions for providing finance. All norms such as assessing the viability of a project or assessing the debt repayment capacity of a nation before providing additional debt to finance a project are measures to avoid this reputation loss. Even when the financing is done by a national development aid agency (such as JICA in Japan), the financing norms are kept transparent in accordance with internationally agreed definitions. Similarly, the Paris Club has norms on providing debt relief.

China has gone completely against the grain of this accumulated wisdom and experience. It has gone ahead unilaterally to announce an ambitious infrastructure development initiative on a global scale. Moreover, it has done so with financing mechanisms that are opaque. It has invested in projects of questionable viability and not adhered to environmental concerns. Many of the projects are in countries that are already saddled with debt, and hence have a low credit rating – the very reason they could not get finance from multilateral institutions. The risk is furthermore in countries that have unstable regimes and poor governance. This lack of risk assessment is inevitably an invitation to bear reputational costs and China is already bearing them. China has probably extrapolated its internal experiences to projects abroad. Opaque procedures, corruption and projects of questionable merit may not get questioned in an authoritarian nation in which events are hidden from external gaze and procedures are not subject to intense scrutiny. The Chinese strategy to build infrastructure first, with the expectation that it will provide the stimulus for demand to catch up, is a high-cost strategy that it could bear. However, when the same strategy is applied to other nations that do not have the requisite economic capacity, it can be a drain on their resources. Such nations need projects that will provide immediate revenue flows rather than drain resources for the promise of future prosperity. There were reports of infrastructure excesses within China but those were not openly visible to the rest of the world. However, when these same opaque procedures, corruption and unviable projects occur in another country, it attracts international scrutiny that the Chinese companies and financial institutions are not accustomed to.

The Belt and Road Initiative

The ubiquitous maps attached to reports of the BRI, apart from the name itself, are misleading. It appears to be a corridor development programme in which corridors with greater connectivity are being developed for the movement of people, power, goods and ideas from and to China. However, the actual content of the BRI so far does not align with this perception.

There is no consensus on which projects constitute the BRI. Once we get past this hurdle of classification by defining our own criteria, the resulting database seems to be a coalescence of numerous projects with Chinese participation, usually undertaken by SOEs and financed by Chinese institutions. These projects are not necessarily for enhancing connectivity or setting up industrial corridors. The projects are dispersed both within the declared "corridors" and outside them. Coherence of thought and strategy, if any, on these multifarious projects is actually difficult to trace. In fact, it is quite chaotic.

The BRI is a concoction of activities by numerous institutions and agencies of China that are not necessarily working in tandem. It is too large and complex in its scope to be described in a few convenient all-encompassing phrases such as "debt trap", howsoever tempting such labels may be. The dynamics varies from country to country and project to project. There has been intense scrutiny of China's overseas loans, and there is a proliferation of reports and databases. Since China does not make public most aspects of its overseas funding, the opacity has made assessment difficult. Unsurprisingly, the estimates and resultant conclusions vary. While intent is always difficult to gauge, it becomes even more difficult with such opacity. A *Harvard Business Review* report of February 2020 concluded that China and its financial institutions have lent $ 1.5 trillion to more than 150 countries between 1949 and 2017.[8] It also estimated that half of China's loans to developing nations go unreported. As of 2016, it estimated that more than $ 200 billion of Chinese lending was unreported.

One estimate is that the total amount disbursed by China since the announcement of the BRI in 2014 till November 2019 was $ 337 billion, way short of the envisaged $ 1 trillion.[9] Another estimate by the American Enterprise Institute (AEI) and the Heritage Chinese Global Investment Tracker (CGIT) put a value of $ 340 billion for the period from 2014 to 2017.[10] As early as in 2018, a report on the BRI by OECD calculated the cumulative value of "troubled" Chinese projects since 2005 at a whopping $ 369.5 billion. The "troubled" assets under BRI were calculated at $ 101.8 billion.[11] The term "troubled" refers to suspended, renegotiated or cancelled projects, and the amounts were calculated using AEI and CGIT databases.

The China Development Bank (CDB) and the China Export-Import Bank (EXIM of China) are the two policy banks that financed a major portion of BRI projects. As per a Rhodium Group report, the peak of BRI financing by these two banks was $ 50-60 billion in 2015-16.[12] However, since 2017, Chinese overseas lending has either remained the same or decelerated in most of the developing and emerging world. China's policy banks are now cutting down on lending overseas since debtor nations are increasingly seeking re-negotiations citing inability to repay.[13] In fact, the number and amount of debt renegotiations had been increasing even before the COVID pandemic. Pre-COVID, the report estimated that 16 per cent of China's overseas lending has been subject to renegotiation. With the COVID pandemic, the situation got worse and another Rhodium Group report of October 2020 estimated that 25 per cent of Chinese overseas lending is under renegotiation.[14]

Let us consider the three corridors that are being developed around India – CPEC, CMEC and Trans Himalayan Multi-dimensional Connectivity Network. The present status of physical connectivity belies the ambitious predictions that were being made at the commencement of the BRI. Connectivity along these corridors is progressing but will take time to materialise. Some ambitious projects like rail lines and pipelines through high mountainous terrain will probably never happen.

The CPEC is supposed to link up Xinjiang Uygur Autonomous Region in China to Gwadar in Pakistan. However, the only linkage that has come up is the fibre optic cable that will provide direct digital connectivity between China and Pakistan, and onwards to Africa. The road link remains weak due to the forbidding topographical challenges around the Karakoram Highway. The highway, though repaired and functional, remains hostage to possible blockages and closes down in winter. Traffic remains low. Building oil pipelines and railways over these high mountains is definitely extremely challenging, strategically vulnerable and not financially viable. Pumping oil from the sea level to over 15,000 feet will require massive pumping facilities. To keep the oil flowing in the cold temperature at high altitude will require heating facilities. The daunting altitude and topography also make it difficult to construct the rail line over the Khunjerab Pass. Even the track-doubling and upgradation of the 1,872 km rail line from Karachi to Peshawar (Main Line 1 or ML1) is still a long way away with finance not yet available for it.[15] At the other end of this corridor is the port of Gwadar that has nothing to suggest that it deserves to be developed commercially. Situated in a location with neither industries nor skilled labour nor even drinking water, it is poorly connected to a hinterland that has no product to offer. Unsurprisingly, the port has seen little traffic and largely lies idle. All projects associated with it are lagging behind schedule. It is not clear which companies will inhabit the SEZ near the port. It is even less clear what commercial use the airport, the largest in Pakistan if completed, will ever have. The CPEC does have projects to improve rail and road linkages within Pakistan. However, an overwhelming majority of projects in the first phase were power projects. The next phase will see the setting up of some SEZs. Overall, there is no indication that there will be a spurt in economic traffic across the Khunjerab Pass. Pakistan has realised that it cannot take more loans and is seeking finance on concessionary terms that China is not willing to provide. The CPEC will never reach the vaunted investment figures of $ 46 billion (some even counted up to $ 100 billion), and is expected to stay closer to the present range of $ 20-25 billion.

The CMEC aims to connect Kunming in China to Kyaukpyu in Myanmar. The gas pipeline became operational in 2013 and the oil pipeline became operational in 2017. In the first two years of its operation, the oil pipeline, touted as a bypass to the Malacca Strait, had operated at only 40 per cent capacity.[16] The port and SEZ project has been renegotiated by Myanmar from $ 7.3 billion to $ 1.3 billion by restricting it to the first phase of construction. The rail connection is yet to cross the Myanmar border. The 328-km rail from Kunming to Dali, in China, became operational in July 2018.[17] Construction of 336 km from Dali to the border town of Ruili began in 2011 and is scheduled to be completed in 2022.[18] On the Myanmar side, the China Railway Erguan Engineering Corporation (CREEG) has started a partial survey for the 431-km rail from Muse across the border from Ruili to Mandalay.[19] The port at Kyaukphyu is situated nearly 400 kilometres from Mandalay. On 10 January 2021, the CREEG and the state-run Myanmar Railways signed an agreement to conduct a feasibility study for the Mandalay-Kyaukphyu railway project.[20] Another line is planned to be extended south to Yangon from Ruili.

The Trans Himalayan Multi-dimensional Connectivity Network (THMCN) is the present nomenclature for connectivity projects between China and Nepal. Nepal has sought to improve its connectivity with China as an alternative to India. In 2016, the two nations signed the Nepal China Transit Transport Agreement that grants Nepal land access to China's ports in its eastern seaboard. It is a highly questionable alternative considering the disparity in distance between ports in India and those in China. In June 2020, China started a weekly freight line from Xian (in Shaanxi province) to Kathmandu.[21] The existing road connectivity is sought to be augmented with rail connectivity. The Qinghai-Lhasa rail line in Tibet was extended till Shigatse in 2014. This line is sought to be extended through Gyirong, near the Nepal border, to Kathmandu, and thereafter to Pokhara and Lumbini in Nepal. The Gyirong-Kathmandu rail line is an extremely ambitious project that seems unlikely to happen soon.[22] Apart from the difficult terrain, environmental issues, and tectonic fault-lines, financing of the project, estimated at $ 5.5 billion, is not clear.[23]

So far, three things are clear about the BRI. First, it is slowing down and actual disbursals of investments are way below the committed amounts. China has over-promised and under-delivered. There is no way that China can finance the entire spectrum of projects envisaged under the BRI. In fact, many projects considered under the BRI are piggy-backing on those being funded by other multilateral institutions. The headwinds faced by the BRI are the result of China's falling economic prowess and awareness about pitfalls in financially weak nations sustaining high debt. Maybe, the Chinese institutions have learnt their lessons the hard way and have deliberately slowed down. However, it is equally clear that since China has committed significant political capital to the BRI, to the point of including it in the CPC Constitution, there is no rolling back. China is recalibrating on the basis of the lessons it has learnt. Third, the flows of investments have shifted from hard infrastructure to digital and telecom infrastructure. Digital connectivity is tangible and more easily established. The narrative is being shifted to other variants – "Green Silk Road" and "Health Silk Road".[24] In any case, these are still early days for the BRI, considering that the final milestone is pegged at 2049. Hence, it is instructive to dwell on the implications in the longer term as the decades roll by.

The BRI has further established the need for providing capital for infrastructure development. Despite the reputational reverses suffered by China due to certain projects, nations have not stopped approaching it to finance their infrastructure projects. In recent times, Indonesia, Sri Lanka and Bangladesh have presented their wish list to China. Nigeria completed the Lagos-Ibadan rail line with a Chinese loan of $ 1.5 billion[25] and is awaiting approval from China of a $ 5.3 billion loan for extending the rail line to Kano.[26] Hence, any rhetoric on the ills of the BRI is futile unless alternative sources of funding for the nations seeking capital are made available to them. Of course, this runs the risk of getting drawn into an ill-advised contest in providing assistance if some nation decides to play both sides to gain maximum advantage. The dual challenge is of providing financial alternatives to the smaller nations even while avoiding an upward spiralling contest to match resources with China.

Alteration of Geography

The Eurasian heartland stayed cut off from the oceans to its south primarily due to the daunting geographical obstacles in between. In Southeast Asia, the highlands extending from the northeast of India to North Vietnam were an obstacle to traverse to the South China Sea. The Himalayan and Karakoram ranges provide a similar hurdle to access the Indian Ocean. China is now striving to overcome this geography. North South travel that was heavily restricted due to the formidable geography is sought to complement the east-west traffic that already exists. This altered geography, as it happens, will bring with it major implications.

China has the largest dredging capacity in the world. This capacity has been put to use to create artificial maritime features in the South China Sea. The dredgers have since moved eastward in search of employment. One of them is the 665-acre Colombo International Financial City Project that will enable the China Harbour Engineering Corporation (CHEC) Port City Colombo Ltd. to have around 116 acres of reclaimed land leased for 99 years.[27] When a revised blueprint of Gwadar was issued, it mentioned a similar Central Business District of reclaimed land called "Chand-Tara" islands that would be the largest in Pakistan.[28] Protests saw it getting eliminated from the blueprint. In any case, Gwadar is supposed to cater for a Chinese population of 500,000 by 2023.[29] These enclaves, especially when leased for decades, provide the space for business and technical activity on the lines of Hong Kong and Macau. In fact, enclaves that enable setting up of companies with ease and provide data centres for business will provide far greater ingress by China in the Indian Ocean than any military base. These can also provide landing stations for undersea cables with implications that we will see ahead.

This alteration of geography coupled with the presence of Chinese populations and Chinese enclaves in the region will buttress the claims of residency of China in the Indian Ocean Region. This will not be surprising considering that it considers itself a "near Arctic nation" while being nowhere in the vicinity of the Arctic region. China already claims to be a neighbour to South Asia or a "near South Asian" nation sharing borders with five of the SAARC members. It has been awarded exploration areas in the Indian Ocean for deep sea exploration by the International Seabed Authority (ISA).[30]

Contracts for exploration exist with the Federal Institute of Geosciences and Natural Resources (Germany), China Ocean Mineral Resources Research and Development Organisation (China), Republic of Korea, and India.

These claims to residency will provide support to be part of all initiatives and forums in the Indian Ocean Region – Indian Ocean Rim Association (IORA), Indian Ocean Naval Symposium (IONS), and similar organisations. The Indian Ocean Region does not have any effective regional governance mechanisms in place. This creates a void waiting to be filed up by any nation that takes a leadership role in forging such mechanisms. China has already demonstrated its capability to engineer divisions in multilateral organisations like ASEAN and EU. It has created alternative regional platforms like the Lanchang-Mekong Cooperation Forum established in 2016. In 2012, ASEAN Foreign Ministers failed to issue a joint communiqué after their annual summit for the first time. It was not the last time it had happened. In June 2017, Greece blocked an EU statement in the UN that sought to criticise China's human rights record. China is already creating the ground for alternative South Asia organisations having convened joint meetings with Afghanistan, Pakistan and Nepal – a Himalayan Quad, in a way. A claim of residency will also provide the reasoning to maintain a permanent military presence in the IOR. Once China establishes its claims as a resident power in the IOR, it could be assumed that it will make a strong case for the region to resolve its problems on its own, keeping out extra-regional powers, as it argues for the South China Sea.

This increasing Chinese presence will result in the relative diminution and overshadowing of India as the major power in the region. However, it needs to be reiterated that this alteration of geography will play out over the next three decades. The north-south corridors are in the primary stages yet and are not economically viable.

Chinese Presence

There are five north-south axes along which the proposed "Belt" from China is planned in the Indo-Pacific region. Moving east to west, they are – through the Mekong region; through Myanmar; to Nepal; through Pakistan; and through Iran. Migration of Chinese nationals and creation of Chinese enclaves have been happening along these routes up to the Mekong region and Myanmar. The migrants are usually workers and businessmen. Places like Mandalay in Myanmar, Vientiane and the northern provinces in Laos, and Sihanoukville in Cambodia have already seen a transformation with the influx of Chinese immigrants. More will be seen in places like the planned "Forest City" project in Malaysia and a planned gated community in Gwadar. China already has more citizens abroad than any other nation. Although the exact numbers are debated, there is a substantial presence of Chinese nationals in Africa.

The increasing presence of Chinese nationals and the increasing Chinese investments in a region make it pertinent for China to take measures for their security. It provides the reasoning for maintaining a permanent military presence in the Indian Ocean Region. There are, of course, additional reasons as well. For example, the largest part of China's oil imports comes from West Asia and Africa. The share of these two regions in Chinese oil imports has oscillated between 63 and 75 per cent between 1995 and 2016.[31] This oil is transported through the Indian Ocean. A significant portion of its raw materials and its exports also traverse the Indian Ocean. Safeguarding these Sea Lines of Communication (SLOCs) is critical for China. As the saying goes – "The flag follows the trade". An increase in Chinese commitments and Chinese population in the region will mean a greater presence of the Chinese state and the PLA Navy in the neighbourhood. In 2004, Hu Jintao's "New Historic Missions" gave the PLA the task of defending China's overseas interests.[32] China made amendments to its National Defence Law that became effective from 1 January 2021. It provides a broader definition of the conditions under which the military can be mobilised. One particular amendment that caught greater attention was that China can undertake mobilisation if its "development interests" are under threat.[33] India will perforce need to get used to this presence in its neighbourhood, and increased interaction with all arms of the Chinese state that it entails. The maritime corridor from the east coast of China to the coast of Africa and the Persian Gulf will inevitably witness a more robust deployment of the PLA Navy in the coming decades. The thrust given to maritime security in the MSR vision document clearly indicates China's willingness to use its maritime power for protection of its expanding maritime interests. China's Defence White Paper of 2015 mentions that "the security of overseas interests concerning energy and resources, strategic sea lines of communication (SLOCs), as well as institutions, personnel and assets abroad, has become an imminent issue" and that safeguarding "the security of China's overseas interests" is one of the strategic tasks of its armed forces.[34] It also declared that "the PLA Navy (PLAN) will gradually shift its focus from "offshore waters defence" to the combination of "offshore waters defence" with "open seas protection". China's Defence White Paper of 2019 also listed safeguarding "China's overseas interests" as one of its aims of national defence.[35] In 2014, a three-ship task force of the PLA Navy conducted exercises south of Java. In 2018, a four-ship task force, which included a destroyer, a frigate, a LPD and a replenishment ship, conducted drills in the eastern Indian Ocean.

The PLA is making its presence felt on the borders of India and Bhutan, as also probably in Gilgit and Baltistan. However, the PLA Navy is far from being a potent force in the Indian Ocean. That is still decades away. However, Chinese influence in India's neighbourhood due to its economic and political heft is already apparent, and has to be contended with.

Chinese Influence

China's influence around India's neighbourhood is already apparent in multiple ways – economic, political, technological, military and industrial. The economic clout of China is of course the most apparent. As the largest exporter and second largest importer in the world, it is the largest trading nation with around 130 nations around the world. All the nations in the region have a trade deficit with China, and are largely dependent on China for supply of a wide range of products. Every nation hopes to attract Foreign Direct Investment (FDI) and, hence, any nation capable of providing it remains an attractive economic partner. Outward Chinese investment was $ 196.1 billion in 2016, $ 158.3 billion in 2017 and $ 143 billion in 2018.[36] In 2017-18, China invested over $ 143 billion in the IOR as per the estimates of the American Enterprise Institute (AEI).[37] Chinese economic clout has been amply demonstrated several times in recent years when it has chosen to use its strength in trade and tourism to coerce nations. Mongolia, Sweden, Japan, South Korea, Canada and Australia are some of the nations that have faced China's ire for different reasons. In each case, China has also been careful to restrict its economic punishment since an all-out attack would hurt it in the long run. India itself faces the quandary of having to stand up to China and yet engage with it economically. There is no way the Indian economy can be expected to grow completely divorced or cut off from the second largest economy in the world. India-China bilateral trade peaked in 2018 at $ 95.7 billion, with a trade deficit of $ 56.95 billion in China's favour.[38] China's share in India's total exports and imports was 9 per cent and 18 per cent, respectively in 2019-20.[39] In 2019, India's imports from China totalled $ 74.72 billion while exports to China amounted to $ 17.95 billion, resulting in a trade deficit of $ 56.77 billion.[40] In 2020, India's imports from China fell to $ 66.7 billion while exports rose to $ 20.86 billion to reduce the trade deficit to $ 45.8 billion, the lowest since 2015.[41] During April 2020 to January 2021, the proportion of imports coming from China was estimated at 15.23 per cent.[42] India has been demanding the opening of China's IT and pharmaceutical sectors to enable it to increase its exports, but there has been no headway. Meanwhile, China has been wooing nations around India's neighbourhood with tariff exemptions.

From July 2020, 8,256 products from Bangladesh, constituting 97 per cent of all products from the nation, were exempted from tariff by China.[43] This concession is under a preferential tariff programme that China has for LDCs since 2002 and applies to 40 other nations.[44] On 17 October 2019, China and Mauritius signed a Free Trade Agreement that committed both countries to reduce tariffs on over 90 per cent of products for each other.[45] In March 2021, China approved a $ 1.54 billion currency swap with Sri Lanka.[46]

Between 2000 and 2010, Chinese companies executed projects worth $ 53.46 billion in India.[47] The growth of Chinese investments in India increased after 2014.[48] Among the main sectors receiving this investment in the 2014-2018 period were infrastructure, automobiles, energy, real estate and consumer goods sectors. Starting from 2016, Chinese private sector technology companies and venture capital players started acquiring stakes in Indian companies.[49] Although the single biggest deal was the $ 1.09 billion acquisition of a 74 per cent stake in Gland Pharma by the Fosun Group in 2017, the investments have largely been in the technology sector, especially Internet startups. Alibaba, Tencent and Xiaomi were the three biggest investors in this trend of Chinese investments and acquisitions that peaked in 2016 and 2017.[50] The total current and planned Chinese investment in India is estimated to be around $ 26 billion.[51] Investments in Indian start-ups, especially in the Fintech sector, have been welcomed but concerns have risen about providing such access to Indian data and financial systems. In the last five years, joint ventures with Chinese companies have been awarded $ 1 billion worth of rail projects in India.[52] Online loan apps, mostly backed by Chinese entities have been flagged by regulatory authorities and state police departments for unlawful lending practices in India.[53]

With the economic clout comes political influence. As China gains greater access and clout with its economic diplomacy, it will play a larger part in the governance and security of the IOR. To conclude that this political influence has, by default, meant an easing out of India is not zero-sum thinking. The implications for India have been reiterated by events in the Maldives and Nepal in recent years, when Indian sensitivities were brushed aside. The rolling back of a contract to GMR to undertake the Male Airport project or putting on hold the Colombo East Terminal project are two such examples. In May 2020, when Nepal protested against India inaugurating a new road through Leipulekh Pass, the Indian Army Chief hinted at the possibility of "these issues being raised at the behest of someone else".[54] In Nepal in particular, China has dispensed with its rule of "non-interference in internal affairs" enshrined in its fabled Panchsheel. The Chinese Ambassador had openly mediated between political parties, and a high-level delegation had landed in Nepal to take stock of political events. The growing economic and military partnership between China and Iran could cast a cloud over India's aspirations to gain access to Afghanistan and Central Asia through Iran.

Proliferation of own technology and standards have emerged as a major point of global influence. The USA and Europe have benefitted as global leaders, but now China has emerged as a rival. Standards are a major source of revenue and 'lock in' the user to buy and use products and services of the standard-setter. Earlier, technical standards were largely driven by industry bodies but China has changed the game by taking it up as a central government-driven aim. In certain emerging technologies like ultra-high voltage power transmission, China is the only country deploying projects on a large scale. In many sectors like high speed rail, it has developed its own standards. It has home-grown social media and cashless payment systems rivalling the Western technology giants. Massive exports of certain Chinese products can make them the *de facto* standards, if accepted standards do not exist in the sector. In recent years, representatives of China have filled global standard-setting bodies like the International Telecommunication Union (ITU).

This race is across all conceivable sectors, and leadership in each sector bring in its portion of influence. For example, the Beidou satellite navigation system seeks to become the global default against the American GPS. It is a dual-use technology with military and non-military applications. Roping in users also means access to more data that can be utilised in AI applications. Another example is the Port Management System which will capture the movement of all ships.

The maritime world is being increasingly governed through cyberspace. Digital trade facilitation seeks to make all stages of cross-border trade paperless. Thus, control and security of cyber assets has implications on the maritime domain. In 2017, Wannacry and NotPetya ransomware struck worldwide, paralysing the container lines and terminals that were hit. It is estimated that APM-Maersk, the world's largest container ship operator, lost $ 300 million in revenue due to the NotPetya attack. In fact, ransomware has hit more top shipping companies since then – COSCO in July 2018, Mediterranean Shipping Company in April 2020 and CMA CGM in September 2020. In February 2021, Recorded Future, a privately held cyber security firm based in London, released a report of cyber attacks on India's critical infrastructure. Among the 12 targeted organisations were the Mumbai Port Trust and the V.O. Chidambaranar Port.[55]

Ninety-five per cent of digital data that travels the globe is carried by undersea cables. Presently, there are around 400 such cables of varying capacity.[56] China's emergence in this field started in 2009 with a joint venture between Huawei and Global Marine of the UK. Huawei went on to lay more than 50,000 km of cable across 90 projects.[57] In 2020, the Hengtong Group, a private company with a history of cooperation with the Chinese military, acquired Huawei Marine Networks and rebranded it as HMN Technologies.[58] This rings true with the historical lessons of the telegram – the influence and advantage of access to cables; the dangers of interception of data by those with access; and the sudden importance of remote and uninhabited locations as landing stations. Alarmed at the ownership of undersea cables passing on to non-European entities, the EU, Norway and Iceland signed the European Data Gateways Ministerial Declaration on 19 March 2021. It seeks to develop four European data gateways. In March 2021, the UK Ministry of defence announced the construction of a new multirole ocean surveillance vessel that will be used to "protect" undersea cables.[59] It is expected to be completed by 2024.

China is the primary supplier to the world for a wide range of products. This was accepted as a characteristic of the interdependence of a globalised world. However, the danger of this interdependence was highlighted whenever China employed coercive tactics to pressurise nations. "Weaponised Interdependence" is a term that has found acceptance in academic circles.[60] However, one need not delve into any theoretical framework to realise that dependence on a potential adversary can be fateful. A Group of Ministers (GoMs) report on boosting manufacturing in India noted that there are 86 'line items' in which India is "critically dependent" on Chinese imports. The 'line items' include consumer electronics, computer hardware, telephone equipment, electronic items, and air conditioners and refrigerators.[61] Indian drug makers import about 70 per cent of their Active Pharmaceutical Ingredients (APIs), which are crucial for the pharmaceutical industry, from China.[62] India is adopting solar power on a massive scale and a major portion of the solar panels are imported from China since they are the cheapest. In 2017-18, when bilateral trade had peaked, China's share in India's imported items included about 73 per cent in telecommunication equipment, about 82 per cent in semiconductor devices, more than 75 per cent for Active Pharmaceutical Ingredients, and about 81 per cent for antibiotics.[63]

China is estimated to be the fifth largest exporter of arms in the world and supplies arms to 53 nations.[64] Considering the sales from 2010 to 2019, Pakistan, Bangladesh and Myanmar are the three largest buyers accounting for around 63 per cent of the sales.[65] In addition, China gifted a type 053 frigate to Sri Lanka in August 2019. For the period from 1999 to 2018, 13 per cent of China's arms exports have gone to Southeast Asian countries accounting for 6.3 per cent of sales in the region.[66] From 2013 and 2018, the total value of arms transfers from China to Pakistan was estimated to be $ 3.5 billion.[67] The sale of military equipment, apart from creating dependency, also provides the opportunity for extended deployment of personnel and equipment in the customer nation for training and equipment lifecycle support purposes.

Rare Earth Elements (REEs) are 17 elements in the Periodic Table of elements that include 15 lanthanides, yttrium, and scandium. They are further sub-divided into Heavy and Light REEs. Though referred to as one group, the elements have varied properties that makes them critical in the manufacturing of a wide array of products that include smart phones, rechargeable batteries, solar panels, cameras, LCD and plasma screens, magnets, missile guidance systems, pharmaceuticals and energy-efficient bulbs, to name a few. Most applications require small amounts of elements and, since they do not degrade, they can be recycled when the equipment is disposed. Although China possesses only about a third of proven reserves of REEs[68], it dominates the global supply of refined REEs. It provides more than 98 per cent of global supply of some elements and close to 90 per cent of the world's permanent magnet alloys.[69]

An unquantifiable arbiter of influence is 'soft power'. It includes the attractiveness of language, education, popular culture, to name only a few. Several private schools in Nepal made learning of Chinese language compulsory after China assured that it will pay the salaries of teachers who teach Mandarin.[70] Thereafter, the Nepalese Ministry of Education signed a Memorandum of Understanding (MoU) for teachers to teach Mandarin in public-funded schools.[71] Young Pakistanis are also learning the language that promises future employment and prosperity.[72] Around 550 Confucius Institutes and 1,172 Confucius Classrooms were established in 162 nations by China's Ministry of Education for propagating the Chinese language and culture.[73] These institutes, established mostly in campuses of educational institutions, came under a cloud for their censorship and conditions of engagement with their host institutions.[74] Several countries have even shut them down. Perhaps in a bid to deflect some of the criticism, in July 2020, these institutes were transferred to a NGO called Chinese International Education Foundation.[75] In August 2020, India reviewed the functioning of seven such institutes established in Indian universities, in addition to 54 MoUs between Indian and Chinese education institutions.[76] However, there is no stopping the Indian yearning for an education degree. Around 7,000 to 8,000 Indian students travel to China every year for an MBBS degree.[77] This is despite the requirement that they must clear an exam in India, after graduation, to practice in India. Out of the 20,310 students who graduated from 86 Chinese medical universities or colleges and took the exam from 2015 to 2018, only 2,369 students or 11.67 per cent passed it.[78] Every year, China offers Pakistani students around 7,000 fully-funded scholarships to Master's and PhD courses.[79]

Maritime Component of BRI

The maritime component of the BRI, or the Maritime Silk Road, has the same misleading impression as the BRI itself. When presented with maps accompanying its description, it too gives an impression of being an endeavour to improve maritime connectivity along certain 'routes' or 'economic passages'. These declared routes have increased from two to four over a period of time. However, the maritime component of the BRI too seems more like a diverse collection of port and SEZ-related projects all across the globe rather than a coherent plan to enhance maritime flows along specific routes. Since there is no master list of projects, any Chinese involvement in any maritime construction or operational activity is liable to be labelled as part of the MSR. Some of the projects are within the declared routes while some are out of it. For example, China has invested in ports in western Africa but they are not part of any of these routes. Even after seven years of its announcement, the MSR does not give an impression of consisting of projects that have been coherently planned as part of some master plan. Will this nebulous collection of maritime projects, by itself, alter maritime trade flows in any significant manner? It certainly does not appear to be so. Not yet at least. North America, Europe and Asia continue to be the continents where the industrial production and prominent markets lie. Africa and South America still do not figure prominently in global trade.[80] International trade will continue to be predominantly borne by ships, and the east-west maritime flow across the Indo-Pacific region will dominate. Global maritime routes are more likely to alter due to geographical changes such as the melting of Arctic ice. The Kra canal will never happen.

The seeming obsession with China needs to be explained. China is building ports abroad. So also are India and Japan, for example. Chinese companies are operating ports throughout the world. So also are state-owned companies like DP World. In fact, in February 2020, DP World became fully state owned.[81] Chinese companies together may be the largest carriers of maritime freight but the largest is AP Moller-Maersk headquartered in Denmark. This pattern of responses can be formed for almost everything China does. However, there are a few factors that force reconsideration whenever there is Chinese involvement. To begin with, the lines between public and private or civil and military in China can be blurred. Chinese State Owned Enterprises are provided with huge capital support by the state that enables them to eliminate competition and even invest in assets that are not financially viable but can be used later for strategic purposes. The fusion between the public and private in China is quite high unlike other democracies. Products and activities by a private company can often have military underpinning. In 1998, the hull of the erstwhile *Varyag* was bought by a Macau-based company. In September 2012, it was commissioned as the first aircraft carrier of the PLA Navy. Setting up of an overseas base and militarisation of the maritime features in South China Sea were denied once upon a time but happened later. Chinese support comes with the baggage of political influence that others, such as Japan, do not indulge in. There is lack of transparency in Chinese agreements, especially with regard to the terms and conditions. Finally, there is assertive Chinese behaviour and the lack of hesitation in using trade, tourism and every other means to hurt any nation that falls on its wrong side.

An infrastructure development project may not always be purely commercial or purely geopolitical. Very often, it will have both factors intertwined to varying degrees. Despite this possibility, it will be useful to consider the commercial and military components separately while considering the implications of China's maritime infrastructure. There must be recognition that all Chinese investments are not the same. Some are purely commercial (like FDI), some purely strategic (like Gwadar) and some have commercial with strategic implications.

Maritime Dominance?

Let us look at the commercial aspect first. Post 2008, the alarm was raised, especially in Europe, when Chinese companies bought stakes in ports. The thinking was that China was gaining undue influence in the maritime industry. Some reports suggested that with China moving into a pole position on all aspects of maritime activity (port ownership and operation, shipping lines, ship building, Navy and Coast Guard, underwater technology), it will be in a position where it can start altering the flow of maritime traffic at will. Nine of the top 20 container ports in the world are in China.[82] China has the largest number of merchant ships in the world and is the third largest in terms of tonnage.[83] China is the largest shipbuilder in the world in terms of tonnage.[84] One example was that of Piraeus port which became profitable after being bought by COSCO, since Chinese container traffic was directed to it.

The global maritime industry is extremely complex. There are different types of ports to cater for different types of cargo. Similarly, there are different types of ships. The reasons for either the success or failure of each port or type of ship can be difficult to predict since it depends on so many factors. Ownership in these multiple types of ports and ships is also highly diffused. The maritime industry is replete with examples of fortunes being made and lost on a regular basis due to change in market conditions. For example, the COVID-19 pandemic has disrupted global supply chains in ways that were completely unexpected. Apart from jamming ports due to shortage of labour, the availability of cargo containers has reached crisis levels. Some ports have an excess of empty containers piled up while many have a critical shortage.[85] With freight rates touching record heights, some shipping companies have scored a bonanza. Another example is the International Maritime Organisation's decision to cut down on emissions. All ships are supposed to shift over to clean fuels but there is no clarity on which clean option will become the most acceptable. Shipping companies are postponing fresh orders on ship construction till there is clarity. In March 2021, a 20,000-TEU container ship, *Ever Given*, ran aground in the Suez Canal blocking traffic completely in the waterway through which 12 per cent of world trade transits. The vessel is owned by a Japanese company, operated by a Taiwanese company, registered in Panama, technically managed by a German company, had a mostly Indian crew, and was shipping cargo from Malaysia to France. Apart from being yet another example of the myriad possible disruptions in maritime trade, it is also an example of how globally diverse the industry is. Hence, without going into the details, it can be declared that no nation has the wherewithal to manipulate maritime flows on its own.

From 2010–2020, container shipping companies sought to expand their services to include shipping, terminal operations and inland logistics to reduce exposure to volatile freight rates and generate alternative revenue streams providing end-to-end logistic solutions.[86] Chinese companies followed this global trend. Obviously, once the port terminal and shipping line is owned by the same company, it will direct its ships to ports owned by it. Hence, the most successful container terminals are those owned by shipping line owners. Examples are APM Terminals and Maersk; Terminal Investment Limited and Mediterranean Shipping Company; Mitsui Osaka Shosen Kaisha Lines; Yang Ming Marine Transport Corporation; HMM and COSCO.[87] In fact, container traffic is now controlled by three major alliances – 2M, Ocean Alliance and The Alliance. The nationalities of the companies in the three alliances are varied and do not coincide with geopolitical mappings. In fact, commercial ties do not often coincide with geopolitical groupings.

China may have the largest number of merchant ships in the world but, in terms of tonnage, it is third behind Greece and Japan, and has just 11.15 per cent of the whole world.[88] COSCO and China Merchant Ports may contribute 18.1 per cent of container throughput worldwide[89] but most of it is within ports in China. Hutchinson Ports is a listed company based in Hong Kong with an international management. The largest shipping company is not Chinese. It is Maersk of Denmark, which serves 343 ports in 121 countries. Its associated port operator company, APM Terminals, has infrastructure in 73 ports and 154 inland locations.[90]

It is estimated that there are around 90 ports around the world that have stakes held by Chinese companies. To give some context to this number, there are around 8,000 ports worldwide.[91] In most of the around 90 cases, Chinese companies own minority stakes. These are purely commercial as they do not allow the companies to influence port operations in any manner. The logical method to identify ports that could possibly come under Chinese influence is to separate those in which the SOEs have majority stakes. Furthermore, the host nation is also important. Chinese companies own majority stakes in terminals in the UAE but they can be considered as commercial since the UAE is a thriving maritime hub. Nobody expects a Chinese base to come up in UAE. However, in Djibouti, although the Chinese company does not own the port fully, it has a Chinese military base. Hence, instead of becoming suspicious of every Chinese commercial venture, it makes sense to look at those that are majority owned by Chinese companies and do not make commercial sense. If this exercise is done for the Indo-Pacific Region, the present candidates emerge clearly in Cambodia (Dara Sokor and Ream), Pakistan and Sri Lanka (Hambantota).

Places and Bases

One of the most debated issues is about the extent to which Chinese port building and port operation activities will be used to support military operations. If the earlier conjecture was that China would be setting up military "bases", now there is greater consensus that it merely requires "places" to support its maritime operations.

If we examine the trend of Chinese activities in the South China Sea, it is quite clear that China follows an incremental approach of ingress, taking care to avoid the threshold that can invite retaliation. It is safe to assume that a similar approach will be followed in the IOR. China will avoid any action that will ratchet up tension beyond a threshold. With the advancement of technology, warships can stay for longer durations of time at sea without major maintenance or refits. All that they require are replenishment of rations, spares and consumables (lubrication oils, cartridges for reverse osmosis plants, and so on). Although they can be supplied at sea, it will be much more expensive. A more suitable alternative is to visit a port where they can be supplied by Chinese logistics companies that have global coverage. There is no 'modification' that is required for a warship to come alongside a jetty meant for general use, except for the usual considerations such as the depth available. Hence, it is entirely possible for the PLA Navy to increase its presence in the IOR, with logistic support provided during visits to foreign ports. Moreover, visits of warships to foreign ports are routine activity and do not contravene international law. Hence, host nations can allow such visits without worries of inviting external pressure. In this model, foreign ports at strategic locations will have terminal and commercial zones operated by Chinese companies. The ports and associated facilities will facilitate Chinese trade and investment with the host nation while also helping the PLA Navy to establish a network of logistics and intelligence hubs across the Indian Ocean Region.

This scenario changes dramatically if either the military presence becomes permanent or hostilities break out. Nations in the IOR will be wary of allowing a permanent Chinese military presence. Some like Sri Lanka and Myanmar have explicitly stated that they are committed to not have any foreign military presence in their territories. Moreover, any permanent Chinese military base will be a vulnerable (and attractive) target for any adversary should hostilities break out. The only nation that can be considered as an exception to this is Pakistan. In its case, it is only a matter of time before it hosts permanent Chinese military presence. There has been conjecture that it could be at either Jiwani or Gwadar. That is just a matter of detail. It is not a coincidence that among the CPEC projects, projects in Gwadar are primarily financed through grants while projects elsewhere are financed through loans. The Pak-China military nexus is well known. It is needless to add that Pakistan has no incentive to bother about Indian security sensitivities. Pakistan can even provide repair and refit infrastructure to enable maintenance and repair of PLA Navy vessels if required. It is inducting frigates and submarines constructed in China, among other equipment, which will increasingly provide compatible infrastructure or an ecosystem for maintenance of Chinese military equipment. Such a presence will significantly constrain India's options against Pakistan in case of outbreak of hostilities.

Publications in China suggest that China should set up "strategic strong points" or "maritime hubs". It will be interesting to see if the government does indeed do so in future. There are numerous examples of China not adhering to its declared intent – bases abroad; militarisation of maritime features in the South China Sea, and provisions of the Hong Kong agreement, to name a few.

Military Implications of Chinese Presence

The PLA Navy's presence in the Indian Ocean commenced in 2008 with the deployment of the first Anti-Piracy Escort Force to the Gulf of Aden. Since then, the deployment of this Escort Force has been used to gain experience in extended deployment, training of crew, proving of logistic arrangements through Chinese companies, and 'showing the flag' around the region. At the time of writing, the 37th Escort Task Force was deployed to the Gulf of Aden. Alarm bells rang when PLA Navy submarines started getting deployed to the region. At least eight submarine missions, both nuclear and conventional, were reported to have been deployed between 2013 and 2018.[92] In 2018, at any point, the PLA Navy had six to eight ships in the Indian Ocean. This included the three ships of the Anti-Piracy Escort Force and three to four survey vessels or satellite tracking ships.[93]

The presence of oceanographic research and survey vessels is of particular concern. Although such vessels can be deployed in a region for legitimate scientific explorations, the data they collect is of dual use. Satellite tracking and control ships may be used for own satellites as well as for tracking launches of long range missiles. Underwater data such as currents, salinity, and temperature at different depths is critically required for submarine operations. Similarly, mapping of the ocean floor and undersea features is useful for submarine operations. Vessels equipped for intelligence collection can eavesdrop on communications, track Indian Navy fleet movements, collect radar signatures of Indian equipment, collect noise signatures of Indian vessels, and assess live firing exercises by the Indian forces at sea. Greater Chinese presence in the region means more vessels that can conduct intelligence, surveillance and reconnaissance missions to better understand regional militaries and gather data on geographical area. India's sea-based nuclear deterrence would be a prime target.

A report of 2018 stated that at any given time, five to 10 Chinese "scientific research vessels" operated beyond Chinese jurisdictional waters in strategically-important areas of the Indo-Pacific.[94] In September 2019, a Chinese research ship *Shiyan-1*, which is owned by the Chinese Academy of Sciences, was spotted carrying out research activities in India's EEZ in the Andaman Sea.[95] In January 2020, it was reported that four to six Chinese research vessels were spotted in the Indian Ocean

Region, and that around 600 Chinese fishing boats are present in the Indian Ocean Region annually since 2015.[96] In August 2020, when tensions rose at the land border in Ladakh, a Yuan Wang class research vessel entered the Indian Ocean and was tracked by the Indian Navy.[97] Survey ship *Xiang Yang Hong 03* is reported to be a regular visitor to the Indian Ocean.[98] In November 2019, it undertook a survey of the region west of Indonesia to the Bay of Bengal. In November 2020, it undertook a survey in the Arabian Sea. Along with its sister ship, *Xiang Yang Hong 01*, it has been surveying "the Ninetyeast Ridge, an underwater mountain range that cuts through the Eastern Indian Ocean from north to south" and "is particularly relevant for submarine operations".[99]

The presence of oceanographic survey vessels can be justified by the exploration region awarded by the ISA, and collaboration in oceanographic studies with nations in South Asia. The China–Sri Lanka Joint Centre for Education and Research for the 21st Century Maritime Silk Road (CSL-CER) was founded in August 2015.[100] Even before the establishment of this centre, Chinese research ship *Shiyan-1* was undertaking an annual scientific expedition in the eastern Indian Ocean since 2010. Chinese research vessels have been undertaking similar joint marine research expeditions in Myanmar's waters since January 2018.[101] The first China-Pakistan joint oceanographic expedition was undertaken off Makran coast onboard the research vessel named *Shiyan 3* in January-February 2018.[102] A longer joint expedition was undertaken onboard the marine geological survey vessel *Haiyang Dizhi-10* in February 2019.[103] Research vessels *Xiang Yang Hong 1*, *Xiang Yang Hong 3* and *Shiyan 3* were reported to have been at Colombo in September-November 2020.[104] There have been 12 'declared' visits by Chinese survey ships to Sri Lankan waters from February 2014 to November 2020.[105] Recent reports by Open Source Intelligence (OSINT) analysts suggest that four of the Xiang Yang Hong class research ships (*Xiang Yang Hong 1, 3, 19 and 6*) have been particularly active in the Eastern Indian Ocean for the last two years.[106]

Some of the Xiang Yang Hong class of ships are capable of deploying Sea Wing underwater gliders. The unmanned gliders have no propulsion power but use a variable buoyancy mechanism to dive down and come up repeatedly while their large wings allow them to glide forward. They can be deployed for months to gather oceanographic data and transmit it to the mother ship through a trailing antenna. It was reported that 12 gliders were launched in the Indian Ocean by survey vessel *Xiang Yang Hong 6* in mid-December 2019 and recovered in February 2020.[107]

In recent times, Indonesia has been discovering that particular attention was being paid to studying its waters. In January 2021, an Indonesian Coast Guard vessel shadowed the *Xiang Yang Hong 3* after its Automated Identification System (AIS) was found to be switched off three times while transiting the archipelago.[108] It was not the only instance of Chinese survey vessels switching off their AIS.[109] Chinese Sea Wing gliders have been recovered from Indonesian waters on at least four occasions,[110] with the latest discovered in late December 2020 near South Sulawesi's Selayar Island.[111] The gliders can take sonar soundings of the ocean floor and capture data like seawater temperature, salinity, turbidity, and chlorophyll and oxygen levels. Such data of the acoustic environment underwater is used by submarines to avoid detection by sonar. If PLA Navy submarines have to transit from the South China Sea to the Indian Ocean submerged and undetected, they will traverse the Sunda Strait or the Ombai-Wetar Strait. Detailed mapping of the contours of the seabed and data on the acoustic and thermal environment underwater (sound propagation underwater) are essential for it. Similar data are also captured by survey vessels and Remotely Operated Vehicles (ROVs). China possesses larger Unmanned Underwater Vehicles (UUVs) like the HSU-001 and Sea Whale 2000 that can travel long distances autonomously and gather environmental data or intelligence.

The Future Role of China's Maritime Forces

China has the largest navy (in terms of number of vessels, not total tonnage), the largest Coast Guard and the largest fishing militia. As the blue water capabilities of its navy continue to be augmented, what could be the operational profile that Chinese maritime forces will adopt? Will the PLA Navy deploy Carrier Task Forces in the far seas like the US Navy or will it restrict its distant operations to a small Task Force as it does now? Will it adopt the 'salami slicing' and gray zone tactics that it has adopted in the South China Sea in other regions, such as the Indian Ocean, as well? Will it spread its Anti-Access Area Denial (A2AD) capabilities further away from its shoreline, perhaps covering the eastern Indian Ocean as well?

It is said that imitation is the best form of flattery. The PLA Navy seems to have followed the path of the US Navy in building up its force structure. Two aircraft carriers have been unveiled, with a plan to have six more of them. The largest destroyers mimic features of those of the US Navy. The destroyers and frigates will form part of the envisaged Carrier Task Forces. Sea lift capability and expeditionary capability is getting enhanced. A marine force has been raised.

Speaking to Rajya Sabha TV in October 2020, Vice Admiral Satish Soni, who retired as a Commander-in-Chief of the Indian Navy, predicted that by 2025 to 2030, the PLA Navy (he called it "CCP Navy") will have its first overseas command with its headquarters at Gwadar. Having a military base in Gwadar makes sense for the PLA Navy, the primary reason being geography and an obliging host nation. A strong presence to India's west can be a good way to keep the focus of the Indian Navy away from the Malacca Strait and the east.

Since 2013, China has reclaimed around 3,200 acres in the Spratlys in the South China Sea. On three of these artificial maritime features (Fiery Cross Reef, Mischief Reef and Subi Reef) there are hardened shelters with retractable roofs believed to be housing surface-to-air missile (SAM) systems. There are hangars capable of accommodating aircraft. There is space to host large numbers of ships. Should the PLAN be tasked with defending access to the Malacca Strait in a crisis, PLAN ships and aircraft based in the Spratlys could respond much more rapidly than forces based further away on Hainan Island or the mainland.[112]

Right now, the priorities of the PLA Navy are around its peripheral waters. Before it moves into the Indian Ocean, it will need to have surveillance capabilities in the region. This may be through space-based assets or Maritime Patrol Aircraft. It will also have to cater for its present weak anti-air and anti-submarine capabilities in the Indian Ocean. When close to home, the PLA Navy has the advantage of operating under the cover of shore-based air defence systems, land-based aircraft, presence of own submarines, and a network of sensors. This advantage is not available to it in the Indian Ocean.

Once the PLA Navy is in a position to have a permanent presence in the Indian Ocean, there will be several implications. The first will be that the PLA Navy will be in a position to be the 'first responder' for rescue and relief operations in the region, a privilege exercised by the Indian Navy as of now. Secondly, its presence can be a threat to Indian assets and island territories. It is quite clear that occupation of territory is very much part of the Chinese world view, even if it is considered an anachronism for the present age. Buffer zones are created and eventually get assimilated. Gray zone warfare and salami slicing are common trends of Chinese behaviour along the borders of India, the East China Sea and the South China Sea. There is nothing to suggest that this behaviour and these tactics will not be repeated in the Indian Ocean Region in the future, when China is in a position to do so. It is already undertaking firing of missiles from container ships and can be expected to progress on miniature/modular versions of its A2AD capabilities. Commentators are already speculating on a scenario of a Chinese occupation of an Indian island territory.[113] Of course, all this is still some time away, maybe at least two decades.

Obviously, the only way to deter the adversary from undertaking any misadventure is to bolster capabilities to undertake punitive measures. These measures are already being put in place by India.

Scenarios

Let me take some creative licence to paint four scenarios moving up the escalation ladder. They are not based on any formal net assessment or simulation exercises but merely to explore future possibilities. Each scenario, for convenience, can be assumed to last a decade. Let me state that as we move up the escalation ladder, the probability of these scenarios happening gets lower.

The first stage is what can be called "Balancing and Signalling". This is already happening. As China is rising, the other powers align together to preserve the balance. China is undertaking a massive naval expansion with significant expeditionary capability – Landing Helicopter Docks (LHDs), Fleet Support vessels and a 100,000-strong marine force. In early 2014, a Chinese Surface Action Group (SAG) carried out a 23-day training exercise spanning the South China Sea (SCS), eastern Indian Ocean, and the Philippine Sea. India, on its part, is conducting exercises with leading navies and the sophistication of these exercises is increasing. Increasing Coordinated Patrols (CORPAT) and bilateral exercises with nations around the Malacca Strait, and bilateral exercises with Vietnam, Australia and Japan indicate a willingness to push east despite capacity constraints. The deterrent signalling of these efforts, along with operational initiatives like Mission Based Deployments[114] is not lost on anyone.

However, at the moment, there is not much cause for friction between the naval forces of India and China. The PLA Navy is tied up with issues of its immediate waters such as Taiwan and the famous chains of islands around it. Its sole aircraft carrier is a training platform for now and lacks a credible naval aircraft. The Indian Navy too is constrained by its capacity to venture beyond the IOR.

The next stage in this build-up will be what I label as "friction". Once the PLA Navy is able to break out of the encumbrances of its immediate waters and operationalise its carrier-based task force, it will seek to move out to distant waters more robustly. As the navies of India and China meet more often, there will be pleasant maritime exchanges and mechanisms need to be adopted, like it has been done for the armies, to ensure that these exchanges do not spiral out of control. The cat-and-mouse game of Chinese submarines and Indian ASW forces will intensify, with India taking all the assistance it can from like-minded navies as it has already started doing.

The support facilities that China is setting up for the nations that procure its equipment (submarines for Pakistan and Bangladesh, for example) can be utilised for support of its forces. Its shipping lines, port operation companies and port ownership are adequate to provide logistics support for its fleet around the globe (in terms of fuel, rations, etc.). This scenario is still a decade away and India has this strategic window to prepare itself.

As the "friction" increases, it will give way to "contestation". If the trajectories of economic growth of both nations continue, there will jostling for natural resources and energy across the globe, more precisely in West Asia and Africa. Problems will be exacerbated if China continues its practice of increasing political influence and hold in the region while pushing back competitors like the USA and India. We already see how successfully it has propped up Pakistan to pin down India. Salami-slicing; two steps forward and one step back; operating below the threshold to attain objectives – call it whatever you want, but these are different names for the same Chinese characteristic that we have seen in the borders with India and Bhutan, and in the South China Sea. They will be manifested once the PLA Navy presence is considered to be strong enough in the IOR. The obvious targets will the island territories strewn across the IOR. What we see today in East Asia, will get replicated in a different avatar in the IOR.

The ultimate stage is "Conflict". It is a stage that nobody desires and is hurtful for all. As I said, as one goes up the escalation ladder, the probability of incidence decreases. The probability of conflict in the IOR between India and China is the least. Maybe, it will not happen in the IOR since events in the SCS may boil over before that, precipitating events that foreclose a stronger PLA Navy presence in the IOR.

Finally, there is the question "Will the order in the Indian Ocean flip over?" A good answer is that it is early days yet. As I have mentioned in the build-up of the four stages, we are in the first stage and the second stage is probably a decade away. The developing scenario is never a straight line and there will be detours, the most important being the growth of the economies of both countries and the second being the growth of their respective navies. The gaps in the Indian Navy's capabilities are well known but the gaps in the PLA Navy, despite the massive expansion, cannot be papered over. For example, how does it provide trained manpower for these numerous frigates and destroyers? What is the status of its aircraft carrier and naval aircraft? Can its famed anti-ship ballistic missiles actually hit moving targets at sea? The situation is evolving and India has a strategic window to prepare itself for it.

Conclusion

This chapter has hopefully conveyed some of the geo-political implications for India with the maritime infrastructure development projects being undertaken in the Indo-Pacific Region. The BRI has not lived up to its initial vaunted reputation. Although financial disbursements are massive, the change on ground is not as fast as it was initially estimated to be. However, Chinese influence in India's neighbourhood is already perceptible. It needs to be reiterated that breathless and alarmist commentaries do not do justice to a game that will unfold over three decades. India needs to be prepared for the long haul. The next two decades are not going to be easy. The next chapter seeks to explore the geopolitical options available to India.

NOTES

1. Ministry of External Affairs (MEA), GoI, "Prime Minister's Remarks at the Commissioning of Offshore Patrol Vessel (OPV) *Barracuda* in Mauritius (March 12, 2015)", 12 March 2015.
2. IANS, "Iranian foreign minister Javad Zarif invites Pakistan, China to join Chabahar Port project with India", *Firstpost*, 13 March 2018.

3. PTI, "Iran's Chabahar and Pakistan's Gwadar are sister ports, says Islamabad", *Hindustan Times*, 16 March 2018.
4. Anirban Bhaumik (DHNS), *Iran goes to Pakistan with Chabahar link plan, Deccan Herald*, 27 May 2019.
5. Amrita Nayak Dutta, "110-km road is final challenge for long-delayed India-Myanmar Kaladan connectivity project", *The Print*, 29 March 2021.
6. Vinitha Revi, "Seychelles and Assumption Island project: Another test for India", *Raisina Debates*, Observer Research Foundation (ORF), 23 May 2020.
7. Constantino Xavier and Riya Sinha, "Land comes in the way of Modi govt's Neighbourhood First and Act East, study shows", *The Print*, 31 August 2020.
8. Sebastian Horn, Carmen M. Rienhart and Christoph Trebesch, "How much money does the world owe China?", *Harvard Business Review*, 26 February 2020.
9. Sheridan Prasso, "One of China's Most Ambitious Projects Becomes a Corridor to Nowhere", *Bloomberg*, 2 March 2020.
10. Cecilia Joy-Perez and Derek Scissors, "The Chinese State funds Belt and Road but does not have trillions to spare", *American Enterprise Institute*, March 2018.
11. OECD, "China's Belt and Road Initiative in the trade, investment and financial landscape", *OECD Business and Finance Outlook*, 2018, 29.
12. Agatha Kratz, Daniel H. Rosen, and Matthew Mingey, "Booster or Brake? COVID and the Belt and Road Initiative", *Rhodium Group*, 15 April 2020.
13. Kratz, Rosen, and Mingey, "Booster or Brake?".
14. Agatha Kratz, Matthew Mingey, and Drew D'Alelio, "Seeking Relief: China's Overseas debt after COVID-19", *Rhodium Group*, 8 October 2020.
15. Adnan Aamir, "China and Pakistan fall out over Belt and Road frameworks", *Nikkei Asia*, 19 January 2021.
16. Richard T. Griffiths, *The Maritime Silk Road: China's Belt and Road at Sea* (International Institute of Asian Studies: 2020), 113.
17. Bertil Lintner, "Full steam ahead for China-Myanmar high-speed railway", *Asia Times*, 21 February 2019.
18. Lintner, "Full steam ahead for China-Myanmar high-speed railway".
19. Lintner, "Full steam ahead for China-Myanmar high-speed railway".
20. Nan Lwin, "Myanmar, China to conduct feasibility study on Mandalay-Kyaukphyu rail link", *The Irrawady*, 11 January 2021.
21. Ramesh Kumar, "New China-Nepal rail corridor: The trans-Himalayan railway line is not built yet, but first weekly Nepal-bound freight train arrives in Xigatse", *Nepal Times*, 5 June 2020.
22. Ramesh Bhusal, "Nepal-China Rail Project: Fantasy or reality?" *thethirdpole.net*, 18 June 2019.
23. Bhusal, "Nepal-China Rail Project: Fantasy or reality?"
24. *Ministry of Foreign Affairs of the People's Republic of China*, "Opening Speech by State Councillor Wang Yi At the Meeting of the Advisory Council of The Belt and Road Forum for International Cooperation, 2020", 18 December 2020.
25. Ronald Lwere Kato, "Nigeria commences Lagos-Ibadan railway operations", *Africa News*, 9 December 2020.
26. Gboyega Akinsanmi, "FG Awaits China to Approve $5.3bn Loan to Execute Ibadan-Kano Rail Project", *This day*, 10 January 2021.
27. "Port President hands over land deed to Colombo City", *Daily FT*, 30 October 2019.
28. Ali Syed, "$10 billion man-made 'Chand Tara' Island to be built in Gwadar", *Daily*

Times, 10 February 2020.

29. Murtaza Ali Shah, "500,000 Chinese professionals expected in Gwadar by 2023", *The News*, 21 October 2017.
30. Map of Indian Ocean Exploration Area in website of International Seabed Authority accessed from https://www.isa.org.jm/map/indian-ocean on 19 January 2021. Contracts for exploration exist with the Federal Institute of Geosciences and Natural Resources (Germany), China Ocean Mineral Resources Research and Development Organisation (China), Republic of Korea, and India.
31. Yves-Heng Lim, "China's rising naval ambitions in the Indian Ocean: aligning ends, ways and means", *Asian Security*, 2020, DOI 10.1080/14799855. 2020.1721469
32. Daniel M. Hartnett, "The "New Historic Missions": Reflections on Hu Jintao's Military Legacy" in Roy Kamphausen, David Lai, and Travis Tanner (Eds.), *Assessing the People's Liberation Army in the Hu Jintao Era* (US Army War College: 2014).
33. Ananth Krishnan, "China amends defence law to boost war preparedness", *The Hindu*, 3 January 2021.
34. The State Council Information Office of the People's Republic of China, *China's Military Strategy*, 2015.
35. The State Council Information Office of the People's Republic of China, *China's National Defence in the New Era*, July 2019.
36. Anantha Krishnan, "Following the Money: China Inc's Growing Stakes in India-China Relations", *Brookings India Impact Series 032020-01*, March 2020, 11.
37. Jeffrey Becker, "Securing China's Lifelines across the Indian Ocean", *China Maritime* Report No. 11, China Maritime Studies Institute, 2020, 3.
38. Embassy of India, Beijing, China, "India-China Trade and Economic Relations" accessed from https://www.eoibeijing.gov.in/economic-and-trade-relation.php on 10 January 2021.
39. Somesh K. Mathur and Anusree Paul, "Covid-19 and India's trade dependency on China: Should we continue our ties?" *The Economic Times*, 12 January 2021.
40. K. J. M. Varma (PTI), "India-China trade dips by nearly $3 billion in 2019", *The Mint*, 14 January 2020.
41. Ananth Krishnan, "India's trade with China falls in 2020, deficit at five-year low", *The Hindu*, 16 January 2021.
42. Vivek Kaul, "India, China and the Quest for Atmanirbharta", *www.vivekkaul.com*, 11 March 2021.
43. PTI, "China woos Bangladesh, provides tariff exemption for 97% of exports from Dhaka", *The Economic Times*, 20 January 2020.
44. Adam Pitman, "China's Stake in Bangladesh Is Overplayed", *The Diplomat*, 8 August 2020.
45. Rosie Wigmore, "Will Africa's First Free Trade Agreement with China actually help Africa?" *Development Reimagined*, 2 October 2020.
46. Waruna Karunatilake and Alasdair Pal, "China approves $1.5 billion currency swap with Sri Lanka", *Reuters*, 10 March 2021.
47. Krishnan, "Following the Money", 10.
48. Krishnan, "Following the Money", 11.
49. Krishnan, "Following the Money", 11.
50. Krishnan, "Following the Money", 20-23.
51. Krishnan, "Following the Money", 5.

52. Pallavi Pengonda, "As India-China border tensions intensify, some key sectors are caught in the crossfire", *Mint*, 29 June 2020.
53. Saloni Shukla and Ashwin Manikandan, "RBI is exploring ways to regulate online loan apps", *The Economic Times*, 12 March 2021.
54. Abhishek Bhalla, "Army chief hints at China's role in Nepal's protest against India's strategic road", *India Today*, 15 May 2020.
55. Recorded Future, "China-Linked Group RedEcho Targets the Indian Power Sector Amid Heightened Border Tensions", *Cyber Threat Analysis China*, 28 February 2021, 8.
56. Jonathan E. Hillman, "Securing the Subsea Network: A Primer for Policymakers", *CSIS Reconnecting Asia Project*, March 2021, 2.
57. Takashi Kawakami, "Huawei to sell undersea cable unit to deflect US spy claims", *Nikkei Asia*, 4 June 2019.
58. Hillman, "Securing the Subsea Network", 18.
59. "New Royal Navy ship to protect 'critical' undersea cables", *BBC*, 21 March 2021.
60. Henry Farrell and Abraham L. Newman, "Weaponized Interdependence: How Global Economic Networks Shape State Coercion", *International Security*, Vol. 44, No. 1 (Summer 2019), pp. 42–79, https://doi.org/10.1162/ISEC_a_00351
61. Remya Nair and Neelam Pandey, "India 'critically dependent' on China in imports across 86 tariff lines, GoM report says", *The Print*, 9 December 2020.
62. Pallavi Pengonda, "As India-China border tensions intensify, some key sectors are caught in the crossfire", *Mint*, 29 June 2020
63. Biswajit Dhar, "Chinese Cheer for Indian Exports", *Business Line*, 4 March 2019.
64. Pieter D. Wezeman, Aude Fleurant, Alexandra Kuimova, Diego Lopes da Silva, Nan Tian and Siemon T. Wezeman, "Trends In International Arms Transfers, 2019", *SIPRI Factsheet*, March 2020.
65. "Importer/exporter TIV Tables", *SIPRI Arms Transfer Database*.
66. Siemon T. Wezeman, "Arms Flow to Southeast Asia", *SIPRI*, December 2019.
67. Filippo Boni, "Protecting the Belt and Road Initiative: China's cooperation with Pakistan to secure CPEC", *Asia Policy*, Vol. 14, No. 2, April 2019, 6.
68. Stratfor, "*The Geopolitics of Rare Earth Elements*", 8 April 2019.
69. Stratfor, "*The Geopolitics of Rare Earth Elements*".
70. Sabitri Dhakal, "Mandarin made compulsory in many schools", *The Himalayan Times*, 15 June 2019.
71. Binod Ghimire, "Government has agreed to promote Mandarin in Nepali schools and not everyone seems pleased", *The Kathmandu Post*, 15 October 2019.
72. Diaa Hadid and Abdul Sattar, "In Pakistan, Learning Chinese Is Cool — And Seen As A Path To Prosperity", *NPR*, 9 October 2019; Sabrina Toppa, "Why Young Pakistanis Are Learning Chinese", *The Atlantic (Pulitzer Centre)*, 14 November 2018.
73. Ananth Krishnan, "The Hindu Explains: What are Confucius Institutes, and why are they under the scanner in India?"*The Hindu*, 9 August 2020.
74. Pratik Jhakar, "Confucius Institutes: The growth of China's controversial cultural branch", *BBC Monitoring*, 6 September 2019.
75. Chen Xi, "New NGO to operate China's Confucius Institutes, 'disperse misinterpretation'," *Global Times*, 5 July 2020.
76. Ananth Krishnan, "The Hindu Explains".
77. Sowmiya Ashok, "Cheaper fees, easy admissions: Indian medical students shift gaze towards China", *The Indian Express*, 29 July 2019.

78. Sowmiya Ashok, "Less than 12% Indian students with Chinese medical degree clear eligibility exam", *The Indian Express*, 30 October 2019.
79. Ehsan Masood, "South Asia's Pivot towards China", *Nature*, Vol. 569, 2 May 2019.
80. UNCTAD, "Review of Maritime Transport 2020" 7.
81. "DP World returns to full state ownership, takes on $8.1 billion debt", *Reuters*, 17 February 2020.
82. UNCTAD, "Review of Maritime Transport 2020", 18.
83. UNCTAD, "Review of Maritime Transport 2020", 40.
84. UNCTAD, "Review of Maritime Transport 2020", 44.
85. Peter S. Goodman, Alexandra Stevenson, Niraj Chokshi, and Michael Corkery, "'I've never seen anything like this': Chaos strikes global shipping", *New York Times*, 6 March 2021.
86. UNCTAD, "Review of Maritime Transport 2020" 58.
87. UNCTAD, "Review of Maritime Transport 2020", 57.
88. UNCTAD, "Review of Maritime Transport 2020", 40.
89. UNCTAD, "Review of Maritime Transport 2020", 58.
90. Deborah Brautigam, "A critical look at Chinese 'debt-trap diplomacy': the rise of a meme", *Area Development and Policy*, Vol. 5, No. 1, 2020, 1-14, DOI 10.1080/23792949.2019.1689828
91. *World Port Index* (National Geospatial Intelligence Agency, USA: 2019).
92. Abhishek Bhalla, "China sent 8 submarines in last 5 yrs that drifted too close to home", *DNA*, 4 December 2018.
93. Video of "Navy Day 2018 Press Conference by CNS Sunil Lanba" accessed from https://www.youtube.com/watch?v=enL0CP42kxM on 19 January 2021.
94. Ryan D. Martinson and Peter A. Dutton, "China's Distant-Ocean Survey Activities: Implications for U.S. National Security", *China Maritime* Report No. 3, China Maritime Studies Institute, U.S. Naval War College, November 2018.
95. ANI, "Indian Navy forced PLA ship to return after it entered Exclusive Economic Zone in Andaman Sea", *Times of India*, 3 December 2019.
96. Shaurya Karanbir Gurung (ET Bureau), "Alarm over Chinese research ships in Indian Ocean Region", *Economic Times*, 30 January 2020.
97. Ajit K. Dubey (ANI), "Indian Navy tracks Chinese research vessel in Indian Ocean amid Ladakh border tension", *Mint*, 17 September 2020.
98. H. I. Sutton, "Chinese Survey Ship Caught 'Running Dark' Give Clues to Underwater Drone Operations", *USNI News*, 16 January 2021.
99. H. I. Sutton, "Two Chinese Survey Ships are Probing a Strategic Section of the Indian Ocean", *USNI News*, 23 March 2021.
100. Luo Yao, Wang Dong-Xiao, Pan Gang, Zhang Zhen-Qiu, Wang Wei-Qiang and Yao Jing-Long, "China–Sri Lanka Joint Centre for Education and Research for the 21st Century Maritime Silk Road", *Atmospheric and Oceanic Science Letters*, 2017 Vol. 10, No. 5, 354–357, https://doi.org/10.1080/16742834.2017.1343085
101. "Chinese research vessel ends fruitful ocean expedition in Myanmar", *CGTN*, 21 January 2018.
102. Faiza Ilyas, "China Pakistan Oceanographic expeditions complete", *Dawn*, 4 February 2018.
103. Gao Yun and Pan Zhaoyi, "Chinese geological survey vessel completes first joint expedition with Pakistan", *CGTN*, 26 February 2019.

104. Srinjoy Chowdhury, "Chinese ships, 'research vessels' on missions to find out more about Indian Ocean", *Times Now*, 4 December 2020.
105. Snehesh Alex Philip, "Chinese research vessels in Sri Lankan waters come under Indian Navy lens", *The Print*, 14 November 2020.
106. H. I. Sutton, "Chinese Ships Seen Mapping Strategic Seabed In Indian Ocean", 21 January 2021 accessed from https://www.navalnews.com/naval-news/2021/01/how-china-is-mapping-the-seabed-of-the-indian-ocean/ on 23 January 2021.
107. H. I. Sutton, "China Deployed 12 Underwater Drones In Indian Ocean", *Forbes*, 22 March 2020.
108. H. I. Sutton, "Chinese Survey Ship Caught 'Running Dark' Give Clues to Underwater Drone Operations", *USNI News*, 16 January 2021.
109. John Mcbeth, "China, Indonesia on a collision course at sea", *Asia Times*, 15 January 2021.
110. Mcbeth, "China, Indonesia on a collision course at sea".
111. Kristin Huang, "China's underwater drones seized in Indonesia expose tech, routes and potential submarine plans", *South China Morning Post*, 10 January 2021.
112. Jeffrey Becker, "Securing China's Lifelines across the Indian Ocean", *China Maritime* Report No. 11, China Maritime Studies Institute, 2020, 3.
113. John Graver, "Limitations on China's ability to understand Indian apprehensions about China's rise as a naval power" in David Brewster (Ed.), *India and China at Sea: Competition for Naval Dominance in the Indian Ocean* (Oxford University Press: 2018), 86.
114. Since 2017, the Indian Navy has been maintaining a permanent presence of warships on patrol in seven regions in the Indian Ocean to keep an eye on all entry and exit routes to and from the Indian Ocean. In addition to these deployments, Long Range Maritime Reconnaissance aircraft fly sorties almost every day. These operations are collectively called Mission Based Deployments.

9

Manoeuvring Through Severely Restricted Waters

Introduction

The next two decades promise to be extremely trying for India as it will have to make tough choices amidst structural change in the global order to secure its national interests. India will have to continue its national mission to provide prosperity and economic well-being to its citizens even while negotiating external forces that will sap its limited resources. So, how does India move ahead in this game of using technology and infrastructure development to further geopolitical ends? The frank answer to that is that it is going to be extremely difficult to further Indian interests against forces that enjoy asymmetric advantages. The options before India seem to be limited. This chapter seeks to explore these limited options. It has to be admitted that it will not offer any magical prescription that is not already known. In fact, much of what this chapter will cover is being pursued by India in some form or the other. It will give a top-to-bottom scan of the choices and paths before India from the strategic to the operational.

The Economy, Stupid

If there is a single mission that should be the top-most national priority, it has to be economic growth. From China to Vietnam to India, it is a proven fact that GDP growth is the most effective way to eradicate poverty. It is also a hard reality that when the national economy grows swiftly and the domestic market becomes attractive, foreign attention focuses on economic ties. The patronising interventions about human rights, environmental protection and all such "value-based" activism shepherded from abroad miraculously move to the background. A growing economy provides revenue for building up the military, providing assistance abroad and claiming a greater say in global affairs. It is not a coincidence that India's diplomatic engagements improved significantly since the turn of the century and coincided with a period of high GDP growth. Unfortunately, the linear forecasts of growth extrapolated from this high growth period have not sustained. The Indian economy has been unable to maintain high growth consistently since the 2008 global financial crisis. Whether India falls back to the sub five per cent GDP growth of the pre-1990s or recovers to move out of the Lower Middle Income Group[1] will be determined by policy choices by the Central government and implementation by the State governments over the next few years. To put things in perspective, even if India's GDP reaches $ 5 trillion by 2024-25, as targeted by the Government of India, it will still be a lower middle-income economy. India will graduate to become an upper middle-income economy only by 2030 when it is expected to become the third largest economy in the world. Sustained economic growth over two decades, if it ever happens, will bring India within striking range of becoming a high-income economy. It is only then that India will need to think in terms of avoiding a "middle income trap". Right now, India is merely avoiding a "lower middle income trap".

The fact that India's population is one of the youngest in the world is seen as its asset. However, this "demographic dividend" is not going to last for ever. This window will be open till around 2035. A November 2019 report of the National Commission of India had some sobering population projections.[2] India is going to age faster than expected due to falling fertility rates.

> *"Between 2011 and 2036 the proportion of population aged under 15 years is projected to decline from 30.8 to 19.8 percent; the proportion of the middle age-group (15-59 years) and the older ages (60 years and above) are set to increase considerably. The youth population in the age-group 15-24 years is expected to increase from 23.3 crore in 2011 to 25.2 crore in 2021 and then continue to decrease to 22.7 crore in 2036. Its proportion to total population is expected to fall from 19.3 per cent in 2011 to 14.9 percent in*

2036. The average age of Indians is expected to be of 34.7 years in 2036 as compared to 24.9 years in 2011".

This means that India has a 15-year window in which it needs to provide skills and finance to its young workforce to enable them to productively join and develop the economy.

The way ahead has been prescribed by many under the umbrella term of "reforms" – enhance ease of doing business, eliminate redundant procedures, reduce discretionary power of government officials, provide policy stability, provide strong regulatory bodies, streamline logistics infrastructure, bring in labour reforms, make land acquisition easier, get rid of loss-making public sector units, invest in better health and education, encourage low-skilled manufacturing to take advantage of availability of low-cost labour, to name a few in a long list. The 158th Report of the Parliamentary Standing Committee on Commerce on attracting investment in the Post-COVID economy also recommends such measures.[3] In July 2020, Teamlease released a report that listed the total number of regulatory laws and compliances that have to be complied with by Indian businesses – 1,536 Acts, 69,233 compliances and 6,618 filings.[4] It is beyond the scope of this book to go into details of the economy and recent economic policy except to say that though some measures towards reforms have been taken in recent times, fears of slipping into old habits remain. India needs to have the confidence to open up its economy to engage with the world. If the Indian economy does not look up, nothing else can be done.

Partnerships

As is often mentioned, China's economy is almost five times that of India and its military expenditure is almost four times that of India. Without getting into details, it is quite clear that India needs to match with a nation that has huge asymmetrical advantages. The only obvious way to be able to do so is to forge partnerships with like-minded nations. Formal military alliances are not the preferred option in present times. With interdependencies of trade and supply chains, nations are exploring mutual alignment over issues rather than formal military alliances. In fact, two nations may find themselves aligned on certain issues while being on opposite sides on other issues. In the past, India and China have been on the same side in issues like climate change and reform of multilateral organisations.

The one grouping that has caught much of the recent attention is the Quadrilateral Dialogue or "Quad" between the USA, India, Japan and Australia. Every meeting of this grouping has been thoroughly analysed and there is much debate about its possible transformation in the future. The Quad, in turn, has an underlay of several trilateral arrangements. India-Japan-USA, Australia-India-Japan, Australia-India-Indonesia, and Australia-France-India are some of the trilateral arrangements that have gained some traction. All these nations also agree on the "centrality of ASEAN" in the Indo-Pacific Region. India has also been upgrading its bilateral relations across the Indo-Pacific Region. It is this network of alignments and partnerships that will have to be cultivated to provide an alternative option to infrastructure development.

India lacks financial capital but has much to offer in terms of human resources, technological capabilities, people-to-people contacts, and historical relations in the Indo-Pacific Region, including Africa. This has a strong complementarity with the USA, Japan, France and the EU that have the financial capital and seek partners to progress projects in regions that are too far away from them but closer to India. As noted in the earlier chapters, some progress has been made in terms of announcements but substantial projects are yet to take off.

It is quite clear that although developing nations have become relatively more careful about the quantum of loans they take and about the viability of projects, they still seek loans from China. This is primarily since adequate capital, at affordable rates, is not available for infrastructure development. The most quoted estimate is that of the Asian Development Bank but there are similar reports of huge gaps in infrastructure funding from multiple agencies – the World Bank, G20's Global Infrastructure Outlook, and McKinsey & Company, to name a few. Unless India, in partnership with other financially capable like-minded nations, provides an alternative, opposition to any other nation that is providing funding is a moot point.

There is also a vacuum in the regional security architecture of the Indian Ocean Region. There is no multilateral platform, with membership across the region, which can be considered as an enabler for forging regional stability. Instead, there are multiple sub-regional organisations. This makes it imperative to forge partnerships with regional and extra-regional nations to maintain regional stability.

Choices – Sooner Rather than Later

Talking about partnerships, India will have to make tough choices in its international partnerships and technological standards, sooner rather than later. India has conventionally followed the ubiquitous "middle path" and rarely moved decisively to one side in the political and economic choices that it made, unless pushed into a corner. Approaching the USA for military help after the 1962 debacle and signing a "Treaty of Peace, Friendship and Cooperation" with the Soviet Union in 1971 would be two such moments. On the sidelines of the G20 Summit held in December 2018 at Buenos Aires (Argentina), Prime Minister Narendra Modi attended the first Trilateral meeting of India-Japan-USA. He christened it as "JAI", meaning success. The same day, he also attended the second Trilateral meeting of Russia-India-China, initiated after a gap of 12 years. It is not clear how far India can travel along such parallel tracks and avoid getting embroiled in great power politics. India assumes that the world is becoming multi-polar with India as one of the poles. The scenario has been described as "a multi-polar world with bipolar characteristics (with the USA and China as the two major poles)".[5] It is an assumption that may not turn out to be correct especially if the Indian economy does not accelerate and if India does not achieve reasonable self-sufficiency in military equipment. The friction between the USA and China is rising, and expanding over multiple domains like trade and technology. While the earlier consensus may have been that India can afford to tread the middle path for some time till it accumulates sufficient comprehensive national power, the events during the outbreak of COVID-19 seem to have fast-forwarded the strategic scenario. China has displayed an unusually impatient streak to leverage the situation along multiple axes. India's moment to make choices may appear sooner than expected.

The choices to be made will not just be political. Increasingly, the choices will be in technology and standards. Connectivity and interoperability across the globe is supported by the universal adoption of standards. However, the deepening global political divide threatens to spill over to the world of technology and standards. The Internet was once eulogised as a "global common" free from the limitations of territorial boundaries. However, it did not take long for nations to attempt reasserting their sovereignty in cyberspace. Questions were raised over the preponderant US influence over the Internet, the role of the Internet Corporation for Assigned Names and Numbers (ICANN), and the control of the Domain Name System (DNS) root servers. As a result of this push, changes in Internet governance took place but the issue is still up for debate. Meanwhile, China established the "Great Firewall" to ring fence its segment of the Internet. Russia has been progressing on its version to isolate the segment of the Internet within its territorial boundaries. Other nations are preparing for an emergency situation where the Internet (for domains under their control, like .in for India) will continue to function within their territory even when isolated from the rest of the world. Huawei has proposed a new Internet Protocol (IP) at gatherings of the International Telecommunication Union (ITU) in September 2019 and February 2020.[6] The proposal seeks to create an Internet that is smarter, more secure and consumes fewer resources but sceptics point out that it entails huge costs and remains silent on the possible impact on civil rights and surveillance.[7] The threat of segmentation of the Internet between competing blocs is real.

As the threat over segmentation of the Internet hangs over the world, the scramble for data ownership has gained momentum. Data is now recognised as a vital resource, and a critical raw material for developing Artificial Intelligence (AI) solutions. One way for nations to assert their sovereignty over data storage and data flows is to ensure its location within their legal jurisdiction, which effectively means within their territory. Hence, there are demands for "data localisation". The international norms for cyberspace and data usage have been under debate in a plethora of platforms but there does not seem to be any convergence of views between the contending parties. For example, the United Nations had to set up two parallel tracks for cyber security to cater for competing parties – an Open Ended Working Group (OEWG) comprising all UN members and a Group of Governmental Experts (UNGGE) comprising 25 members.

There is also a movement to do away with monopolies that provide undue leverage to one nation, the USA in particular. One example is the Society for Worldwide Interbank Financial Telecommunications (SWIFT) payment messaging system that is behind most international money and financial security transfers. Although there are similar messaging systems, SWIFT continues to be the dominant one. The USA has considerable control over SWIFT since a majority of members running it are American. Similarly, the US dollar continues to be the major reserve currency of the world. These monopolies give the USA the leverage to implement sanctions against other nations, like Iran. Nations that want to bypass these sanctions and continue trade and transactions with Iran struggle to do so. China, and to some extent Russia, are keen to work on alternative platforms and standards.

The most visible of these tussles is over capturing 5G standards, and implicitly, the telecom market. Huawei stunned its competitors by offering end-to-end 5G solutions, thereby offering the template for the default standard. The pushback since then has been intense but varied. Some nations have declared an outright ban on Huawei 5G, some have moved back and forth on their decision, some have declared a partial ban while some, like India, have postponed the decision. India seems to be in no hurry to set up its 5G network. The first step of selecting frequency bands for 5G in India is pending. Perhaps, the sense is that India can afford to take its time in adopting 5G. Hopefully by then, the 5G standards debate would have settled down and India too would have developed adequate home-grown technology. The 5G game will play out over the next two years in which Huawei (read China) will try to capitalise on its head start and its competitors (read the West and its allies) will try to stall it till they catch up. The role of technology in determining international relations will continue to increase rather than decrease. The MEA has already set up a New, Emerging and Strategic Technologies (NEST) Division to deal with this. When "techno-alliances" come up in various emerging technologies of the future, India will have to take a call on which one it intends to join. Not joining any will hardly be a choice.

Similar choices need to be made in international trade. In November 2020, 15 nations signed the Regional Comprehensive Economic Partnership (RCEP), the world's largest Free Trade Agreement (FTA). India had withdrawn from the RCEP negotiations in November 2019 over fears of getting flooded with cheaper Chinese imports and concerns about the impact on certain domestic sectors like agriculture, dairy and textiles.[8] India proposed an auto-trigger mechanism to impose tariffs when imports crossed a certain threshold, but the proposal was not agreed to. India has entered into numerous bilateral and regional trading agreements over the years. These include Preferential Trade Agreements (PTAs), Free Trade Agreements (FTAs), and Comprehensive Economic Cooperation Agreements (CECAs) or Comprehensive Economic Partnership Agreements (CEPAs).[9] However, a study by NITI Aayog has indicated that the percentage of India's international trade routed through its PTA/FTA routes is very low and that Indian exports to FTA partner-countries have grown at the same pace as to non-partner countries.[10] Ideally, under the arrangement of the World Trade Organisation (WTO), a key rule of multilateral trade is that reduction in trade barriers should be applied, on a Most Favoured Nation (MFN) basis, to all members. This means that if lower customs duty is offered by one member-country to another, it has to be offered to all the members. However, there are provisions in WTO Agreements that stipulate conditions under which member-nations can enter into separate agreements like PTAs and FTAs.[11] Increasingly, the MFN route has been subverted with the number of Regional Trade Agreements (RTAs) increasing over the years. RTAs now account for more than half of international trade.[12] India is negotiating around 12 such trade agreements. If India wants to be an important member in the global value chain by becoming an important centre for manufacturing, it will have to make its economy competitive and lower tariffs. About 70 per cent of international trade is part of the global value chain.[13]

This emergence of potential blocs in international politics, cyberspace, trade, technology and standards has reignited discussions on a new Cold War. While extending present-day competitions to a Cold War scenario may be a stretch, there is no doubt that ultimately India will have to make difficult choices in each case. The middle path that India loves to tread is getting eroded fast. As some commentators often say, alluding to India's characteristic ambivalence, "sitting on a wall is never comfortable". This does not mean that India is either incapable of making tough choices or has never been unequivocal. When India took a stand against the BRI, it was the sole protestor. Over the following months, many nations endorsed India's line of thought. In 2020, India banned Chinese apps, including Tiktok, over multiple tranches. The USA followed India in banning Tiktok. Shorn of all nuances and diplomatic language, the choice before India could come down to choosing between either being subservient to China or accepting a transactional partnership with the USA. An optimistic third path could be of "Middle Powers" in Europe and Asia coming together to safeguard their mutual national interests. This option is not easy to forge and past events have shown that the larger the multilateral grouping, the more difficult it is to decide on a common path and the easier it is to break consensus within the grouping. Thus, the choices in international politics, trade and technology that India will make over the next two decades will not be easy ones. The choices will deeply affect India's journey over this century. The option of not choosing one over the other will get harder as the years go by.

Coming down from the stratospheric heights of the international order that provides the larger background, we can now examine how India can proceed to enhance infrastructure and improve connectivity for itself and other nations that require it for the benefit of all.

Build India

As noted earlier in this book, before India steps up its endeavour to provide infrastructure and connectivity in the region, it needs to do it at home. As home to the world's second largest population and the fifth largest economy, clearing the domestic clog of transport and logistics has international ramifications. Goods will need to move faster within India to make it an attractive production destination. As we saw in the chapter on maritime history, overseas trade in the Maurya Empire and the Gupta Empire flourished not just due to the availability of ports but due to the connectivity provided by highways and governance structures provided in terms of laws, public services and taxes. India has immense capability but has limited capacity to execute its vision. Hence, any measure to improve India's response has to begin with enhancing India's capacity within the country. There has to be an upgradation of India's own maritime infrastructure and connectivity with the hinterland has to be enhanced. As has been covered in Chapter Seven, this is a lacuna that has been recognised and work on it has been accelerating over the last two decades. Some of the largest infrastructure projects in the world are in progress within India.

Foremost among India's weaknesses is the internal state of logistics. Logistics play an important role in determining competitiveness. There is a need to reduce the average logistics costs in India that is estimated to be around 40 per cent higher than the global benchmark. Average logistics costs in India are about 15 per cent of GDP compared to 8 per cent in Germany and 11 per cent in Japan.[14] India intends to bring it below 10 per cent by 2022. The World Bank maintains a Logistics Performance Index (LPI) of all nations. In recent years, India has been a top performer in improvement of logistics and is placed at 44th position in the 2018 report (up from 54th position in 2014). Of course, such ratings are not sacrosanct and can be 'gamed' towards improvement. India's LPI ranking was 39 in 2007. The Economic Survey of the Government of India, released annually along with the Union Budget, acknowledges this requirement. Case studies illustrate the bottlenecks in connectivity and movement of goods within India. They also make several pertinent points. The Economic Survey 2017-18 estimated that a 10 per cent decrease in indirect logistics cost can contribute to around 5-8 per cent of extra exports, since the cost of the products being exported will come down.[15] Soft infrastructure matters as much as hard infrastructure. Interoperable procedures and systems that work seamlessly throughout India are essential. These in turn need to work seamlessly with international systems and procedures. Ports, airports and border check points are the major points of coagulation that need to be unclogged. Much of the heavy lifting has to be done by individual state governments. Finally, it is governance at the level of the state governments that is often the final determinant between success and failure.

The total cost of export-import container movement in India is significantly higher than in other countries. The transit time is highly variable (seven to 17 days) making it difficult to plan delivery to customers. The high transit time results in higher levels of inventory along the supply chain.[16] Some of the reasons for this sub-optimal container movement are skewed modal mix (e.g., long distance transport by road rather than railways), complicated and time-consuming procedures, and infrastructure bottlenecks at ports and Inland container depots. Hence, optimising time and cost for export containers would improve the competitiveness of exports.[17]

Like everything else in life, infrastructure development requires finance. The availability of affordable finance to a nation from external sources is directly related to the international credit rating. The lower the credit rating, the more difficult it is to access finance since lenders will charge a higher rate of interest. Multilateral financial institutions too have conditions, like viability of the project and repayment capacity of the government, to be fulfilled to disburse loans at concessional rates. India is one of the few developing nations that can fulfil the conditions of multilateral financial institutions and access low cost capital. Its huge population and large market provides the scale to create viable connectivity projects. In addition, there are other avenues. India is the largest recipient of funds from Japan International Cooperation Agency (JICA). Sovereign funds of West Asian nations are now keener to deploy their massive reserves in Asia rather than in the financial markets in the West.[18]

The weighted average for distance between the manufacturing hinterlands and ports in India is 700 to 800 km compared to 150 to 300 km in China.[19] Export-oriented industries that are logistics-intensive (where transportation cost is a high proportion of cost or timely delivery is critical) have to be near ports. Six sectors have been identified as having the most potential – electronics, furniture, automobiles, apparel, leather and footwear.[20]

Initially, there were some who felt that India will miss out on the benefits of the BRI if it does not join. It is not clear what benefits the BRI provides. If the connectivity sought to be provided is between the member-nations and China, the only advantage to be accrued will be with respect to trade with China. India has no dearth of sources of funding that range from multilateral institutions to sovereign wealth funds. The Indian market is an attractive proposition for the BRI rather than the other way around. Moreover, it would be incorrect to think that the BRI, by itself, will provide the sinews for connectivity world-wide. Despite the enormity of its scope, it will still be a drop in the ocean. The baggage that comes along with it cannot be ignored. Hence, India has no great incentive to sign up to the BRI. On the other hand, it can be argued that the north-south BRI corridors on either sides of India can be financially viable only if India becomes part of the corridor. Moreover, past events have shown that there is little correlation between signing the BRI Memorandum of Understanding (MoU) and getting Chinese investments. In March 2019, President Xi Jinping visited Italy and France. Italy signed a non-binding agreement to join the BRI. Chinese and Italian companies signed deals worth € 2.5 billion ($ 2.8 billion), way short of the expected € 7 billion.[21] On the other hand, in France, 15 business deals totalling about € 40 billion ($ 45 billion) were signed, including an order for 300 Airbus planes estimated at € 30 billion.[22] This happened without France joining the BRI and despite the French President questioning some aspects of China's policies during the visit. Not signing on for the BRI has not stopped Chinese companies from either getting contracts to work in India or investing in India. The checks and balances that may emerge after Indian policy calibration on Chinese investment, after the border incidents in 2020, is another issue but it will be an Indian decision, not a Chinese one.

Development of Island Territories

The need for development of India's island territories has been recognised and, as discussed earlier, some progress has been made. It is also recognised that islands have a crucial role in supporting maritime security but we will come to that later.

The island territories can be springboards in connectivity. As always, execution is a weak point. Construction of a trans-shipment port in Car Nicobar has been under consideration for the last five years. Then, there is a stated goal to create 'smart islands'. The India-Japan Joint Statement of 11 November 2016 stated that the two nations had decided "to identify technologies, infrastructure, development strategies and management processes that would facilitate development of smart islands".[23] Nothing has been heard of it thereafter. In August 2018, the NITI Aayog organised an event to get private investors for "ready to launch" sustainable eco-tourism projects for which environmental clearances have been obtained. However, there have been few takers till date.[24] The difficulty of enhancing infrastructure in far-flung island territories is high but India has to persist.

Neighbourhood First

Along with enhancing connectivity at home, it is equally important to plug in the world to this domestic network as seamlessly as possible. This is especially true for India's immediate neighbourhood. It has to be its priority region. India needs to connect to its immediate neighbourhood, both land and maritime, as it builds its own infrastructure. There is little that can be done with the western neighbour but there is much to be done with everyone else. It makes sense to build up regional interdependencies and to offer the benefits of connecting up to the large Indian market. The linking of people, goods and services is the most preferred option to increase India's influence around its periphery. It will be incongruent for India to step up and connect to the world without first connecting up to its immediate neighbourhood. Regional integration, with economic openness and interdependence, is in India's interests. As one of the least connected regions in the world with intra-regional trade that is one-fifth of that in Southeast Asia, there is much that remains to be done. India's structural relations with its neighbouring nations will need to be strong enough to overcome the vagaries of the domestic politics of those nations. The process is already underway and needs to be continued. Local eco-systems need to be nurtured between India's border states and the neighbouring nations. The state governments have to become part of this connectivity initiative. In 2017, the Government of Assam set up a Department of Act East Policy Affairs.

The steps being taken in this regard have been covered in Chapter Seven – Integrated Border Posts; using the rivers of Bangladesh to transport goods to the Northeast; use of ports of Bangladesh by India; air connectivity between the Northeast and nations in South East Asia; direct shipping lines between India and neighbouring countries; multi-modal transport from Bhutan to Bangladesh through the Brahmaputra river; multi-modal transport from Nepal to Kolkata through India's inland waterways; Maritime agreements for direct shipping lines; a common South Asia electricity grid; improvement of road connectivity with international assistance; oil and gas pipelines across borders; and reviving and opening up of old rail lines between India-Nepal and India-Bangladesh. All this is still work in progress. In many cases, only trial runs have been done. The trick will be to scale it up to viable commercial options. Multi-modal transport involves loading and unloading of cargo at multiple points. This requires standardisation of containers and procedures to avoid delays.

As India links up with its immediate neighbourhood over land, air and water, it will have to stretch out similarly to its extended neighbourhood. However, there is often a gap between intent and result on the ground. Since 2012, there has been a proposal referred to as the Mekong-India Economic Corridor. It envisaged a shipping line between Chennai (India) and Dawei (Myanmar), and a road link thereafter up to Vietnam. This link is yet to materialise since the Dawei Port-SEZ project itself is floundering. Indian ports have limited direct calls with ports in ASEAN countries despite discussions on a maritime agreement for many years. In September 2017, when the External Affairs Minister Sushma Swaraj visited Vladivostok, there was talk of a Chennai-Vladivostok shipping line. In September 2019, when Prime Minister Narendra Modi visited Vladivostok, a Memorandum of Intent was signed.

It also has to be kept in mind that the smaller nations welcome having alternatives to seeking assistance. There is a misconception that the smaller nations lack agency. In fact, events in the Indian Ocean Region show that smaller nations often find it useful that they now have more options in engagement (read 'China') to extract benefits than earlier. Bangladesh has adroitly accepted assistance from India, Japan and China. Since President Solih took office in the Maldives in November 2018, it has received financial assistance exceeding $ 2 billion from India in the form of budgetary support, grants, currency swap agreements and concessional lines of credit. In September 2020, India provided $ 250 million on concessional terms to help the country tackle the economic hardship that followed the COVID-19 pandemic. In May 2020, Sri Lanka had sought India's assistance for a $ 400 million currency swap under SAARC arrangements, and an additional $ 1.1 billion currency swap, bilaterally. The $ 400 million currency swap agreement was signed in July 2020 (and settled in February 2021). The $ 1.1 billion currency swap under bilateral arrangements was not offered. In March 2021, China approved a $ 1.54 billion currency swap with Sri Lanka.[25] In October 2019, China and Mauritius signed a FTA that came into effect in January 2021. In February 2021, India and Mauritius signed a Comprehensive Economic Cooperation and Partnership Agreement (CECPA), the first by India with an African nation.

There are some genuine security concerns in opening up. However, illegal activities never stopped due to physical restrictions. The challenge now is to monitor and enforce the rule of law even while keeping the borders open for trade and transit.

The India Way

It is neither advisable nor affordable for India to invest in massive infrastructure development abroad. The smaller nations in the region do see China as an alternative to gain benefits. However, India cannot fall into the trap of matching China step-by-step. The India Way is not to build "brick and mortar" structures that may not be economically viable. The India Way is to cater for the genuine requirements of the smaller nations in consultation and participation of the local population – economic prosperity, sustainable development, protection from natural calamities, halting rising sea levels due to climate change, protection of national resources in Exclusive Economic Zones (EEZs), and enhancement of national capacity in security and governance.

Indian engagement abroad seeks to reflect this approach. Speaking about India's development partnerships in Africa, Prime Minister Narendra Modi said that "our development partnership will be guided by your priorities. It will be on terms that will be comfortable for you, that will liberate your potential and not constrain your future. We will rely on African talent and skills. We will build as much local capacity and create as many local opportunities as possible".[26]

India's approach to the whole issue of infrastructure and connectivity is best summarised by the reasons given for it not joining the BRI.[27] India has the "firm belief that connectivity initiatives must be based on universally recognised international norms, good governance, rule of law, openness, transparency and equality. Connectivity initiatives must follow principles of financial responsibility to avoid projects that could create unsustainable debt burden for communities; balanced ecological and environmental protection and preservation standards; transparent assessment of project costs; and skill and technology transfer to help long-term running and maintenance of the assets created by local communities. Connectivity projects must be pursued in a manner that respects sovereignty and territorial integrity...it should bring greater economic benefits to all in an equitable and balanced manner". India will have to live up to these public pronouncements with its actions. Not acting as per stated policy can have deleterious effects on national reputation. India's engagements will have to continue as per its strengths rather than its weaknesses - providing infrastructure as per requirement; keeping it quiet rather than grandiose; promising less and delivering more rather than not living up to promises; enhancing capacity and capability; providing without reciprocation; ensuring inclusiveness and transparency; and focusing on human resources and people-to-people contacts. These are some of the mantras of the Indian engagement that have to be pursued.

India's advocacy of the International Solar Alliance (ISA) that seeks to promote solar energy and the Coalition for Disaster Resilient Infrastructure (CDRI) that seeks to promote disaster resilient infrastructure reflect this commitment. The fact that India is on track not just to fulfil the targets set by the Paris Agreement (on climate change) but exceed them makes its commitment to the cause more credible. India's development partnership programme focuses on India's immediate neighbourhood and Africa. Capacity enhancement is enabled by providing training and resources. This is complemented by India's commitment to be the first responder in providing Humanitarian Assistance and Disaster Relief (HADR) in emergencies and natural disasters in the region. The Indian initiatives of Security and Growth for All in the Region (SAGAR) and Indo-Pacific Oceans Initiative (IPOI) reflect this free, open, and inclusive security and development mindset.

Although India is still a low middle income economy and fares low in human development indices, it still has a lot of capabilities to offer. A lot of these pockets of excellence are related to providing public goods. A world-class payment gateway system, a model for providing direct cash benefits to the poor (the trinity of Aadhar, Jan Dhan Yojana and mobile phones), a frugal but cutting edge space programme with space assets directly contributing to development, a thriving pharmaceutical industry that manufactures drugs at the lowest cost, an efficient national election mechanism, a stock and money market using the latest technologies, and a major shift towards renewable energies, are some of the examples. India can offer these to the world. One example of this is the Pan Africa e-network set up over the last decade that links 48 African nations and is the backbone for e-education and tele-medicine. Another is the tsunami warning system for the Indian Ocean Region. In fact, there are some sectors in which India was looked up to by developing nations for support even way back in the 1960s but India has since fallen back in the development of those sectors. It needs to reclaim this ability to provide expertise in railways, agriculture, dairy development and other sectors related to development. The higher education system that lies broken and deficient resulting in Indian students flocking to foreign shores for a degree has the potential to be turned around for foreign students, especially in India's neighbourhood, to come to India.

The COVID-19 pandemic too gave a demonstration of India's capability to offer public goods. By May 2020, India had spent $ 16 million to send essential medicines and test kits to 90 nations.[28] India supplied essential medicines, test kits and Personal Protective Equipment (PPE) to over 150 countries, with assistance to 80 countries given as grants.[29] Medical teams were deployed to the Maldives, Kuwait, Mauritius and Comoros. Indian manufacturing capacity in PPE, N95 masks, medical syringes and ventilators expanded within months. By December 2020, India had exported 40 million N95 masks and 20 million PPE suits.[30] Vaccines developed in India are now available to the world. By February

2021, India had supplied 36 million doses around the world, with 20 per cent of them provided as grants.[31] It is striking that even as the rich nations grabbed and hoarded vaccines, a low middle income nation stepped up to offer them to developing nations. It is not an overnight achievement. Indian capacity in generic drugs and vaccine manufacturing has been built over decades. It accounts for 20 per cent of global production in generic medicines and 62 per cent in vaccines.

If India has to step up globally, it will need to develop home-grown technology and standards. The Indian space-based navigation system, development of Standards Essential Patents (SEPs) on 5G,[32] and the RuPay payment system are such examples. India is already working with Australia, Bahrain, Bhutan, the Maldives, Myanmar, Saudi Arabia, Singapore and South Korea to ensure that RuPay cards are integrated with their local payment systems. Crucial technologies that India lacks include gas turbines (jet engines) and semiconductor manufacturing.

Rule-setting and rule-making in international law for use of the global commons has become a critical requirement. For far too long, India has been a responsible complying state, offering its opinions to proposals made in international forums by others. It is time for India to create clusters of legal minds and domain experts to draft legal interpretations and norms that can be proposed to the world. East Asia and Southeast Asia have been grappling with issues related to Laws of the Sea and "code of conduct" at sea. India has resorted to 'value-based diplomacy' by stating some norms in joint statements with like-minded nations. "Freedom of Navigation" is one such term. However, the Indian position of the presence of foreign vessels in the EEZ as per its interpretation of UNCLOS, is closer to that of China than that of the USA. Norms on cyber and data usage are open to debate. India has the requisite expertise to build up arguments and interpretations on all these issues and offer them to the world.

Myanmar is using the services of a Swiss consultancy firm to scrutinise the Chinese offer for the Muse-Mandalay railway line project.[33] It has also hired a German consultancy firm to scrutinise counter-offers from other firms to the Chinese offer for New Yangon City project.[34] This indicates yet another service that Indian companies can offer.

Finally, the core of 'the India Way' is to be a responsible power. India has demonstrated this consistently and needs to adhere to this path.

India's commitment to international maritime law mechanisms can be seen in its consistent stand across three verdicts of the PCA – India-Bangladesh Maritime boundary in 2014, Chagos Islands in 2015, and maritime features in South China Sea in 2016. In each case, India supported the verdict. Many nations that advocate adherence to international law and order have not been this consistent. In April 2015, India undertook Operation Rahat to evacuate its nationals from Yemen. Over 1,783 Indian citizens were evacuated. In addition, 1,291 foreign nationals from 37 countries were also evacuated.[35] In October 2020, India and South Africa jointly proposed at the WTO for the temporary waiver of Intellectual Property Rights (IPR) and patent laws for COVID vaccines, medical devices and protective kits to make them accessible to all countries. This strand of global responsibility can be traced to many of India's commitments – adhering to the Paris targets on climate change; advocacy of CDRI and ISA; Neighbourhood First policy; first responder to provide humanitarian assistance and disaster relief in the IOR; and medical assistance.

Execution Capacity

As has been reiterated several times in this book, infrastructure development tends to be messy. Hence, it is not desirable for any government to commit itself directly to it. It is one thing for a Public Sector Company like ONGC or Oil India Ltd. to execute a contract abroad, and it is quite another for officials of the Ministry of External Affairs to be directly involved in projects abroad. The Minister of State for External Affairs gave an account of delays in development projects in a reply in the Lok Sabha.[36]

> *"These are mainly long gestation and/or large infrastructure projects in sectors such as power, roads, railways, industrial units, etc. There are several possible factors which may, and do cause delays, many of which, are under the partner countries own sphere of responsibility and not necessarily due to delays from our side. The type of delays which are normally faced, result from issues such as security threats, political or socioeconomic crisis in the partner countries, delays in land acquisition, local permits, internal approvals or finalization of Detailed Project Report (DPR) by the host government, lack of capacity to provide data or certain facilities, change in scope of projects by host government, natural calamity or geological factors such as difficult terrain or excessive rains that do not allow for work during the monsoon months in the host country, or issues such as delays in*

> *mobilization of manpower and resources on (the) part of the Indian contractors".*

Meanwhile, infrastructure building and connectivity continues to grow as part of India's development partnership programme. Some recent commitments are significant. The Greater Male Connectivity Project (GMCP) in the Maldives is financed by a $ 100 million grant and $ 400 million Line of Credit (LoC). India has committed to an LoC of $ 1 billion for physical and digital connectivity projects with ASEAN. There is another commitment of a LoC of $ 1 billion for development of Russia's Far East region. The partnership programme covers nations from the Caribbean to the South Pacific Island nations. Of the 54 nations in Africa, India has development projects in 51.[37] Since India has to shoulder greater responsibilities, it needs to augment its capacity to execute them. India could set up a separate agency, by hiving off the Development Partnership Administration (DPA) Division from the MEA. This will enable employing domain-knowledge experts from all relevant disciplines to deal with infrastructure development abroad. It is well known that India has a shortage of officers in its Foreign Ministry compared to the tasks on hand.

As mentioned earlier, it is essential for India to join hands with like-minded partners to provide alternatives and execute projects in third nations. India has stated such intentions with Japan,[38] the USA[39] and the EU[40]. However, asymmetries in technical capability and mismatch in priorities can drag implementation. The idea of the Asia Africa Growth Corridor (AAGC) emerged in the India-Japan Joint Statement of November 2016. The vision document of the AAGC was released in May 2017. The three organisations that were to determine the detailed work plan (RIS, ERIA and IDE-JETRO) seem to have been unable to agree on one. Nothing has been heard of the AAGC for three years.

The Softness of Soft Power

While skill development and scholarships for students are useful avenues to enhance the capacity of the smaller nations, it should not get swamped by the quest for 'soft power'.

New Delhi has sought to show its historical ownership of maritime links with Southeast Asia by showcasing cultural links and the influence of Indian culture visible across Southeast Asia. The Mausam Initiative was one such (mis)endeavour. When initiated, it was mistaken as an Indian response to the BRI. It has since become Project Mausam that seeks nomination of a transnational (39 nations) route in the Indian Ocean as a UNESCO World Heritage site.[41] Focusing on common cultural links too has its limitations. The endeavour may be to allude to belonging to a common collective heritage of yore. However, it has to be kept in mind that every nation has a certain sense of identity. There is only a particular level to which it can be elaborated that the language, culture, arts and architecture has been influenced by India. Nations around India, in particular, would like to emphasise the uniqueness of their national identity rather than allow it to be swamped by Indian cultural narratives.

Aspirations to be "Vishwa Guru" (World Leader) may resonate in the domestic election campaign trail but can be jarring as part of foreign policy.

Supply Chain Reliability

Recent events have highlighted the dangers of dependency on a single nation. This has prompted a rethink. There is global recognition that supply chains need to diversify. Japan, India, and Australia have jointly launched a Supply Chain Resilience Initiative for securing supply chains end to end. The Foreign Secretary has started mentioning "supply chain resilience" as part of SAGAR.[42] While it is true that dependencies in critical sectors on a potential adversary is not advisable, it is equally true that the Indian economy cannot move ahead divorced from the second largest economy in the world. There are numerous small and medium enterprises in India whose business model rests on the cheap and varied products available from China. If the proportion of Indian imports coming from China has increased from 0.11 per cent in 1991-92 to 16.4 per cent in 2017-18, it was because Chinese productivity improved year on year.[43] China is central to many global supply chains and it will not be easy to lower dependence on China dramatically. As the tussle between China and the USA on IT chips in the last few years has shown, a complete de-coupling is not going to be easy due to many economic and technical issues.

It makes sense to identify the critical sectors and ring-fence them rather than think of a complete decoupling that is not possible. India will need to wean away from dependencies in critical sectors like pharma, power, cyber, and telecom. A managed and selective decoupling is the way ahead. India has already launched efforts to revive manufacturing of Active Pharmaceutical Ingredients for the pharmaceutical industry. Selective decoupling can be seen in the Production Linked Initiative (PLI) of the Government of India that seeks to enhance India's manufacturing capabilities and exports in 10 key sectors – Advance Chemistry Cell (ACC) Battery, Electronic/Technology Products, Automobiles and Auto Components, Pharmaceuticals and Drugs, Telecom and Networking Products, Textile Products: MMF segment and technical textiles, Food Products, High Efficiency Solar PV Modules, White Goods (ACs & LED) and Specialty Steel.[44]

East vs. West

There is also an East vs. West conundrum for India. The factors that determine the importance of either direction of India depends on several factors – sources of trade, sources of energy and natural resources, and sources of threats. India's trade and energy requirements depend critically on transport by the seas and these routes need to be secured. Hence, naval deployment too will depend on this assessment. This section will merely highlight the factors that determine India's "Act East" and "Think West".

Fifty-five per cent of India's trade is to its east.[45] The impact of Africa and Latin America and the Caribbean (LAC) to global maritime flows remains marginal. In 2019, Africa accounted for only 7 per cent of imports and 5 per cent of exports, when taken as a percentage share in total tonnage in the maritime trade.[46] Asia, on the other hand, has become the maritime hub of the world with 41 per cent of the total goods exported and 62 per cent of total goods imported.[47] In container throughputs at ports worldwide, Africa and LAC contributed around 10 per cent while Asia contributed around 65 per cent.[48] Inter-regional trade within Asia is increasing. The green shoots of economic growth can be seen in Africa but there is still a lot that bedevils the continent. It will be some time before the global gaze turns south. Indian companies have the DNA to prosper in Africa and LAC that have similar socio-economic environments like India.

In the case of energy sources, there is a clear tilt towards the west. In crude oil imports, 59 per cent is from West Asia and 16 per cent is from Africa. In addition, 11 per cent crude oil comes from Venezuela and Mexico, also to the west. Similarly, in Liquefied Natural Gas (LNG) imports, 56 per cent comes from West Asia and 23 per cent from Africa. In 2014-15, the Indian economy consumed around 227 MTPA of crude oil, of which 189 MTPA was imported. Sixty-five per cent of this imported crude was handled by the Gujarat cluster of Vadinar, Mundra and Sikka. Mumbai, New Mangalore and Paradip accounted for 7-8 per cent each. Chennai, Kochi and Visakhapatnam accounted for 4-5 per cent each.[49]

The acute worries in the past about supplies of fossil fuels drying up have been belied. Import-dependent nations like China and India deployed resources world-wide to diversify and secure sources of supply. In the early 2000s, worries of India losing access to adequate energy resources were expressed when Chinese companies outbid Indian companies in several instances. Since then, there has been a realisation that competition is counter-productive. In fact, both nations have switched tack to leverage their position as the largest buyers in the market. Supply of energy resources is now considered to be stable although price fluctuations cannot be ruled out and fluctuations in supply may occur due to geopolitical disturbances. India is building up its strategic crude oil reserves to eventually comply with the International Energy Agency (IEA) stipulation to maintain emergency oil reserves equivalent to 90 days of imports.[50] India is now considering building up strategic gas reserves as well.[51]

In terms of traffic at Indian ports, the tilt is towards the west. In 2015, Indian ports handled around 1,050 MTPA. Of this, around 655 MTPA was handled by ports on the western coast while around 390 MTPA was handled by those on the eastern coast.[52]

While access to oil and gas is crucial for traditional energy security, access to minerals is crucial for manufacturing industries. Of course, there are resources like coal that can be put in either category. For ease of explanation, access to minerals can be explained by broadly classifying them into three categories. The first are minerals like iron ore, bauxite, copper, and zinc that are used in numerous traditional manufacturing industries. The second are Rare Earth Elements (REEs) used in numerous industries. The third are minerals required for new-age industries keeping transitions for the future in mind, like cobalt and lithium. The "Strategic Minerals" to be given priority have been listed in successive reports of government agencies like the erstwhile Planning Commission,[53] Ministry of Mines[54] and Ministry of Science and Technology.[55] In August 2019, the

Khanij Bidesh India Ltd (KABIL) was set up. It is a joint venture of three public sector units (PSUs) – National Aluminium Company (NALCO), Hindustan Copper Ltd. (HCL) and Mineral Exploration Corporation Ltd. (MECL). Its objective is to undertake identification, acquisition, exploration, development, mining, and processing of strategic minerals overseas for commercial use and for meeting the country's requirements of these minerals. These strategic minerals include cobalt, lithium, germanium, gallium, indium, beryllium, niobium, tantalum, tungsten, bismuth, and selenium.

When we map these sources of trade, and sources of energy and natural resources, we can establish the relative importance of the sea lanes that reach either side of India. The endeavour would be to protect them from threats – traditional and non-traditional. This is not a static situation. The flow in maritime routes can change due to a change in market locations (on account of GDP growth); a change in sources of raw materials, energy and food; a change in ship propulsion technology; and a change in taxes and tariffs.

Maritime India

The maritime domain covers many sectors – ship building, ports, merchant shipping, fishing, security, scientific exploration, tourism, etc. Except for the ship-breaking industry and merchant shipping manpower, India lags in all sectors of the maritime domain. The Sagarmala Project documents and the MIV 2030 adequately highlight all the issues relevant to the maritime sector. It is useful to have a relook at them since most of these issues often tend to be 'out of sight out of mind'.

India has 32 ship building/repair companies with eight of them in the public sector.[56] However, the Indian ship building industry is dominated by public sector shipyards. In 2007, several private shipyards showed promise.[57] Some of them went on to bag orders from the Indian Navy. However, most of them failed. India's share in global shipbuilding is just 1 per cent.[58] It is ranked 21st globally. Over 90 per cent of global shipbuilding happens in China, South Korea and Japan. With its low labour costs, India should have performed better in ship building. However, the competitiveness and efficiency of Indian shipyards continues to be low.[59]

Port infrastructure is sought to be enhanced under Sagarmala. Only two container ports of India figure in the top 50 container ports of the world – Jawaharlal Nehru Port Trust (5.05 million TEU in 2018) at 29th position and Mundra Port (4.44 million TEU in 2018) at 34th position.[60] One important element is the improvement of the operational efficiency of Indian ports. There are several parameters on which the efficiency of ports is judged. One important indicator of operational efficiency of ports is the turnaround time or Turn Round Time (TRT). It is "defined as the time spent by a vessel at the port from its arrival at the reporting station to its departure from there".[61] The average turnaround time of major ports of India was about 5.3 days in 2010-11 and fell to 3.4 days in 2016-17.[62] As per the Ministry of Shipping's 2018 Year End Review, it was 82.32 hours in 2016-17, 64.32 hours in 2017-18 and improved further to 60.48 hours.[63] It has further improved to 59.51 hours during 2018-19.[64] However, even with this fall, it is still more than two times the TRT level of the best performing ports of the world. Moreover, within Indian ports, there is a wide variation. This means that there is still considerable scope for improvement in their efficiency. It is intuitive that efficiency in port efficient will result in greater cargo throughput, more profits, and greater volume of merchandise trade.

In FY 2019, the capacity for Indian ports stood at 2,377 MTPA while it handled traffic of 1,281 MTPA. Twelve major ports accounted for 1,514 MTPA capacity and handled 699 MTPA traffic, leading to utilisation of a mere 46.2 per cent. Non-major ports, which account for 863 MTPA of capacity, handled 582 MTPA traffic—an utilisation of 67 per cent. Thus, key enhancements in policy, investment, operations and technology are critical to bring India to the forefront of global maritime trade.[65]

Indian ports are generally small, and most lack the draught to handle the largest (cape size) vessels. In 2018, only five ports had cape size handling capability. Currently, India has five major ports and two non-major ports with capacity greater than 100 MTPA. The average size of a container vessel calling at Indian ports is around 5,000 TEU while for China it is 12,000 TEU. At JNPT, India's largest container port, draught is 14 m while an average cape size vessel requires more than 16 m.[66]

Dwell time for exports in global mega ports is approximately 40 per cent lower than Indian ports, thus highlighting the necessity of having an efficient evacuation network to move high volumes of cargo.[67]

In 2019, the total throughput of Indian container terminals reached approximately 16 million TEUs. More than 70 per cent of the country's containers are handled at the West Coast ports. While India currently is at less than 30 per cent containerization levels, other developing and developed nations have reached more than 65 per cent containerization levels.[68]

A trans-shipment port is an intermediate destination where containers are shifted from a larger vessel (mother ships) to many smaller vessels (feeder vessels) or vice versa. Currently, nearly 75 per cent of India's trans-shipped cargo is handled at ports outside India like Colombo, Singapore, Klang, Salalah and Dubai. Colombo port alone handles 60 per cent of India's trans-shipment cargo. Trans-shipment through other countries adds to additional port handling costs to the tune of $ 80-100 per TEU.[69] Apart from adding to costs, it also increases transit time of cargo by five-seven days.[70] In 2011, the Vallarpadam International Container Trans-shipment Terminal (ICTT) of Cochin Port Trust was established as the first international trans-shipment hub of the country. The terminal is operated by Dubai Ports World under a Public-Private Partnership (PPP) agreement for 30 years with Cochin Port Trust. The terminal has struggled and a Rs. 400 crore plan to deepen the channel from the present 14.5 metres to 16 metres is not moving ahead due to paucity of funding.[71] In FY 20, ICTT handled 620,000 TEUs, of which only 36,000 TEUs or 5.9 per cent were trans-shipment containers while the remaining 584,000 TEUs were origin-destination containers.[72] In 2015, a feasibility report was prepared for a trans-shipment port at Enayam in Tamil Nadu. In July 2016, the Union Cabinet accorded in-principle approval for building the new port in three phases with an investment of Rs. 27,570 crore to handle 127 MTPA.[73] Following resistance from local fishermen groups, the plan was cancelled in 2017. A trans-shipment port is under construction at Vizhinjam in Kerala under Public-Private Partnership (PPP). The contract for constructing the port and operating it for 40 years has been awarded to Adani Ports and Special Economic Zone Ltd. (APSEZ). The project is entitled to receive a Viability Grant Funding (VGF) of Rs. 1,635 crore to be shared equally by the Central and Kerala governments to boost its viability, making it the first port project to be offered such a grant.[74] Of this amount, Rs. 1,227 crore will be given during the construction phase itself. India has been planning to set up a trans-shipment port in Great Nicobar. The latest endeavour is to build a greenfield port and container trans-shipment hub near Kanyakumari, nestled between Kovalam and Keelamanakudi villages, through the PPP route.[75] In February 2021, Expression of Interest was sought from port developers and shipping lines to build a 6.5 million TEU capacity trans-shipment hub. Kanniyakumari Port Ltd., a Special Purpose Vehicle floated by V.O. Chidambaranar Port Trust, Chennai Port Trust and Cochin Port Trust has been tasked with helming the new port project.

In February 2020, the Union Cabinet cleared the proposal for a deep water port at Vadhavan at a cost of $ 9 billion. The location has a natural water depth of 20 metres that can take vessels of 25,000 TEU capacity. If built, it will be India's 13th major port. However, the project has faced protests from local communities immediately after its announcement.

India is 18th in the world in ownership of vessels when considered as per tonnage (1.26 per cent of the world).[76] It is not in the top 25 when ranked as per value of vessels.[77] As on 30 September 2019, 41.99 per cent of the Indian fleet was over 20 years of age and 12.49 per cent in the age group of 16-20 years as per the Directorate General of Shipping.[78] As on 1 July 2019, the average age of ships globally was 15.04 years. While India's overseas seaborne trade has been growing exponentially over the years, there is a sharp decline in the share of Indian ships in the carriage of India's overseas trade from about 40 per cent in the late 1980s to 7.9 per cent in 2018-19.[79] The operating cost of Indian ships is on an average 20 per cent higher than foreign flagged ships, primarily on account of taxation, blockage of tax credits, and higher cost of capital.[80]

In December 2020, with 69 ships, The Great Eastern Shipping Co. Ltd. overtook the public sector Shipping Corporation of India (SCI), which has 59 ships, to become India's biggest ship owner by fleet size. But SCI is still ahead when it comes to dead weight tonnage. SCI's 59 ships add up to a total of 5.3 million dwt, representing 35 per cent of India's total tonnage.[81] The world leader, APM-Maersk, operates more than 700 vessels with most of them of much larger size.

One of the major policy issues has been of cabotage. Cabotage is the transport of goods or passengers between two places in the same country by a transport operator from another country. As per Indian Cabotage law, only Indian registered ships are allowed to ply on local routes for carrying cargo. However, in 2018, the law was relaxed by the Ministry of Shipping to allow foreign flagged ships to transport export-import laden containers meant for trans-shipment, empty containers meant for re-positioning, agriculture, horticulture, fisheries, fertiliser and animal husbandry commodities on domestic routes without a licence from the DG Shipping.[82]

India is at the top of the charts in only two areas – ship-breaking and merchant shipping crews. In 2018 and 2019, 1,418 ships were dismantled worldwide. Of these, 453 ships (8,584,610 gross tonnage) were dismantled at Alang in India. This is the second largest volume in the world after Chattogram in Bangladesh.[83] In 2019, Bangladesh undertook 54.7 per cent of ship recycling of the world while India was second at 26.6 per cent.[84] India now provides 9.35 per cent of the global seafarers and ranks third in the list of the large seafarers-supplying nation to the world maritime industry.

With ships and ports becoming better connected and further integrated into IT networks, the implementation and strengthening of cybersecurity measures are becoming essential. All the issues highlighted in this section have to be addressed if India intends to move ahead in the global maritime sector.

Military Issues

Military issues are vast enough to become the subject of a separate book. However, some general points can be made.

It is obvious that the Indian Navy and Coast Guard will need to expand proportionately to take up greater responsibilities. However, budgetary constraints will always be an issue. The Indian Navy (IN) presently operates about 140 warships and 235 aircraft. As per the Maritime Capability Perspective Plan (2012-2027), it is likely to have a 175-warship and 320-aircraft force by 2027. The Indian Coast Guard (ICG) operates about 136 vessels and 62 aircraft. Its Long Term Perspective Plan (2012-2027) envisages 190 ships and 100 aircraft by 2023.

As seen in the earlier chapter, it is vital for the Indian Navy to possess adequate capability for punitive measures to deter misadventure in the Indian Ocean. Maritime Domain Awareness, including Underwater Domain Awareness, will always be a vital aim. India's island territories are critical elements in its maritime security. They are useful but vulnerable as well. The Andaman and Nicobar Islands provide the vantage staging point in the east close to the choke points of the Malacca

Strait and the Indonesian archipelago. The upgradation of military facilities in these islands will, of course, need to continue. The progressive augmentation of infrastructure for aircraft and sea vessels will enable a larger permanent military deployment of all arms in the islands. The military posture can be further strengthened by deployment of long-range weapons and sensors, such as Brahmos SSMs and weaponised drones. The islands will also be nodal points for maritime security interactions with other navies. The Milan series of exercises has already institutionalised regional maritime cooperation around these waters. Mutual logistics arrangements will enable ships and aircraft of the USA, France, Japan, Australia and ROK to access replenishment facilities.

One of India's major deficiencies is that technological self-sufficiency has not been achieved in all critical areas of military equipment. Moreover, military technology is constantly evolving and new domains of cyber and space have emerged. There is a shift towards the use of Unmanned Underwater Vehicles and drones.

The evolution of the Indian Fleet will always be a matter of debate. However, it is obvious that this will depend primarily on the role envisaged for the military forces. For example, if being the 'first responder' in the region is seen as a primary requirement, the Indian Navy will need an adequate number of Landing Platform Docks (LPDs) and helicopters to fulfil that requirement. Similarly, if maintaining a presence all across the region is the requirement, Offshore Patrol Vessels (OPVs) will be required in large numbers.

As the probability of the Indian Navy and the PLA Navy coming into contact at sea increases, it is imperative that mechanisms to avoid untoward incidents at sea are put in place.

The Indian military has proven to be very useful in India's engagements abroad and military diplomacy needs to be enhanced.

Non-Traditional Security

Although Non-Traditional Security issues have been placed at the end of the chapter, there should probably have been a separate chapter for it. For many of the island nations, issues like climate change are existential threats that are far more important than great power rivalry.

The ravages of climate change are the most significant threat looming ahead, particularly for maritime infrastructure and communities. Rising water levels threaten to play havoc with the maritime infrastructure that has been discussed so far. The island nations have massive EEZs that they are in no position to protect on their own. They need to save their resources from Illegal, Unreported, Unregulated (IUU) fishing. Marine pollution too threatens to devastate these rich natural resources. Higher absorption of carbon dioxide by the oceans and increasing water temperatures has already caused such devastation. Vast stretches of the seas, including in the Bay of Bengal, have become "dead zones" in which no fishing exists. The proliferation of plastic products has resulted in their ending up in the world's oceans and threatening marine species.

Non-traditional security issues require all nations to come together to jointly address them for a better future.

Conclusion

India is already doing much of all that is discussed in this chapter at multiple degrees. However, India's problems are limitations in capacity and speed of execution. India needs to build institutional structures to get rid of these two infirmities. All visions and initiatives are tied to the precondition of the performance of the Indian economy. It is only when the Indian economy performs that India can step up in the world. Along with economic performance, India will have to seek partners and make choices in politics, technology and trade. India will have to address the deficiencies in its maritime sector.

NOTES

1. The World Bank classifies income groups of nations on the basis of Gross National Income per person (GNI per capita). Adjusted to prices on 1 July 2019, lower middle-income economies are those with GNI per capita between $ 1,026 and $ 3,995; upper middle-income are those between $ 3,996 and $ 12,375; high income economies are those above $ 12,376.
2. National Commission on Population, "Population Projection for India and States (2011-2036)", 6-7.
3. Rajya Sabha Secretariat, "Attracting investment in post-Covid Economy: Challenges and Opportunities for India", 158th Report, *Parliamentary Standing Committee on Commerce*, February 2021.
4. Remya Nair, "Ease of doing business? India still has 1,536 Acts, 69,233 compliances for firms to follow", *The Print*, 8 July 2020.
5. Remarks of External Affairs Minister on "Geopolitics of Opportunity: As World Rebalances, How should India Capitalise?" accessed from https://www.youtube.com/watch?v=9jJ3fccQ5rQ on 11 February 2021.

6. Madhumita Murgia and Anna Gross, "Inside China's controversial mission to reinvent the internet", *Financial Times*, 20 March 2020.
7. Aroon Deep, "What Huawei And China's New IP Proposal Is All About", *Medianama*, 7 October 2020 accessed from https://www.medianama.com/2020/10/223-new-ip-huawei-china/ on 21 January 2021.
8. Ila Patnaik and Radhika Pandey, "RCEP would've led to flood of imports into India. Reform is a better way to boost exports", *The Print*, 20 November 2020.
9. Explanation of each type of agreement is available in "Free Trade Agreements: Frequently Asked Questions (FAQs)" of the Ministry of Commerce, Govt. of India, accessed from https://commerce.gov.in/wp-content/uploads/2020/02/FAQ_on_FTA_ 9 April 2014.pdf on 21 January 2021.
10. Dr. V. K. Saraswat, Prachi Priya and Annirudha Ghosh, "A Note on Free Trade Agreements and their costs", *NITI Aayog*, accessed from https://www.niti.gov.in/writereaddata/files/document_publication/FTA-NITI-FINAL.pdf on 21 January 2021.
11. Most notable are Article XXIV of the General Agreement on Tariffs and Trade (GATT), for trade in goods, and Article V of the General Agreement on Trade in Services (GATS), for trade in services.
12. Saraswat, et al., "A Note on Free Trade Agreements and their costs".
13. UNCTAD, "Review of Maritime Transport 2020", 22.
14. Shariq Khan, "India can add 8% to its exports if it puts its last mile connect in the fast lane", *Economic Times*, 22 August 2019.
15. Department of Economic Affairs, "Economic Survey 2017-18", Vol. II, 92.
16. Ministry of Shipping, GoI, "Sagarmala National Perspective Plan", Executive Summary, April 2016, vi.
17. Ministry of Shipping, "Sagarmala National Perspective Plan", viii.
18. Parag Khanna, *The Future is Asia* (Simon & Schuster: 2019).
19. Ministry of Shipping, "Sagarmala National Perspective Plan", viii.
20. Ministry of Shipping, "Sagarmala National Perspective Plan", viii.
21. Shanon Tiezzi, "Xi Jinping in Europe: A Tale of 2 Countries", *The Diplomat*, 27 March 2019.
22. Marine Pennetier and John Irish, "France seals multi-billion dollar deals with China, but questions Belt and Road project", *Reuters*, 25 March 2019.
23. Ministry of External Affairs, "India-Japan Joint Statement during the visit of Prime Minister to Japan", 11 November 2016.
24. Anisha Dutta, "Govt looks to develop Great Nicobar island using PPP model", 28 September 2020; Maitri Porecha and TV Jayan, "NITI Aayog's push for island tourism has no takers", *The Hindu Businessline*, 21 January 2020.
25. Waruna Karunatilake and Alasdair Pal, "China approves $1.5 billion currency swap with Sri Lanka", *Reuters*, 10 March 2021.
26. Ministry of External Affairs, "Prime Minister's address at Parliament of Uganda during his State Visit to Uganda", 25 July 2018.
27. Ministry of External Affairs (MEA), "Official Spokesperson's response to a query on participation of India in OBOR/BRI Forum", 13 May 2017.
28. Roremary Marandi and Rajkumar Sharma, "India sends hydroxychloroquine to Africa in war on coronavirus", *Nikkei Asia*, 18 May 2020.
29. Ministry of External Affairs, "Foreign Secretary's Address on "Leveraging Strategic

Autonomy in a Turbulent World""at the *Diamond Jubilee Seminar of the National Defence College*, 5 November 2020.

30. Kritika Suneja, "Over 40 million N-95 masks, 20 million PPEs exported till now: Smriti Irani", *The Economic Times*, 11 December 2020.
31. Shoumojit Banerjee, "Need to reset trade ties with China, says Foreign Secretary Shringla", *The Hindu*, 28 February 2021.
32. Vishwa Mohan (TNN), "IIT scientists present India's first 5G patent before global body", *Times of India*, 16 June 2017.
33. Nan Lwin, "Myanmar Pulls Swiss Firm to Scrutinize China's BRI Project", *The Irrawady*, 11 June 2020.
34. Nan Lwin, "Myanmar Hires German Firm to Oversee Bidding in Initial Phase of China-Backed New Yangon City", *The Irrawady*, 7 September 2020.
35. Ministry of Defence (MoD), "Annual Report 2015-16", 153.
36. Ministry of External Affairs, "Lok Sabha Question No. 1426 Developmental Assistance Programme", 19 December 2018.
37. Remarks of External Affairs Minister on "Geopolitics of Opportunity: As World Rebalances, How should India Capitalise?" accessed from https://www.youtube.com/watch?v=9jJ3fccQ5rQ on 11 February 2021.
38. Ministry of External Affairs, "India-Japan Vision Statement", 29 October 2018.
39. Ministry of External Affairs, "Joint Statement on the third India-U.S. 2+2 Ministerial Dialogue", 27 October 2020.
40. Ministry of External Affairs, "India-EU Strategic Partnership: A Roadmap to 2025", 15 July 2020.
41. Madhu Bhalla, "Thinking About the Indian Ocean and the Mausam Initiative", *India Quarterly*, 1–14, 2020, DOI: 10.1177/0974928420936106; Madhu Bhalla, "India Should Revive the Mausam Initiative – But Not as it Stands Now", *The Wire*, 20 July 2020.
42. Ministry of External Affairs, "Foreign Secretary's Introductory Remarks at the India-France-Japan Workshop on the Indo-Pacific", 19 January 2021.
43. Vivek Kaul, "India, China and the Quest for Atmanirbharta", *www.vivekkaul.com*, 11 March 2021.
44. Press Information Bureau, "Cabinet approves PLI Scheme to 10 key Sectors for Enhancing India's Manufacturing Capabilities and Enhancing Exports – Atmanirbhar Bharat", 11 November 2020.
45. Ministry of External Affairs, "Question No. 808 Trade through South China Sea", 9 February 2017.
46. UNCTAD, *Review of Maritime Transport 2020*, 7.
47. UNCTAD, *Review of Maritime Transport 2020*, 7.
48. UNCTAD, *Review of Maritime Transport 2020*, 16.
49. Ministry of Shipping, "Sagarmala National Perspective Plan", 4.
50. Utpal Bhaskar, "Companies may get grant to set up strategic oil reserves", *The Mint*, 11 January 2021.
51. IANS, "India now looks to build strategic gas reserve", *The Economic Times*, 11 January 2021.
52. Ministry of Shipping, "Sagarmala National Perspective Plan", xii.
53. Planning Commission, Government of India, "*Report of Working Group on Mineral Exploration and Development (Other Than Coal & Lignite) for the XII Five Year Plan (2012-17)*", 2011.

54. Ministry of Mines, Government of India, "*National Mineral Exploration Policy (Non-Fuel And Non-Coal Minerals)*", 2016.
55. Vaibhav Gupta, Tirtha Biswas, and Karthik Ganesan, "*Critical Non-Fuel Mineral Resources for India's Manufacturing Sector: A Vision for 2030*", CEEW, July 2016.
56. Transport Research Wing, Ministry of Shipping, "Statistics of India's Ship Building and Ship Repairing Industry 2018-19", February 2020.
57. Swaminathan S. Anklesaria Aiyar, "Ship-building", *The Times of India*, 7 April 2007.
58. Uday Mahurkar, "Cochin Shipyard now makes for the world", *India Today*, 18 August 2020.
59. Ministry of Ports, Shipping and Waterways, GoI, *Maritime India Vision 2030* (2021), 149.
60. World Shipping Council, "Top 50 Container Ports" accessed from https://www.worldshipping.org/about-the-industry/global-trade/top-50-world-container-ports on 25 January 2020.
61. Bishwanath Goldar and Mahua Paul, "How operational efficiency of India's ports impacts its manufacturing exports", 10 June 2019, accessed from https://www.ideasforindia.in/topics/trade/how-operational-efficiency-of-indias-ports-impacts-its-manufacturing-exports.html on 11 March 2020.
62. Goldar and Paul, "How operational efficiency of India's ports impacts its manufacturing exports".
63. PIB, "Year End Review 2018 – Ministry of Shipping", 13 December 2018.
64. Ministry of Shipping, Government of India, "Annual Report 2019-20", 10.
65. Mansukh Mandaviya, "Charting course for maritime growth", *Financial Express*, 5 March 2021.
66. Ministry of Shipping, "Sagarmala National Perspective Plan", xi.
67. Ministry of Ports, Shipping and Waterways, GoI, *Maritime India Vision 2030* (2021), 49.
68. Ministry of Ports, Shipping and Waterways, GoI, *Maritime India Vision 2030* (2021), 33.
69. Ministry of Ports, Shipping and Waterways, GoI, *Maritime India Vision 2030* (2021), 54.
70. Shehzad Poonawala and Riya Sinha, "Will Vizhinjam port fulfil India's maritime dream?", 14 December 2015 accessed from https://www.rediff.com/business/column/will-vizhinjam-port-fulfill-indias-maritime-dream/20151214.htm on 25 January 2021.
71. P. Manoj, "Last ditch effort underway to salvage DP World-run box transshipment terminal in Cochin Port", *The Hindu Businessline*, 22 March 2021.
72. P. Manoj, "Vallarpadam ICTT to stick to its original plan", *The Hindu Businessline*, 15 July 2020.
73. P. Manoj, "Centre makes fresh attempt to build transshipment port at Kanyakumari", *The Hindu Businessline*, 22 February 2021.
74. P. Manoj, "Last ditch effort underway to salvage DP World-run box transshipment terminal in Cochin Port", *The Hindu Businessline*, 22 March 2021.
75. Manoj, "Centre makes fresh attempt to build transshipment port at Kanyakumari".
76. UNCTAD, *Review of Maritime Transport 2020*, 40.
77. UNCTAD, *Review of Maritime Transport 2020*, 41.
78. Ministry of Shipping, Government of India, "Annual Report 2019-20", 14.

79. Ministry of Shipping, Government of India, "Annual Report 2019-20", 14.
80. Ministry of Ports, Shipping and Waterways, GoI, *Maritime India Vision 2030* (2021), 138.
81. Ankur Kundu, "Great Eastern Becomes India's Biggest Shipowner by Vessel Count", *The Maritime Executive*, 31 December 2020.
82. P. Manoj, "In 'Atmanirbhar' quest, Shipping Ministry may reinstate cabotage restrictions", *The Hindu Businessline*, 3 June 2020.
83. NGO *Shipbreaking Platform*, "Impact Report 2018-2019".
84. UNCTAD, *Review of Maritime Transport 2020*, 45.

Conclusion

The idea of this book was to focus on infrastructure building in the Indo-Pacific Region, especially in the maritime domain, to comprehend the geo-political implications developing for India. Since the time the project was initiated, much has been written on the Belt and Road Initiative but there is little clarity on its maritime component. Many reports that emanated early, though alarmist in tone, were vague about the implications. Three years down the line, some things have become clearer while many things are yet to play themselves out. It is a fluid and emerging situation in which compilations of data and status of projects get dated rather quickly.

The first and foremost theme that needs to be reiterated, as has been done several times in this book, is that this is a long-term game. Advances in infrastructure building and technology deployment have always been inextricably linked with geopolitics. The high-profile roll-out of the BRI highlighted this aspect to the world. The Chinese also put a date to this long-term game – 2049. Expecting to compress an accurate prognosis of the next three decades in a book chapter is an impossible task, irrespective of the level of analytical skill and clairvoyance. Yet, the trends across the region are discernible. The COVID-19 pandemic seems to have further fast-forwarded these trends. Second, it is clear that the Chinese are not the only ones undertaking infrastructure projects. They may have managed to capture the imagination in recent years with their eye-popping commitments, but endeavours of infrastructure development and connectivity are visible all across the Indo-Pacific Region and Eurasia. A lot of the infrastructure projects now subsumed under the labelling of the BRI actually commenced many years before its announcement. Japan and the Asian Development Bank have been financing infrastructure development across Asia since the 1990s when the Japanese economy was booming. Even now, Japan outperforms China in infrastructure funding in many nations across the Indo-Pacific. Moreover, many of the routes of the BRI are getting enabled due to initiatives that are not Chinese. A majority of the much-publicised China-Europe trains are running through the northern route of Russia and Belarus with the speed of transit facilitated by arrangements of the Eurasian Economic Union (EEU). Connectivity through the Caucasus and Caspian Sea region to Europe, including pipelines, is getting enabled through numerous regional initiatives like Transport Corridor Europe-Caucasus-Asia (TRACECA) and Ashgabat Agreement. The Trans-European Transport Network (TEN-T) policy is implementing connectivity across Europe in two phases ending in 2030 and 2050. Chinese goods are moving north from the Greek port of Piraeus on the European network that already existed. However, it is a fact that China has emerged as the largest lender in the world and spends more on its infrastructure development than any other nation. Infrastructure is seen as a panacea to economic stagnancy and is an attractive marketing tool for political leaders to showcase progress under their stewardship. Numerous nations, big and small, have an infrastructure vision with a catchy slogan. The post-COVID era will see a spurt in such announcements as spending on infrastructure is seen as an effective stimulus to renew growth in economies reeling under the after-effects of lockdown.[1] This brings up the next vital point – finance. All global endeavours have been bedevilled by gaps in finance, be it in achieving the Sustainable Development Goals (SDG) 2030 or the commitments to combat climate change and its impact. Infrastructure is no exception. Getting finance is especially difficult for nations that have a low credit rating due to their poor economic, political or social parameters.[2] These are the nations that have especially looked up to the BRI for finance and these are the nations that need to be provided alternatives.

The BRI, since its advent, meant many things to many people. On one hand of the spectrum, it was seen as an opportunity accorded to nations to upgrade their infrastructure. On the other hand, it was seen as the playing out of China's Grand Strategy. Despite the diversity in views, in the initial years, it was widely expected that China had a well-thought out master plan for the BRI. Now, after seven years, the world is none the wiser about it. There has been an avalanche of publications and databases but some basic questions remain unanswered. For example, there is no clarity on the basis of labelling a project as part of the BRI and financial details are still opaque. It is no wonder that each study reaches its own conclusions based on the database of projects and financial data that it chooses to analyse. Numerous databases that seek to collate information on Chinese projects and financing have proliferated in academic institutions, private consultancy companies and think-tanks around the world.[3] Their data varies, as do the conclusions of the studies based on them. There are contradictory views on "debt trap strategy", usefulness of BRI projects, and China's financial commitments, with many tainted by a confirmation bias. The BRI is a mix of 'top down' and 'bottom up' effects. The top leadership announced an ambitious endeavour and marked it as a national priority while keeping the policy contours blurred. The lower level of provincial governments, state-owned enterprises and banks competed to show their loyalty and capture a share of the pie. The end result has been the commitment of a huge amount of finance, which has not yet been quantified, on a whole range of projects, many without either adequate viability study or implementation oversight. It seems that China sought to replicate its internal policy of building first ahead of demand, with the hope that it will stimulate growth and demand will catch up. Many of the incorrect practices followed domestically, and shielded in an authoritarian system, were replicated abroad and got exposed under international scrutiny. Finally, even the massive financial capacity of China is not limitless. Funding for the BRI has fallen. Nations that have received debt are now seeking reprieve in repayment, especially after getting hit by COVID-19. China is faced with a situation of "damned if you do and damned if you do not".

It is correct to assume that there are linkages between infrastructure development and influence in a nation. However, it is equally incorrect to assume that any nation that receives assistance automatically becomes beholden to all the demands of the provider. Recent events have shown that even small nations do have agency and can negotiate between competing states to derive benefits for themselves. Every nation is different and a broad-brushed approach to analyse influence will not work. For example, the 54 nations in Africa are very different from each other in terms of political stability, economic performance and development indices but are often clubbed together. Around India's neighbourhood, the mechanisms of China's influence work very differently in each nation. However, the one big change in recent years with respect to influence is that of telecommunications and digital domain. A fight has broken out for ownership of the virtual world, the physical media through which it operates and the data that is generated. Thanks to the spread of social media, it is now possible to influence a nation's population even without entering it. Surveillance technology is particularly double-edged, being equally effective in combating crime and in aiding repression. Much of the geopolitics related to infrastructure is now in the arena of the virtual world.

The north-south corridors of the BRI that reach South Asia are still work in progress and do not promise to be commercially viable. However, these corridors to Nepal and into the Indian Ocean, whenever they are established, will create an alteration of geography. Along with the creation of Chinese enclaves in the Indian Ocean Region, this alteration of geography will buttress Chinese claims of being an Indian Ocean nation. It will not be a tall claim to make for a nation that considers itself a "near Arctic state" while not being situated anywhere near the Arctic Circle. This claim of residency will be the licence to participate in, and perhaps even forge, regional platforms. As Chinese investments and the Chinese population increases in the region, it will provide the reason for it to enhance its permanent military presence in the region. This augmentation of military presence may still be a decade or two away but China's political and economic influence is already discernible around India's neighbourhood. If recent events are anything to go by, increase in China's influence has, almost by default, meant the easing out of Indian interests.

The vision of the Maritime Component of the BRI, like the BRI itself, has been on a 'build as we move along' mode. The maps that get published along with reports of this maritime component give the misleading impression that it is a coherent plan to improve connectivity along pre-determined corridors. The declared routes of the maritime component have expanded from two routes to four, but these declared routes still do not cover Chinese investments in western Africa. Now, every Chinese investment or operation, by either SOEs or private companies, in any port-related infrastructure anywhere in the world is considered as part of the fabled MSR. It will be more appropriate to discern the commercial and military aspects separately.

Taking the commercial angle first, there was a spurt of literature that suggested that China was acquiring leverage to control international maritime flows based on its shipbuilding capacity, strength of merchant fleet, and investments and operation of ports worldwide. However, it can be concluded at the moment that the factors that affect the success and failure of ports, ships and shipping lines are too diverse and unpredictable for any one country to wield authoritative power over maritime commerce. Ownership in ships and ports in international maritime trade is too diffused for any one nation to control the flow of traffic. Some of the projects mentioned by the reports either did not commence or got halted or scrapped. This includes Melaka Gateway (Malaysia) and Bagamoyo port (Tanzania). To study the possibility of dual use, it is necessary to sift through the around 90 ports around the world that have Chinese investments. The ones that do not follow commercial logic are the ones in Cambodia, Pakistan (Gwadar) and Sri Lanka (Hambantota).

Moving on to the military aspect, it is important to reiterate that the PLA Navy is not following the US example of setting up military bases overseas. It is following the approach followed during peace time wherein ships can dock at a port overseas, get requisite supplies and spares provided through own logistics arrangements, and remain deployed in a region. This arrangement will get disrupted in the event of war since the host nation will hesitate to provide access. Hence, the PLA Navy will continue such arrangements till it is in a position to get a more permanent presence in the Indian Ocean Region. The only exception to this is Pakistan. It is only a matter of 'when' and not 'if' for the PLA Navy to have a permanent military presence in Pakistan. By all indications, Pakistan will welcome such a move since it will be an insurance against India. There is a body of Chinese literature advocating the setting up of "strategic strong points" or "maritime hubs" overseas supporting PLA Navy operations.[4] It will be interesting to see if these "strategic strong points" do get set up in the future.

The expansion of the PLA Navy is the most rapid in recent history. In many ways, it seems to be replicating the US Navy while seeking to build six aircraft carriers and heavy destroyers and frigates that can be part of a Carrier Task Force. It is also augmenting its sea lift and expeditionary capabilities. However, the PLA Navy will continue to remain engaged within the immediate periphery of China for the time being. Before it can consider having a greater presence in the Indian Ocean, it will need to establish surveillance or Maritime Domain

Awareness (MDA) capabilities through satellites and Maritime Patrol Aircraft. Meanwhile, its Anti-Piracy Task Force continues to be deployed in the Indian Ocean to enable the PLA Navy to enhance its long-term deployment capabilities. Deployment of oceanographic research vessels and surveillance ships are enabling the PLA Navy to collect underwater data for submarine operations, snoop on Indian naval movements and exercises, and collect intelligence. UUVs that can be deployed for long durations and can transmit data through satellite communications are already reported to have been deployed in the region. Chinese fishermen are already in the Indian Ocean. These activities will provide the groundwork for the PLA Navy to set up a permanent presence in the Indian Ocean Region once it is in a position to establish adequate sea control around its peripheral seas.

What about India? First, some of the largest infrastructure development projects in the world are being implemented within India itself. In the last two decades, India has been increasing its spending on infrastructure. Like everything else in India, it has had its fair share of problems in execution. However, there is awareness that infrastructure and connectivity, both hard and soft, needs to be enhanced, within India and in the neighbourhood. India does not face any dearth of funding. In fact, it faces the problem of being unable to absorb all avenues of funding due to its capacity constraints. For example, in August 2015, the UAE committed to invest $ 75 billion towards infrastructure building in India through a UAE-India Infrastructure Investment Fund.[5] However, disbursement was impeded by India's delay in setting up the requisite institutional structures to support it.[6] Private investment, which had swelled in the first decade of this century, has collapsed and companies have run up high debts that they are unable to service. As for the conjecture about whether India should sign on to the BRI, clearly there is no reason for India to do so. It has no dearth of funding. The benefits of signing the BRI MoU are also not clear. The texts of the MoUs, a few of which have been made public, have the same open-ended language of the BRI vision documents. Signing on does not automatically ensure a stream of Chinese funding as countries like the Philippines have realised. On the other hand, Chinese investment flowed into Indian businesses and Chinese companies bagged contracts in India without any BRI labelling attached to them. It can be argued that the north-south corridors that China is planning in the Indian Ocean Region can be commercially viable only if India joins in. Along with development of its own infrastructure, India is also trying to improve connectivity in its immediate neighbourhood by land, water and air.

From the strategic point of view, India's foremost aim is to grow economically. If the Indian economy does not perform, India might as well forget all its global ambitions. India will need to make choices, not just politically but also technologically and economically. The choices are not going to be easy and room for manoeuvring will be narrow. Faced against an asymmetric power, India will need to seek partnerships. It will need to up the ante with its own contribution. To become a stakeholder in global dialogues on instituting norms for technology, India will need to become a developer of standards and systems rather than just a user. India has capability in 'frugal engineering' and proven capability in delivering public goods through technology. It needs to offer them to the world. As for infrastructure and connectivity, India will need to improve 'hard' and 'soft' infrastructure, and connectivity within its territory and with its neighbours. It will also have to contribute to improving connectivity across the Indo-Pacific and Eurasian regions. However, infrastructure projects can be messy. Getting entangled in the uncertainties of infrastructure development can seriously hurt national reputation. Hence, it is advisable to undertake such projects with partners and through multilateral agencies. Bilateral projects, if undertaken, should follow international best practices and norms of transparency already in vogue. It will be useful to have a separate agency, with multi-disciplinary staff, to undertake all international aid, development partnerships and infrastructure projects abroad. The 'India Way' is not to create brick-and-mortar infrastructure that may neither be economically viable nor provide sustainable development. The 'India Way' is to understand the requirements for sustainable economic development and security concerns in the region, and provide relevant solutions accordingly. India cannot afford to get into a race in distributing freebies in a delusionary quest for influence. However, India can provide capability and enhance capacity of the nations in the region while offering them the benefits of the Indian market.

The maritime domain has numerous facets – ports, merchant navy fleet, port operations, shipping lines, ship building, scientific research, fishing, offshore energy and natural resources, tourism, international maritime law, and protection of all maritime assets and resources. It is a no-brainer that India needs to progress in all these sectors. India does not figure highly on a global scale in most of the maritime sectors either in terms of scale or efficiency.

Deployment of Indian maritime forces will be decided on three factors – the routes of India's trade flows, the routes for sourcing energy, food and natural resources, and the sources of threats. The Indian Ocean Region will see a greater presence of regional and extra-regional navies in the future. Hence, there is a need to institute measures to avoid unintended consequences or escalation when these forces interact at sea.

There is a significant gap between what India considers its destined status in the world and what it actually is. The next two decades are going to be particularly difficult for India to navigate.

NOTES

1. "Getting off the ground: Is an infrastructure boom in the works?", *The Economist*, 2 January 2021, has reported that USA's President-elect, Joe Biden, has pledged to spend $ 2 trn on roads, bridges and electric-car charging points; Green projects make up 30 % of the European Union's $ 918 bn recovery fund; and China has set aside $ 1.5 trn for new projects.
2. International Monetary Fund, Standard & Poor's (S&Ps), Moody's and Fitch are some of the organizations that provide Sovereign credit ratings.
3. Reconnecting Asia of CSIS; MacroPolo of Paulson Institute (Chicago); SAIS-CARI of John Hopkins University (Washington DC); China Power of CSIS; China Global Investment Tracker of AEI; China Investment Monitor of Rhodium Group; Mercator Institute of China Studies (MERICS); AidData of William & Mary.
4. Mathieu Duchatel, "Naval bases: From Djibouti to a Global Network?", in *China Trends # 2, China's Port Investment: The Flag behind the trade*, Institut Montaigne, June 2019.
5. Ministry of External Affairs (MEA), "Joint Statement between the United Arab Emirates and the Republic of India", 17 August 2015.
6. FE Bureau, "Despite PM Narendra Modi's push, mega UAE-India infrastructure fund plan at risk", *Financial Express*, 27 January 2017.

Bibliography

Books

Bruno Macaes, *Belt and Road – A Chinese World Order* (Penguin Random House India, 2019).

B. S. Das, *Studies in the Economic History of Orissa: From Ancient Times to 1833* (Calcutta: Firma KLM Pvt. Ltd., 1978).

Daniel Moran and James A. Russel (Eds.), *Maritime Strategy and Global Order: Markets, Resources, Security*, (Washington, DC: Georgetown University Press, 2016).

Daniel R. Headrick, *The Tools of Empire: Technology and European Imperialism in the Nineteenth Century* (New York and Oxford: Oxford University Press, 1981).

Daniel R. Headrick, *Power Over Peoples: Technology, Environments and Western Imperialism, 1400 to the present* (Princeton and Oxford: Princeton University Press, 2010).

David Brewster (Ed.), *India and China at Sea: Competition for Naval Dominance in the Indian Ocean* (Oxford University Press: 2018).

Edward Mead Earle, *Turkey, the Great Powers and the Bagdad Railways: A study in Imperialism* (New York, The Macmillan Company: 1924).

Greame Smith and Terence Wesley-Smith, *The China Alternative: Changing regional order in the Pacific Islands* (ANU Press: 2021).

Indo-Pacific Report 2019 (New Delhi: National Maritime Foundation, 2019).

John Hurd and Ian J. Kerr, *India's Railway History: A Research Handbook*, (Brill: 2012).

Jonathan E. Hillman, *The Emperor's New Road: China and the project of the Century*, (New Haven and London: Yale University Press, 2020).

Kalidas Nag, *India and the Pacific World* (Calcutta: Book Company Ltd., 1941).

Kalidas Nag, *Greater India* (Bombay: The Book Centre Private Ltd., 1960).

Kenneth McPherson, *The Indian Ocean: A history of people and the sea* (New York: Oxford University Press, 1993).

K. N. Chaudhuri, *Trade and Civilisation in the Indian Ocean: An Economic History from the Rise of Islam to 1750* (Cambridge University Press, 1985).

K. S. Behera (Ed.) *Maritime Heritage of India*, (New Delhi: Aryan Books International, 1999).

Louise Levanthes, *When China Ruled the Waves* (Oxford University Press, 1994).

Mark Elvin, *The Pattern of the Chinese Past* (Stanford: Stanford University Press, 1973).

M. N. Das, *Glimpses of Kalinga History* (Calcutta: Century Publishers, 1949).

Murray Hiebert, Under Beijing's Shadow: Southeast Asia's China Challenge (CSIS: 2020).

Nadege Rolland, *China's Eurasian Century? Political and Strategic Implications of the Belt and Road Initiative* (USA: National Bureau of Asian Research, 2017), reprinted by New Delhi: Pentagon Press.

Parag Khanna, *The Future is Asia* (Simon & Schuster: 2019).

Philippe Beaujard, *The Worlds of the Indian Ocean: A Global History*, Volume 1 (Cambridge: Cambridge University Press, 2012).

Raffaello Pantucci and Sarah Lain, "China's Eurasian Pivot – The Silk Road Economic Belt", *Whitehall Paper 88*, RUSI, 2017.

Rear Adm K. Sridharan, *A Maritime History of India, Second edition* (New Delhi: Publications Division, GoI, 1982).

Richard T. Griffiths, *The Maritime Silk Road: China's Belt and Road at Sea* (International Institute of Asian Studies: 2020).

R. K. Mookerji, *Indian Shipping*, Kitab Mahal (Allahabad), 1962.

Roy Kamphausen, David Lai, and Travis Tanner (Eds.), *Assessing the People's Liberation Army in the Hu Jintao Era* (US Army War College: 2014).

Sanjeev Sanyal, *The Ocean of Churn: How the Indian Ocean Shaped Human History* (India: Penguin Books, 2016).

Srikanth Kondapalli, *China's Naval Power* (New Delhi: Knowledge World, 2001).

World Port Index (National Geospatial Intelligence Agency, USA: 2019).

Selected Papers

Andrew Selth, "Burma, China and the Myth of Military Bases", *Asian Security*, Vol. 3, No. 3, 2007, 279-307, DOI: 10.1080/14799850701568929

C. A. Gibson Hill, "The Steamers employed in Asian Waters, 1819-39", *Journal of the Malayan Branch of the Royal Asiatic Society*, Vol. 27, No. 1 (165) (May,1954), 120-162.

Carolien Stolte and Harald Fischer-Tine, "Imagining Asia in India: Nationalism and Internationalism", *Comparative Studies in Society and History*, 2012; 54 (1); 65-92.

Craig A. Lockard, ""The Sea Common to All": Maritime Frontiers, Port Cities, and Chinese Traders in the Southeast Asian Age of Commerce, ca. 1400-1750", *Journal of World History*, Vol. 21, No. 2 (June 2010), 219-247.

Deborah Brautigam, "A critical look at Chinese 'debt-trap diplomacy': the rise of a meme", *Area Development and Policy*, Vol. 5, No. 1, 2020, 1-14, DOI 10.1080/23792949.2019.1689828

Filippo Boni, "Protecting the Belt and Road Initiative: China's cooperation with Pakistan to secure CPEC", *Asia Policy*, Vol. 14, No. 2, April 2019.

Geoff Wade, "The Zheng He Voyages: A Reassessment", *Journal of the Malaysian Branch of the Royal Asiatic Society*, Vol. 78, No. 1 (288), (2005), 37-58.

Geoff Wade, "Engaging the South: Ming China and Southeast Asia in the Fifteenth Century", *Journal of the Economic and Social History of the Orient*, Vol. 51, No. 4 (2008), 578-638.

Geoff Wade, "An Early Age of Commerce in Southeast Asia, 900–1300 CE", *Journal of Southeast Asian Studies*, Volume 40, Issue 2 (June 2009), 221–265.

Henry Farrell and Abraham L. Newman, "Weaponized Interdependence: How Global Economic Networks Shape State Coercion", *International Security*, Vol. 44, No. 1 (Summer 2019), pp. 42–79, https://doi.org/10.1162/ISEC_a_00351

Hong Zhang, "Beyond "Debt-Trap Diplomacy: The Dissemination of PRC State Capitalism", *China Brief*, Vol. 19, Issue. 1, The Jamestone Foundation, 5 January 2019.

Ian Kerr, "The building of the Bhor Ghat Railway incline in western India in The mid-19th century" in *Railroads in historical context: Construction, costs and consequences*, (Eds.) Anne Mccants, Eduardo Beira, Jose M. Lopes Cordeiro, and Paulo Lourenco, Vol. I (MIT Portugal: 2011), 343-346.

Jeremy Garlick and Radka Havlova, "The dragon dithers: assessing the cautious implementation of China's Belt and road Initiative in Iran", *Eurasian Geography and Economics*, 2020, DOI 10.1080/15387216.2020.1822197

Jonathan Fulton, "China-Saudi Arabia relations through the '1+2+3' cooperation pattern", *Asian Journal of Middle Eastern and Islamic Studies*, DOI 10.1080/25765949.2020.1841991

Luo Yao, Wang Dong-Xiao, Pan Gang, Zhang Zhen-Qiu, Wang Wei-Qiang and Yao Jing-Long, "China–Sri Lanka Joint Center for Education and Research for the 21st Century Maritime Silk Road", *Atmospheric and Oceanic Science Letters*, 2017 Vol. 10, No. 5, 354–357 DOI: 10.1080/16742834.2017.1343085

Madhu Bhalla, "Thinking About the Indian Ocean and the Mausam Initiative", *India Quarterly*, 1–14, 2020, DOI: 10.1177/0974928420936106

Manjeet S. Pardesi, "The Indo-Pacific: a 'new' region or the return of history?" *Australian Journal of International Affairs*, 2019, DOI: 10.1080/10357718.2019.1693496

Richard Pearson, Li Min and Li Guo, "Quanzhou Archaeology: A brief review", *International Journal of Historical Archaeology*, Vol. 6, No. 1 (March 2002).

Ruosui Zhang, "To suspend or not to suspend: A cost benefit analysis of three Chinese mega-projects in Myanmar", *The Pacific Review*, DOI: 10.1080/09512748, 2020.1776757, 2 and 17.

Tansen Sen, "Maritime Southeast Asia between South Asia and China to the Sixteenth Century", *TRaNS: Trans-Regional and National Studies of Southeast Asia*, Volume 2, Issue 1(January 2014), 31–59.

Tirta Nugraha Mursitama and Yi Ying, "Indonesia's perception and strategy toward China's OBOR", *The Chinese Economy*, DOI 10.1080/10971475.2020.1809816

Wada Haruko, "The Indo-Pacific Concept: Geographical adjustments and their implications", *RSIS Working Paper* No. 326, 16 March 2020.

Weidong Liu, Yajing Zhang and Wei Xiong, "Financing the Belt and Road Initiative", *Eurasian Geography and Economics*, 2020, DOI 10.1080/15387216.2020.1716822

Yves-Heng Lim, "China's rising naval ambitions in the Indian Ocean: aligning ends, ways and means", *Asian Security*, 2020, DOI 10.1080/14799855.2020.1721469

Selected Reports

Agatha Kratz, Daniel H. Rosen, and Matthew Mingey, "Booster or Brake? COVID and the Belt and Road Initiative", *Rhodium Group*, 15 April 2020.

Agatha Kratz, Matthew Mingey, and Drew D'Alelio, "Seeking Relief: China's Overseas debt after COVID-19", *Rhodium Group*, 8 October 2020.

Anantha Krishnan, "Following the Money: China Inc's Growing Stakes in India-China Relations", *Brookings India Impact Series* 032020-01, March 2020.

Asian Development Bank, "Meeting Asia's Infrastructure Needs", February 2017.

"China Trends # 2, China's Port Investment: The Flag behind the trade", Institut Montaigne, June 2019.

Debasish Mallick, "Inland waterways – positive impact on economy", *ORF*, 20 January 2020.

Deborah Brautigam and Meg Rithmire, "The Chinese 'Debt Trap' Is a Myth", *The Atlantic*, 6 February 2021.

Derek Scissors, "China's global investment vanishes under COVID-19", *American Enterprise Institute*, July 2020.

Cecilia Joy-Perez and Derek Scissors, "The Chinese State funds Belt and Road but does not have trillions to spare", *American Enterprise Institute*, March 2018.

Francis Hutchinson and Tham Siew Yean, "The BRI in Malaysia's Port Sector: Drivers of Success and Failure", *Economics Working Paper* No. 2020-10, *ISEAS-Yusof Ishak Institute*, November 2020.

Jeff M. Smith, "China's Belt and road Initiative: Strategic Implications and International Opposition", *The Heritage Foundation*, 9 August 2018.

Jeffrey Becker, "Securing China's Lifelines across the Indian Ocean", *China Maritime Report* No. 11, China Maritime Studies Institute, 2020.

John Hurley, et al., "Examining the Debt implications of the Belt and Road Initiative from a Policy Perspective", *Centre for Global Development*, March 2018.

Jonathan E. Hillman, *Influence and Infrastructure: The strategic stake of foreign projects*, (Washington, DC: Centre for Strategic and International Studies (CSIS), 2019).

Jonathan E. Hillman, "Securing the Subsea Network: A Primer for Policymakers", *CSIS Reconnecting Asia Project*, March 2021.

Luis Andres, Dan Biller, and Matias Herrera Dappe, "Infrastructure Gap in South Asia: Infrastructure Needs, Prioritization, and Financing", *Policy Research Working Paper* No. 7032, *World Bank Group*, September 2014.

Mathew Mingey and Agatha Kratz, "China's Belt and road: Down but not out", *Rhodium Group*, 4 January 2021.

Nicholas Szechenyi (Ed.), *China's Maritime Silk Road – Strategic and economic Implications for the Indo-Pacific* (CSIS: March 2018).

OECD, "China's Belt and Road Initiative in the trade, investment and financial landscape", *OECD Business and Finance Outlook*, 2018.

Peter A. Dutton, Isaac B. Kardon and Conor M. Kennedy, "Djibouti: China's first overseas strategic strongpoint", *China Maritime Report* No. 6, China Maritime Studies Institute, April 2020.

Peter A. Dutton, Isaac B. Kardon and Conor M. Kennedy, "Gwadar: China's potential strategic strongpoint in Pakistan", *China Maritime Report* No. 7, China Maritime Studies Institute, April 2020.

Recorded Future, "China-Linked Group RedEcho Targets the Indian Power Sector Amid Heightened Border Tensions", *Cyber Threat Analysis China*, 28 February 2021.

Richard Ghiasy and Jiayi Zhou, *The Silk Road economic Belt: Considering security implications and EU-China cooperation prospects* (Stockholm: SIPRI, February 2017).

Richard Ghiasy, et al., *The 21st Century Maritime Silk Road – Security Implications and ways forward for the European Union*, (SIPRI: 2018).

Richard Javad Heydarian, "The 21st Century Silk Road – Perils and Opportunities of China's Belt and Road Initiative", *ADR Publications*, 2018.

RIS et al., "Asia Africa Growth Corridor – Partnership for Sustainable and Innovative Development", May 2017.

Ryan D. Martinson and Peter A. Dutton, "China's Distant-Ocean Survey Activities: Implications for U.S. National Security", *China Maritime Report* No. 3, China Maritime Studies Institute, U.S. Naval War College, November 2018.

Sebastian Horn, Carmen M. Rienhart and Christoph Trebesch, "How much money does the world owe China?", *Harvard Business Review*, 26 February 2020.

Shikha Jha and Rosa Mia Arao, "Infrastructure Financing in South Asia", *South Asia Working Papers* (59), Asian Development Bank, September 2018.

UNCTAD, "Review of Maritime Transport 2020".

Vaibhav Gupta, Tirtha Biswas, and Karthik Ganesan, "*Critical Non-Fuel Mineral Resources for India's Manufacturing Sector: A Vision for 2030*", CEEW, July 2016.

Selected Government Publications

Australia

Australian Government, "Australia in the Asian Century", White Paper, October 2012.

Department of Defence, Australian Government, "Defence White Paper 2013".

Australian Government, "2017 Foreign Policy White Paper".

China

Ministry of Foreign Affairs, People's Republic of China, "Xi Jinping: Let the Sense of Community of Common Destiny Take Deep Root in Neighbouring Countries", 25 October 2013.

The State Council Information Office of the People's Republic of China, "China's Military Strategy", 2015.

National Development and Reform Commission (NDRC), et al., "Vision and Actions on Jointly Building Silk Road Economic Belt and 21st Century Maritime Silk Road", 28 March 2015.

Ministry of Foreign Affairs of the People's Republic of China, "China's Arab Policy Paper", 13 January 2016.

State Council Information Office, People's Republic of China, "China's Policy on Asia-Pacific Security Cooperation", January 2017.

NDRC and SAO, People's Republic of China, "Vision for Maritime Cooperation under the Belt and Road Initiative", 20 June 2017.

The State Council Information Office, People's Republic of China, "China's Arctic Policy", 26 January 2018.

Ministry of Foreign Affairs, PRC, "Joint Communiqué of the Leaders' Roundtable of the 2nd Belt and Road Forum for International Cooperation", 27 April 2019.

The State Council Information Office of the People's Republic of China, "China's National Defense in the New Era", July 2019.

Europe

European Commission, "Connecting Europe and Asia – Building Blocks for a New Strategy", 19 September 2018.

France

Ministry of Defence, France, "France and Security in the Indo-Pacific", 2018.

Ministry for Europe and Foreign Affairs, Republic of France, "French Strategy in the Indo-Pacific "for and inclusive Indo-Pacific", updated August 2019.

Germany

The Federal Government, "Policy Guidelines for the Indo-Pacific: Germany-Europe-Asia: Shaping the 21st century together", 2020.

India

Department of Economic Affairs, "Economic Survey 2017-18", Vol. II.

Department of Economic Affairs, Government of India, "Report of the Task Force on National Infrastructure Pipeline", Vol. I, April 2020.

Ministry of Commerce, Govt. of India, "Free Trade Agreements: Frequently Asked Questions (FAQs)".

Ministry of Finance, Government of India, "Economic Survey 2019-20", Vol. 2.

Ministry of Mines, Government of India, *"National Mineral Exploration Policy (Non-Fuel And Non-Coal Minerals)"*, 2016.

Ministry of Ports, Shipping and Waterways, GoI, *Maritime India Vision 2030* (2021).

Ministry of Railways, GoI, "National Rail Plan", December 2020.

Ministry of Shipping, "Final Report for Sagarmala", Vol. VI.

Ministry of Shipping, GoI, "Sagarmala National Perspective Plan", April 2016.

Ministry of Shipping, Government of India, "Annual Report 2019-20".

National Commission on Population, "Population Projection for India and States (2011-2036)", 2020.

Planning Commission, Government of India, *"Report of Working Group on Mineral Exploration and Development (Other Than Coal & Lignite) for the XII Five Year Plan (2012-17)"*, 2011.

Rajya Sabha Secretariat, "Attracting investment in post-Covid Economy: Challenges and Opportunities for India", *158th Report, Parliamentary Standing Committee on Commerce*, February 2021.

Transport Research Wing, Ministry of Shipping, "Statistics of India's Ship Building and Ship Repairing Industry 2018-19", February 2020.

USA

Department of State (USA), "A Free and Open Indo-Pacific: Advancing a shared vision", 4 November 2019.

Index

*